Abraham Jaeger

Mind and Heart in Religion

Judaism and Christianity

Abraham Jaeger

Mind and Heart in Religion
Judaism and Christianity

ISBN/EAN: 9783744731744

Printed in Europe, USA, Canada, Australia, Japan

Cover: Foto ©Lupo / pixelio.de

More available books at **www.hansebooks.com**

Mind and Heart in Religion;

OR,

JUDAISM AND CHRISTIANITY.

A HEART'S EXPERIENCE

AND

A POPULAR RESEARCH INTO THE TRUE RELIGION
OF THE BIBLE.

BY

ABRAHAM JAEGER.

———•———

Published for the Author by Goodspeed's Publishing House.
NEW YORK.   CHICAGO.
NEW ORLEANS.
1873.

OPINIONS.

Chicago, November 4th, 1872.

"Rev. Mr. Jaeger,

Dear Bro:—I have read the first seventy-six pages of your book on 'Mind and Heart in Religion,' with the deepest interest, and I may truly say that I was fascinated and thrilled by its rapid unfolding of your experience as a Jew, and your saving knowledge of Jesus Christ. I should like to see the work in every house in America, and to hear that everybody has read it."

I am Yours Truly, E. J. GOODSPEED,
Pastor 2nd Baptist Church, Chicago.

"After reading in manuscript and in proof the book 'Mind and Heart in Religion,' by Rev. A. Jaeger, late Rabbi of the Jewish Congregation of Mobile. I cheerfully express my opinion that it is a book which Christians must hail with gratification. It is not only a remarkably able production, indicating scholarship of rare excellence, and defending the cause of the truth with clearness of thought and keenness of argument, but with his glowing zeal, and his originality of expression, Mr. Jaeger has made it a work such as is very seldom, and in some respects never, offered to the community. It is my hope and belief that it is destined to do great good. It will be a refreshment to every Christian heart. It is adapted to awaken slumbering souls, to stir up the indifferent, and to pierce the heart of every reader as with those arrows of truth which heal while they wound. It moves and convinces. I have read it again and again, and every time with increased enjoyment."

J. A. SMITH,
Editor of the Standard.

"I have read more than 200 pages in manuscript and about 100 pages in print, of the book of Rabbi Jaeger referred to above by Rev. Dr. Smith. I fully agree with Dr. Smith in the commendation given by him. I deem it a book of rare merit, adapted to do important service in honor of Christ and his truth. I wish it could be placed universally in our families. It is a fresh view of the claims of Christ and his blessed gospel."

R. E. PATTISON,
Prof. Bap. Union Seminary.

"We have examined the work and fully concur in the above commendation of Dr. Pattison, and in the hope that it may obtain a wide circulation."

A. N. ARNOLD,   E. C. MITCHELL,
  Prof. Bap. Union Theo. Sem.   Prof. Bap. Union Theo. Sem.
W W EVERTS,   G. W. NORTHRUP,
  Pastor 1st Bap. Church.   Pres. B. U. T. Sem.

"I fully concur in the above, and cordially commend the work, and Mr. Jaeger, personally, to the confidence of Christian men."

J. B. THOMAS,
Pastor Mich. Ave. Bap. Church.

"So far as I have read I cordially approve."

C. D. HELMER,
Pastor Union Park Cong. Church.

"I cheerfully endorse the above." S. McCHESNEY,
Pastor Trinity M. E. Church, Chicago.

DR. DANDY,
Presiding Elder M. E. Church, Chicago District.

PREFACE.

In this book I venture to place before the public, not the result of any theological studies or scientific investigations, but my individual view of Judaism and Christianity, as the result of the observations of my own heart, guided by the principles of Scripture. My object is not polemic but apologetic. Since the Twentieth of August, 1872, when I wrote the letter which forms the introductory of this book, I have, in the midst of manifold trials and interruptions, tried to express my thoughts and feelings about religion as well as I could in a language foreign to me, and in which I am not in the habit of writing. I had neither the time nor the opportunity to make any scientific investigations, and have intentionally avoided to bring such subjects into discussion which might render the book unintelligible to the common reader. Every man with common sense should be able to judge in a cause which concerns every single individual, and which is of the very highest importance to his welfare and happiness. My request to every reader is: not to critisize or judge single chapters or passages, but to take into account the entire scope of the book; examine, read carefully and think before you judge.

I must yet guard myself against a misunderstanding, as if I had any intention to write against the people to which I belong, and of which I am proud. This book has nothing to do with men, but with their religion. I fully appreciate the character of my people as *men*. I love my people, while I see their religious error.

At this day I am the reproach of my brethren, and must therefore expect that my words will be an offense to them. But as there is a sure promise that they will one day find their hope, and will glory in the One whom they despise now, so I have the sure hope that they will some day read my words and bless the writer.

CHICAGO, January, 1873.　　　　　　　　　　　A. J.

CONTENTS.

	PAGE
AN OPEN LETTER TO REV. DR. ISAAC M. WISE,	13
Chapter I—RELIGION,	21
" II—THE JEWISH REFORM,	27
" III—THE HEART'S STRUGGLE,	34
" IV—THE BIBLE,	41
" V—THE WANDERING JEW,	45
" VI—THE NEW TESTAMENT,	52
" VII—HUMAN DEPRAVITY,	65
" VIII—JUDAISM,	78
" IX—THE RABBINICAL LAW,	102
" X—CAUSE AND ERROR OF THE REFORM,	133
" XI—TRINITY,	152
" XII—CHRIST,	171
" XIII—THE MESSIAH OF THE BIBLE,	229
XIV—THE DIVINE REDEEMER,	261
" XV—THE BIBLICAL ATONEMENT,	286

Mind and Heart in Religion;

OR,

JUDAISM AND CHRISTIANITY.

INTRODUCTORY.

AN

OPEN LETTER TO REV. DR. ISAAC M. WISE,

Editor of "The Israelite," Cincinnati, O.

DEAR SIR:

Your attack and challenge in your "Israelite" of July 12th, coming to my notice, have made it necessary for me to address you in the following chapters, entering into the subject at more length than I at first proposed.

It is very unpleasant for me to have controversies with you, as you were my friend once, and I am yours yet, and believe I ever shall be. It is not my object to defend myself personally, or to blame you or any of my people for their attacks upon me. Such attacks I expected, and can blame no one on account of them. I can easily place myself in your position, and I know that you must consider it your duty to say all manner of evil against me. A year ago I hated and despised nobody so much as a converted Jew. I could never believe he was anything but a base hypocrite, for I then thought as you do now.

If, in reply to your challenge, I write the following few chapters, it is only in view of my duty to the religion I have embraced of my own free will. Perhaps I shall convince you that a converted Jew, who once followed the flag of the so-called Rationalists must not necessarily be a base hypocrite, as you presume. But, for the sake of the truth, let me correct some mistakes you made in your "Israelite" of July 12th.

You say that I never was a Rabbi and never was considered so by anybody. But, my dear sir, I actually occupied the rabbinical office in Selma and in Mobile; and when the congregation advertised a service in the synagogue they always remarked, "Rev. A. Jaeger, Rabbi," or Minister. I also have the papers of election from the congregation. You also say, that you only advised and recommended me to teach and occasionally to preach. Why, Doctor, you know that we never thought of my being a teacher, and that in Selma I acted as minister only, as the congregation there had no school, and I never taught there one minute.

You know that for many centuries the Jews have had no ordination, but the testimony of Rabbis to a man's learning and the election of a congregation make him a Rabbi. Well, in your "Israelite" and "Deborah" you often gave assurance of my "profound rabbinical learning." Am I now less learned because I confess Christianity?

Between you and me, Dr. Wise, do you, although one of the most influential Rabbis in this country, affirm that you know more of the rabbinical lore than I do? If you say so I shall have to believe you; but look around you in this country, where men who do not even understand the Pentateuch in the original language assume the title of "Rabbi," where you consider many as such, well knowing that they could profit very much by going to school to me for rabbinical instruction. And you say "Jaeger was not a Rabbi"? However, you say that I hold no papers to this effect. My dear sir, I do hold many a paper to this very effect. I shall only copy one here, which ought to be sufficient for you. I have a paper in my hands which reads as follows:

"The undersigned herewith testifies, that Rev. A. Jaeger is known to him as an excellent Talmudist and Hebraist, fully competent to preach our sacred religion, and to discharge the rabbinical duties to the glory of God and the honor of his worshipers in light and in truth. ISAAC M. WISE.
"CINCINNATI, Sep., 1870."

Well, my friend, is not that a sufficient paper for you, or any of my Jewish friends? I have, besides, a letter in my possession, written by you to a gentleman in Selma, in which, speaking of me as "your friend, whom you esteem highly," you say, "As far as rabbinical learning, ability and character are concerned, *he is second to none.*"

In your "Deborah" of June 23, 1871, you say, "Die Wahl des Herrn Jaeger als *Rabbiner* der Gemeinde zu Mobile, was uns erst jetzt augezeigt wurde, ist fuer die Gemeinde als eine bedeutende Errungenschaft zu betrachten, denn Herr Jaeger ist ein ernster und gelehrter Mann und ein denkender heller Kopf. Wir gratuliren der Gemeinde." That means, in English, "The election of Mr. Jaeger as RABBI of the congregation at Mobile, of which fact we had no notice until now, is to be considered an important acquisition for the congregation, for Mr. Jaeger is an earnest and learned man, with a thinking, clear head. We congratulate the congregation."

I can cite many similar passages of your own "Israelite" and "Deborah," in which you speak of me as a Rabbi, and give assurances of my learning. But I presume that what I have cited is sufficient. And your papers are not the only ones which spoke favorably of me. I never courted any publicity or puffing of papers, nor did I even anticipate that you were to pay me such compliments in your papers as you did. But is it not astonishing when you say, now, that I never was a Rabbi, or considered so by anybody? Concerning myself, I care nothing about what you call me, and have not the least ambition to be considered a learned man. As your friend, I am even sorry that I am obliged to expose your contradictions, but you compelled me to do it. Nevertheless, you may rest assured that you have not a more sincere friend on this earth than I am to you. As I said, I can very easily believe that you only mean to do your duty.

Now, it seems that a man can change his mind. You prove it by your different statements concerning me. Why cannot you believe, then, that I have changed my mind about Christianity, as thousands have done before me since the days of Saul of Tarsus?

Your enemies are trying to use the fact of my conversion to your disadvantage, upon the idea that you are the only one who recommended me. But you may tell them that I have papers of Rabbis belonging to every party and rite (Minhag) of the different shades of reform, as well as of orthodoxy. Every truly intelligent Jew who knew me never doubted my rabbinical learning, ability and character. Should your enemies not cease to attack you on account of my conversion, I shall have to publish my letters of recommendation from their party, in order to defend you.

Do not feel embarrassed by the matter. This Jaeger was considered an honest, upright, sincere and good-hearted Jew, of firm character, by all who knew him. No man could ever suspect me of such base hypocrisy as to sell my religion. Nor has this Jaeger even the ability to play the masked man if he wanted to.

You say that I sold my birthright because I could not make my living among the Jews, and had some to support whom, you say, you do not wish to name. You had better name them, Doctor. You may say that I always have spent my last cent to support my old mother; was that wrong? I also have occasionally helped my other relatives, and I am not ashamed of it. And I thank God that these relatives are now able and liberal enough to assist me, now that I have ruined myself pecuniarily by embracing Christianity. No matter how much they feel offended by my conversion, they know that I cannot be a hypocrite, but am sincere. But, again, why should not I be able to make a living among the Jews, where I had a large circle of friends, and enjoyed a good reputation, but should succeed better among the Christians, where I am a perfect stranger? Can any of my acquaintances accuse me of any willful wrong or baseness, or selfishness, or love of money? You, Dr. Wise, know me pretty well. Is it possible, according to your knowledge of human nature, that a man, such as you took me to be, should change his religion for money? If so, what made me give up my situation with its ample remuneration before my time expired? And have you really any other reason to assert that I received any pecuniary benefit, but the fact that I embraced Christianity? Do you know that I received anything? Why do you affirm that I sold my birthright, then, if you do not know it? It is true, that after I joined the church the members, seeing that I had ruined myself, pecuniarily, were kind enough to offer me a purse, but I emphatically declined receiving any favors. I am a proud son of Abraham, and with my ancestor I said, "I have lifted up mine hand unto the Lord, the most high God, the possessor of heaven and earth, that I will not take from a thread even to a shoe-latchet." You may rest assured that I shall never receive but what I earn.

Oh, Dr. Wise, you are so blinded as to believe the most absurd stories about me; and you publish the foolish inventions of some in Mobile. that I claimed to have seen Christ in the flesh, and the Devil in person. Do you not suppose that the Christians would send me to a lunatic asylum after such assertions?

As an old friend let me confide to you that I never labored under such pecuniary embarrassment as I do now. My only hope and prospect for a living is a kind Providence. I have never been so alone, so friendless in the world as I am now. I expected nothing better, but sacrificed myself to my convictions.

Let this suffice as regards myself. You shall now have the privilege of abusing me, and of saying all manner of evil and detailing all sorts of absurd stories against me. You may deride and ridicule me. I shall never contradict you about any thing concerning myself personally.

You pay me the compliment, though, of having been as thorough a rationalist as there is in this country, and you conclude, therefore, that I cannot possibly believe one word of Christianity, and challenge me to come out and defend it. I must surely answer you in that respect, and therefore I have undertaken to write this little book, in order to defend what I feel and know to be true. But let me confess that I feel my knowledge is inadequate to the task. I have never studied one book of Christian theology. All the knowledge I may have acquired of it is by reading books opposed to Christianity, and mainly, besides the Old and New Testaments, the rabbinical literature. Another disadvantage under which I labor is the fact that I am entirely without the necessary library for such a work. But still I shall give you the necessary reasons and the history of my conversion as well as I can. I shall try to express what I think and feel to be true, and how I came to my present thoughts and feelings. It will be for you, then, either to take back what you have said, namely, that I must either be insane or a base hypocrite; or to show me why, if you still maintain what you said. I only request you and every other reader of these pages to read carefully, and examine well, before you judge. As I know by experience that a Jew is very apt to get angry in hearing proofs of Christianity, I beg you to keep calm, and let your mind examine before your heart yields to passion.

CHAPTER I.

RELIGION.

"The just shall live by his faith." HABAKKUK ii: 4.

To defend Judaism, or Christianity, with the principle of the so-called Rationalists, that is, the principle not to believe anything you cannot understand, is, according to my humble view, a thing impossible. I was not converted because I found out that Christianity must be true according to natural philosophy and metaphysics, because I comprehended the fundamental doctrines of Christianity by my reason; I only concluded that there must be something between man and God which my reason cannot comprehend; that my reason does not lead me to truth, or to happiness; that there is something necessary for human happiness which is above reason; and that, therefore, I cannot understand everything, and must have a belief.

Religion means *belief* in matters of God, the soul and eternity. As these subjects are above nature and above reason, we cannot understand, but must believe. Could everything necessary for human happiness be reached by reason, through science, then there would really be no need for religion at all. The schools would suffice, and the learned man must become perfect, while the common man, or the one with little brain, would be at a great disadvantage. Reason can only tell if there is any necessity for the acceptance of belief; if the things comprehensible do satisfy our souls, or if we must believe what is told to us about things incomprehensible and be guided by them, in order to have peace of soul and hope for a future. If reason ascertains that it is not sufficient of itself to make man happy, and that something supernatural, incomprehensible, is necessary for our happiness, then it has also ascertained that we must have a religion, that we must believe. It remains, now, for reason to discern if there is anything incomprehensible deserving our belief, and what we should believe.

If, again, human reason cannot supply us with the things necessary for our felicity. we must look for something which God supplies, that is, we must look for a religion from God; for, a religion not from God is not worth having; as we said that we must first find reason inadequate in order to look for a religion. Now reason must find the religion which God teaches. In short, reason tells first that we need a religion; second, that the religion must be from God; third, which religion is from God. But as soon as reason has ascertained that there is a religion from God, and this religion teaches things which are absurd, according to reason, contradictory according to logic, impossible according to the laws of nature, that can be no hinderance to accepting it, for

God is above reason, logic and nature. The incomprehensibilities can be no hinderance with a religion from God, as God himself is incomprehensible, and as we can only decide to embrace any religion because we see that the comprehensible things are not sufficient, and we look for an incomprehensible way to God.

Let us fall prostrate into the dust; let us bring our vain hearts and haughty minds down in humility; let reason be silent; let the laws of nature cease to work; let philosophy bashfully veil her face; let all the sciences give up their principles; let the universe tremble and listen, when the Lord God, the Lord of Hosts, the God of Israel speaks. And He speaks, speaks through his word, the Bible, and we must listen and believe,—even if we do not comprehend. Philosophy of *religion* can only show us our own spiritual impotence, and lead us to believe.

We do not say that we give up reason because we embrace an incomprehensible religion; nor do we believe anything really *against* reason. We cannot embrace any religion before reason tells us that it is true, that it is from God; but then we can believe God if even his word seems to be against reason. It appears only against reason because it is above it, and reason can easily find that there are things above it.

The efforts of the Jewish philosophers to reconcile the Bible with philosophy were not to prove the revelations a logical necessity, *i. e.*, that they must have happened according to the visible laws of the universe; but that a first cause, a free Being is above the laws of nature, who because above the laws of nature is above our comprehension, and whose revelations have occurred in spite of the visible laws of the universe.

God, as revealed in nature and history, cannot have divided the Red Sea and wrought other miracles which are against natural laws; but still the revelations and miracles are *historical* facts, and the Jewish philosopher believed them, not understood them. Why did he believe? Because the living Jewish nation, in whose presence the miracles were wrought, was a witness; because the marvelous preservation of that nation, against the laws of history, notwithstanding their scattered and persecuted condition, shows that the Bible which predicted their fate must be of divine origin; because the depravity of mankind, notwithstanding moral laws, convinces that mankind needs a supernatural revelation; and because the Bible, of itself, its power and influence, proves itself to be the word of God. The Jewish philosopher saw the conflict between Bible and science, and he only proved that there is something above, not against science and reason; consequently, the testimonies of the Jewish nation and their Bible are credible in spite of philosophy. For God's word needs not to be comprehensible in order to be credible; it is enough to know that God spake it in order to believe it.

So the Jewish philosopher admitted that God cannot be understood, and that He had revealed Himself and worked miracles not according to the laws of nature, but above them. He did not try to understand how it was possible that God should speak or should divide the Red

Sea, but he *believed* that God did speak and that the Bible was His word. Thus we find the old Jewish philosophers all believing, from Saadyah down to Mendelsohn.

It is true, that some introduced a sort of Rationalism into the Jewish theology, by trying to understand God's word, where it deals with God's mysteries, and to find natural reasons for his commandments. That was an inconsistency, and they failed. For if we cannot understand God and believe Him, we cannot understand what He says about Himself, but must accept God's revelations and commandments as they are, without reason. If everything God said was according to science, there was no necessity for His revelations. Had the prophets been teachers of metaphysics merely, then no prophecy was necessary for that. There are but two ways; either you believe and accept everything in the Bible, regardless of reason, or you reject and do not believe. If you believe you must admit that you believe God and He is incomprehensible, and if you again treat His word rationally then you are inconsistent. Just see Maimonides on the vision of Ezekiel about God's chariot (Maasseh Merkabah); is it not ridiculous? In his reasons for God's commandments he also failed. He takes the Talmudical terms, "Maasseh Merkabah," "works of the chariot," and Maaseh Bereshith, "works of the creation," or "beginning," as alluding to metaphysics and natural philosophy, which is an obvious mistake; for any one conversant with the Talmud must see that the Rabbis understood by the above-mentioned terms nothing but some Cabalistic mysteries, which they claimed to have traditionally received from the times of the prophets, and considering them very sacred traditions they committed them to only a very few chosen scholars. "Merkabah" and "Bereshith" was a kind of gnostic knowledge, and they expected that one who knew those mysteries could even work miracles, as they tell of some who understood the "works of creation"; that they created a calf on every Friday for the use of the Sabbath.

Maimonides believed the Bible at the same time that he thought everything could be understood by study. The way of perfection was with him the work of the brain. He was too rational for his belief, and therefore inconsistent. He tried to lift the sacred veil and to look upon the visions with the eyes of reason, and failed. Notwithstanding his orthodox belief, he laid the first foundation for the Bible-denying movement of this century. The germ was slumbering until this century, when the Jews of Germany, becoming acquainted with profane knowledge, cultivated what Maimonides planted, until that poisonous, demoralizing, anti-religious, Bible-denying system which they call Reform, grew up.

CHAPTER II.

THE JEWISH REFORM.

"For the wisdom of their wise men shall perish, and the understanding of their prudent men shall be hid." Is. xxix: 14.

I cannot accuse the Reformed Jews who followed the Rationalists of this century of being inconsistent in the sense in which I had accused Maimonides of being so. The reformers do not try to understand supernatural things, but they deny them. There is no necessity for them to enter into the visions, to understand all the Bible, as they do not believe it to be of divine origin. They think that they have found the true light; human reason and unbelief are their lights. That is really consistent, for if we must understand all we believe, then we cannot believe the Bible, as it is partly incomprehensible; and, as I will show below, it even contains absurdities according to human reason. With the Reformers the Bible is a venerable book, and they criticise it like any other ancient book. Miracles are legends and tales; Moses is a sort of Lycurgus; Aaron a Pope; David something like Alexander the Great; Isaiah the

Jewish Demosthenes; Jeremiah and all the prophets are only a kind of orators or bards (market singers). The source of Jewish theology is sought among the old Egyptians, and in an old Persian literature, which does not even exist. The Urim and Thumim become a kind of Delphinian oracle. The history of Israel is compared with that of Poland, and revelation is a kind of imagination. The Reformers would not even admit that Israel is dispersed for their sins, a thing which is so plainly predicted and taught by Moses and the prophets.

I speak of my own experience. I published articles in which I denied the Sinaitic revelation, the division of the Red Sea and all other miracles, but still I considered myself an adherent of the Old Testament. I thought I was a Jew and a Reformer. These my articles had the approval of every Reformed Jew, and even recommended me for the rabbinical office. That is the Reform, the consequence of refusing to believe anything which is not according to reason, if it is even taught in the Bible. So far the Reformers are consistent.

But on another point they are most absurdly inconsistent. For, what reason have they to keep up synagogues? In what respect are they Jews according to religion? In what respect can they even claim to have a religion if they depend on their own reason and morality only? They claim to be Reformers, but are rejecters of Judaism. God's chosen people they claim to be, and boast of a Bible which in reality they do not believe. What a God-chosen people is that, with whom Moses was a human law-giver, who even blinded his people by making them believe he could work miracles; Joshua and David generals, conquerors; the prophets, bards. What a Bible, with lies, and tales, and doctrines taken from the idolators. That is a horrible chosen people, but exactly according to the reform. If the Bible is not literally the word of God and our ancestors were not distingished by God's grace in speaking to them, then the Grecians and Romans were more chosen than the Israelites. They excelled us in generals, in conquerors, in philosophers, in poets and orators, in everything, if we deny God's revelation, and that he dwelt among us and worked supernatural miracles for us. Why are we chosen? You answer, that the Jews in their wandering might give the Bible to the nations. Firstly, the wandering and dispersion of the Jews is predicted by Moses and the prophets as a curse, a punishment to them, not that they were chosen for that; secondly, the Reformers do not believe the Bible themselves, and only talk about the blessing the nations received with their Bible. (Even the believing Jews do not read the Bible, with exception of the pentateuch; the learned ones study the Talmud, and consider it too trifling a matter to study the Bible.) Thirdly, where are the nations who received the Bible from the Jews? Those Jews only who came in the name of Christ have given and taught the Bible to the Gentiles, and such you do not consider as Jews. You Reformers say that you had the noble mission to teach monotheism to the Gentiles. Show me the Gentiles who listen to you. Wherever the Gentiles listen to the teachings of the God of

Israel it is in a Christian church; when they call to the one God of Abraham they are taught to do so by the apostles of Christ. When did the Jews, especially the Reformers, ever convert a nation to God? It is a sad fact, that the Jews were persecuted and driven away by the nations, not that they learned from them. On the contrary, they always despised their teachings. Where the Jews were tolerated they have surely not influenced the religious life of the Gentiles, nor do they influence it to-day. Secondly, according to the Jewish opinion, the nations do not believe in monotheism as long as they believe in a Trinity; consequently only those Gentiles who reject the Trinity are converted to monotheism. But it is a fact that such nations do not believe even the Old Testament, and deny Judaism as well as Christianity; besides, that they never learned their infidelism from the Jews.

Where are your Monotheists according to your doctrine? The German rationalists have not learned from you, but actually the Reformed Jews learned from them. Even the manner of explicating and criticising Scripture now adopted by the Reformers originated with the German infidels. You learned your reform from them. Consequently, the blessing God gave to Abraham, that in his seed all the nations of the earth should be blessed, is fulfilled in the seed of the old Teutons, not of Abraham. You ought to change the name of Abraham in the Bible for that of Herman, the Cherusksian's ancestor.

If, according to the doctrine of the Reform, it is only necessary to believe in one God, as he is revealed in nature and history, the God of reason, why is it that the world never came to that God without the Bible? For before Christ they were all idolaters. If God is only to be believed according to his revelation to reason, then surely he has not chosen Israel, as the Gentiles had greater philosophers. And why should he choose one nation? Where is the necessity to be Jews for this alone? What need is there of a Pentateuch for the God of the philosophers?

If your monotheism is the monotheism of philosophy, what connection have you with Moses? Did Moses bring any other proof for the existence of God but the miracles? Did he teach philosophy? In his exhortations he says, "Take heed that ye forget not the things which thy *eyes have seen.*" He reminds his people that God delivered them from Egypt with a strong hand, with signs and miracles. If he reminds us not to forget the miracles then we must believe them first.

Oh, the Reformers have forgotten what God has done for them. The God of Abraham and Moses is not the God of the Reformers and rationalists. The God of Moses and Abraham is an absurd, a cruel God in the eyes of rationalists. And you Reformers claim to be Jews while you are rationalists.

The Reformers also sometimes claim, it to be a Jewish mission to teach the world civilization, culture, humanity and other good things. Show me the nation civilized by Jewish teaching or influence; show me the Jewish schools and universities to teach mankind; show me the Jewish civilization and culture. If there is such a thing as a Jewish civilization, why are not the Jews of Africa like those of Germany? the Jews of Russia like those of France? History proves that even the heathen were more civilized than the Jews. And to-day we see in every country the Jews only civilized according to the civilization of the country they live in. What is the mission of the Jews, then?

The real Judaism, as it is handed down to you, is not the so-called Reform. Down to this century, and until a few years ago, you could find no single congregation, no single Rabbi teaching such a curious Judaism as you Reformers do. Judaism teaches that every word of the prophets must be believed, all the miracles and visions; that the law of Moses is obligatory upon every Israelite; that a Messiah will come to redeem Israel, as he is plainly promised in Isaiah, Jeremiah, Ezekiel, Hosea, Micah, Zechariah and Malachi. If you say that the promises of the Messiah are fulfilled in King Hezekiah, that could only be the case with the promises of Isaiah and Hosea. The other prophets lived even after the destruction of the temple, and they predict plainly that Israel's help will come out of the house of David, as I will show below. How can you claim to be an adherent of the Bible and not expect a Messiah? If you believe God spoke on Sinai why don't you keep the Sabbath? If you do not believe it, what makes you keep a sham Sabbath? What madness makes you circumcise your children, if you do not believe it to be literally true that God spoke to Abraham? And if you do believe it, how can you understand it upon rational principles? What few commandments you Reformers keep cannot be defended by reason, but by belief. Therefore, if a Reformer were consistent, he would either have nothing to do with the synagogue and Judaism, or accept the Bible and believe. Should a Reformer get tired of the inconsistency and change to be an orthodox Jew he cannot do it upon the ground that he finds Judaism agreeing with rationalism, but because he concluded to give up the so-called rationalism and believe the Bible; and so I concluded.

I concluded that the Bible is true, and my rationalism was folly, that it is Israel's mission not to teach philosophy, or civilization, or humanity, or science, but religion. Israel are only chosen for religious purposes, and their religion is in the Bible, and as long as they do not come up to their mission they are not true Israelites. Now I will show how I came to that conclusion.

CHAPTER III.

THE HEART'S STRUGGLES.

"And he went on frowardly in the way of his heart." Is. lvii: 17.

Once, in my youth, I was a zealous Jew. I believed every Rabbi, and my days and nights were devoted to talmudical studies. I tried to keep the rabbinical law, and labored anxiously to be good according to prescription. My heart was pressed, my soul in fetters, I never was satisfied. Who can keep all the law? And what I kept gave me no joy, no inner reward. What a life, whose end is death and judgment, and only a law for justification, and that law daily broken. With me a law to torture, before me death to terrify. What a burden! Always sighs and tears. God I knew from hearing, by reputation; I never felt him in my heart. I feared him and knew it was my duty to love him. I was born with religious propensities. As a young boy, I often wept bitterly before God. I wanted to be good, I wanted perfection. The Rabbis told me that the only way to acquire perfection before God, is an everlasting study of the Talmud, and the full keeping of the rabbinical code—that cold, frozen, crazy law.

"Study the Talmud," I heard when I opened my eyes in the morning, and "Study the Talmud," was reverberated in my dreams. "Be a learned Rabbi, then you are a holy man," I often heard and repeated. So that a man with much brain and talmudical knowledge I considered a holy man; the poor in spirit, and the humble, a child of hell. What a reverence I felt for a greatly learned talmudist. So I tried to pile much talmudical knowledge in my head, and with that I fulfilled the main religious duty. Of taming my passions I never thought. "The peevish man cannot be a school-teacher," is a proverb of the fathers, and as a Jewish school-teacher was not the one I envied, so there was no necessity to tame my naturally hot temper. "The jealousy of the learned increases the wisdom," is another proverb. So the teacher was glad to see his scholars vain about their good lessons, or jealous of those better than themselves. In order that my wisdom should increase it was necessary to have me vain and jealous! My heart grew wild, my passions entirely out of my control.

The utmost extremes of anger and passion never gave me any pangs of conscience, for I considered it no sin. It is indeed mentioned in the talmudical moral sayings, that wrath is like idolatry; but these moral sayings are not binding laws; especially if one has a good brain and is a good talmudical scholar, then it is immaterial what kind of a temper he has. To tell a lie, of course, was not right, but it is surely better to say a million of lies every day than to eat one piece of pork, or even to use the same utensil for milk which was used for meat before. Sometimes we must say lies any way, for there are a class of lies considered allowed, especially in business. The Talmud gives permission to tell lies for the sake of peace (mipne darke shalom).

I was also instructed that I must pray at certain hours. When the hour had passed I had lost my chance, and that was a fearful sin. To be sure, every prayer was from the prayer-book, written in Hebrew, and there are very, very few who understand that language; but still they must pray in Hebrew. Luckily enough I understood the Hebrew when I was very young. Before and after every thing you eat you must say a blessing, and before certain kinds of food you must also wash your hands. How often was I almost choked with a piece of apple, when reminded that I forgot to say the blessing, and then I said it quickly while the piece was in my throat. How many sad hours of unavailing penance embittered my youth, when I forgot an evening prayer, or a blessing before an apple, or a certain piece of prayer to be inserted at certain days or new moons. I never shall forget the terror and contrition I felt for carelessly taking one raspberry into my mouth on the anniversary of the destruction of Jerusalem, when I had to fast. I once forgot and carried my handkerchief in my pocket on the day of atonement, which is forbidden, because it is said "Ye shall carry no *load* out of your houses on the Sabbath day." I thought that I must surely die that very year on account of such a fearful sin.

So I labored under the law, until a little secular knowledge and the study of the old Jewish philosophers made me examine the Talmud with a critical eye; and I suspected, finally concluded, that the rabbinical law was not of divine but of human origin; that the spirit of the Talmud was not the one of the Bible. Love of the world and a wild temper made me break the law entirely and publicly; I studied now for the sake of knowledge. The rabbinical law was dead for me, and I partly despised those who had made it. But not even here did it end. The modern critics of the Bible made me treat the Bible as I would any other ancient book. I had no religion, and so made one for myself. I was a rationalist, a Reformer. The blood only made my nation dear to me; the influence of youth or the inner power of it made me love the Bible. But it was an inconsistency. I deceived myself. I never was satisfied with the spirit of the Jews, and had no right to claim to be a believer in the Bible, more than any reform Rabbi has.

The breaking of the law and the free criticism of it after a life of Jewish orthodoxy, looked like freedom. But I did by no means feel free. The soul is only free when it is subjected to God. In God is freedom. I was in business, and worked in the world, and also tried to enjoy it. I often even forgot myself in it, and lived not in accordance with my own principles. I did not maintain the position in society as I ought to have done. I made myself low with the low men of this world, who think themselves high. In short, I did not lead the life I was destined to lead by my education. I failed very much. But the most of my nights were taken up for reading and study. I was thinking almost incessantly.

I was not satisfied, I was miserable. I finally entered the Jewish ministry of this country. It became my business now to think and to study about the relations between man and God, and my misery increased. I believed in God, in an immortal soul, in judgment, and what did I have? The religious and spiritual condition of my people brought me to despair. I could feel and preach that we were bad, that we have no religion, but could I show the way how to be good? Who can? I praised the Bible, and perverted it. My heart told me I had no business with the Bible. What shall a Jew do with a Bible, when he sees that the law does not make him happy, or even better?

I got sick of the world, I felt miserable and sometimes I did not even know why. Is not every body unhappy? Is there not a certain yearning and longing after something unknown in every human heart? There is an aiming without an end. Who is happy? I also was considered good-hearted, honest, and to myself I said that I was a miserable wretch. Conscience always torments. Who has a perfectly clear conscience? Who does not complain of himself? Conscience is a more reliable judge than public opinion. We can hear mankind sighing; there is one sigh going through every human heart. Why?

Believing in God, I had good reason to fear him, to fear death, which brings me before his throne. I thought I saw the light, I was a rationalist; but did rationalism settle the account between me and my great all-loving, rihgteous Creator? I often thought I could die without fear, but when I saw others dying, or was myself sick,. then I felt a trembling soul in me. Let people boast about courage to die; everybody feels he must go before his God and trembles. We can see mankind tremble. What will be our end? Think!

Dear reader, ask your own heart. It will tell you whether I am wrong, whether I speak in accordance with your own heart. Are you happy? Is your conscience clear? Have you peace of soul and peace of mind? Is there peace between you and your God? Is your soul perfectly at rest? Can you meet death with a smile? Can you meet God's judgment without fear? Ask yourselves these questions. Perhaps some say they do not believe in God or in immortality, but just ask your heart. You will feel that you do believe, that you are miserable and tremble. Do not deceive yourself.

I was troubled, awfully troubled. I studied, and searched, and thought all the time, about the cause of human misery, and I will show you below that I found the real cause, and I hope you will find that I am right. I tried to be good, to improve my ways, I made the best resolutions. All in vain. The more I tried to be good, the worse I got. I found no rest for my soul. Weakness overcame good intentions, raging passions overpowered the best will. The spirit is willing, but the flesh is weak. Moral proverbs and the best intentions give no *power* to be good. I knew that I was bad but weak. Thus I was restless. Single good actions gave me no peace. I suffered fearfully. I had no aim but this world; I ran after it, and still I could find no satisfaction in it; I despised it.

Peace of heart and mind was my most ardent desire, was all I wanted. It became my constant prayer. But I prayed to the God of philosophy, and he does not hear; the God of nature has immutable, merciless laws. and is not engaged in hearing prayers; the God of history laughs you to scorn and says, "Reap what you sow."

Whenever I addressed the God of nature and history as the God of Israel; whenever I, the Reformer and rationalist, dared to pray to the God of Israel, then I felt I was a stranger to him. I was ashamed and frightened, for I saw the staff of Moses and heard the thunders of Sinai. The God of Israel is a terror to a rationalist, for he points to the Bible. Notwithstanding my treating and criticising the Bible as I would any other ancient book, it always exercised a great power over my heart, and I often, as if involuntarily, sought to find consolation in it.

CHAPTER IV.

THE BIBLE.

"The law of the Lord is perfect, converting the soul." Ps. xix, 7.

So I tried to make the Bible the refuge of my soul. It is always a relief for every burdened heart to read that Bible. Often it gave me consolation. But the ears of my soul were opened and heard the voice of God speaking from that book; I involuntarily examined whether I had the right system of explicating what the Bible says. Many commandments appeared to me binding forever, and I did not keep them. Moses spoke decidedly in the name of God; so that it suffers no spiritual interpretation. Some commandments are against common sense, against humanity and cannot be defended by reason, or justified because of the olden time. Especially the doctrine of the Divinity as taught by Moses is entirely different from what philosophy teaches. I saw that we must simply accept mysteries, if we accept the Bible, for Moses' monotheism is a mysterious one. I used to think I spiritualized the miracles because I took them to be poetical expressions. The old Jewish bard related the facts of

Israel's history in the form of a miracle. That method I, like all the reformers, learned from the German Gentiles, but in reading the Bible, *feeling* it as the word of God, we lose the appetite for such reformed explanations, especially as we see the language is too prosaic, the description of the miracles too specific. For instance, the miracle with the manna can either be taken as a natural phenomenon, or a tale, if we do not accept a miracle. But the Bible says that every one had an omer per head, no matter if he gathered more or less, and that it bred worms if left for the next day, except for the Sabbath day. [Ex. xvi.] And besides that, Moses reminds his people of the miracles they saw, and gives it as the only proof for the existence of God and his providence. We also find in the latter ages of the Bible that the historian mentions the miracle of the manna. The Psalmist reminds Israel of the fact that God gave them manna.

We must, then, take it as a fact—as something supernatural, but a fact. It can not be poetry, but either a lie, in which case the Bible is the meanest of humbugs, or a fact, and then it is the word of God. Again, the Bible tells us that when many Israelites died because they were bitten by serpents, Moses, by God's command, made a brazen serpent, that the one who was bitten might be healed by looking at it. Reformers consider this a tale. But we find in the Bible that many centuries after Moses, King Hezekiah destroyed that very brazen serpent, because the Israelites worshiped it as an idol. Could Hezekiah destroy a serpent which existed in a tale only? The most radical rationalist, like Mr. Strauss, would say that the Israelites made up the tale; because the serpent was found, therefore they said that Moses made it by the command of God. Thus the serpent made God's command, not the command the serpent. But if we say so, then we deny the Bible entirely, and have no part in Israel whatever; and if the Israelites were not deceivers, then they were fools, in keeping such a Bible. And still the Bible had such an influence as to make the most civilized heathen accept it, and through it believe in one God, a thing which the philosophy of a Socrates, Plato and Aristotle did not accomplish. Besides this, I could not reject the Bible entirely, for the reason I will show in the next chapter. And if I should accept the infidel method of explaining the occurrence with the brazen serpent, what must I do with the manna? There are numerous miracles related in the Bible which can not possibly be explained [rationally, even with the method of Strauss, and they are so related that we must either believe them to be facts, and then we believe in incomprehensible miracles, or if we do not believe we must in consequence reject the Bible and despise it beyond any written book. That the Bible can only be either a made-up humbug or the word of God, is a fact which no *really* rational man can deny.

After I had such a conviction about the Bible, I was very much troubled, and even in despair. Where am I? A minister of a Reformed Synagogue, who does not keep a single word of the law, and that Bible literally true? What is my rationalism good for, then? I became wavering in my mind, and I still had ideas of giving up religion and the Bible entirely. For I saw that there was no way between, but either to believe more than I liked to, or nothing.

Naturally, men are inclined to go after the world and the flesh. Every man makes up a kind of a philosophical system of his own, because he would rather consider himself free than bring his neck under the yoke of the Bible. It is only a very weak voice of the heart which makes him still hold on to a shade of religion, which voice is the propensity of the poor struggling soul. This is also the case with the Jewish Reformers; they go after the inclination of the heart, hating the yoke of religion, religion is not a matter of much consideration with them. No one of the so-called Reformed Jews ever reads the Bible, or thinks of examining it. They know nothing of it, save as an abstract of Biblical history which they learned as children. Still they choose to be Reformers, in order to be able to go freely after their hearts' desires, and not to be troubled by religion. They keep up a synagogue, (which they very seldom visit,) in order to pacify their soul's desire for a religion, and they make themselves believe that attention to business in order to support their families is all their Creator demands of them. So was I also somewhat disposed to give up the Bible, go into business, and be a free-thinker.

CHAPTER V.

THE WANDERING JEW.

" Ye are my witnesses, saith the Lord. " Is. xliii, 10.

As I said, I was tempted to reject the Bible entirely. But I could not do it. I examined my heart, the Bible and the history of my people, and the result was, that I could not reject the Bible.

Doubting whether I should reject all belief in supernatural things, and give up the Bible, according to the infidel principle in which I am posted, I met that old man who is commonly known under the name of " Wandering Jew." I spoke to him about the troubles of my heart and mind. " It is pretty hard to believe anything against reason, against science," said I. "Science is exact and sure, you can rely on it, but supernatural things always seem to be doubtful. We must always prefer a certain thing to an uncertain. How can a man believe, in this enlightened century, after such heroes of the scientific world. If anybody does believe, he is considered a fool or a hypocrite. 'Attend to your business,' is the common motto of every one of my people. I am especially very much troubled now about the new method of using the Bible. According to the latest discoveries, for example, the Bible ought to be taken quite differently from the way in which they used to take it. They used to take it as it is, now the world is advanced; they have meat extract, and milk extract, and they also have *Bible extract.*

"That Bible extract is a very saleable article in this country, and also in Germany. Our people, the Jews, buy it. They do not use it, but they pay for it. Every Jew in this country speaks of it; they call it also reform. They mostly import it from Germany. There is a man there, a wholesale spiritual druggist and chemist; his name is, translated into English, 'Fiddler.' He is a splendid spiritual chemist; by chemistry he can make almost every spiritual thing; and he sells it for genuine. He makes religion and manufactures history. Many who understand the business accuse him of using a surrogate, called hypothesis, for history. He recommends the extract of Bible highly.

"Also in this country there are manufacturers of extract of Bible, and they say it all agrees with science, and the beauty of it is, it gives those who take it no trouble whatever. The shops where Bible extract is sold are only open on Saturday. You know this is the business day. Almost all the Jews pay their money, but do not even take the trouble to go and look at the article. They call it humbug, themselves, and still pay for it. When you ask them, 'If Bible-extract is humbug, why do you pay for it? why do you not rather buy Bible by the pound?' they answer you, 'Bible by the pound is out of fashion; we want to be fashionable according to the time, and are Reformers.'

"Honest dealers in Bible by the pound are rare, but there are plenty selling the extract. There are very many of them unfit for the business, and have a bogus article. Many never learned the business, but because they can sing a little, or they have a good pronunciation, and wear spectacles, or because they understand French or another language, they think they are able to manufacture and sell extract of Bible. Their own customers trouble them awfully, for they neither respect them nor their article. If a little dealer has sixty customers, every one wants an article of his own, and usually a customer who does not understand the goods can never be satisfied; and those able, genuine little dealers suffer more trouble than the one with his singing, spectacles and French. You have no idea what the poor extract seller suffers from his customers. If he is not pliable, like a Jesuit, but does stick to a principle, then he is surely lost. The customers do not care for a real honest man, but he must please them. The dealer again despises the customers in return, and suffers everything from them, so long as they pay.

"There are also some leading men in that business, the most of whom are able, and they mainly work for fame, for they are extremely ambitious and want great names. So they are very jealous and hateful to one another, always in the name of the Almighty. They all sell a manufactured article; none gives Bible by the pound, and still every one most zealously *protests* against the article offered by the others. What is the difference, if none is genuine?

"Well, excuse me, Mr. Wandering Jew, for getting off my topic. I thought it might interest you," continued I, "but I want you to give me your candid opinion about believing supernatural things and miracles. I am inclined not to believe at all, and since that Bible-extract flourishes, people do not believe any way. Why should we deceive ourselves. Rather let us give up everything."

Old Mr. Wandering Jew smiled, and then looked seriously; he looked in my face and I saw something like pearls in his eyes. "My son," said he,—he always calls me "son" and I love him like a father. "My son, thou knowest me well, dost thou?"

"Certainly I know you," I replied, weeping. "Your language is my language, your people are my people; you are my bone and my flesh. Your name was dear to me from my childhood. I learned to love you from my cradle. I love you more dearly than my own life. You are suffering, poor old man. I wish I could give my life a ransom for you, dear old man. You have such a kind, noble heart, and look so venerable, but still are suffering, restless and low."

"Be quiet, my son;" answered he, "wipe thy tears, and let me tell thee my own story. The story of my life will teach enough about what men ought to believe.

"I am old, very old, and have seen different days, and expect a glorious future yet. But my sorrows and troubles are not undeserved. I am the son of a nobleman; my blood is the purest and noblest on earth. I was brought up under the special care of the mightiest king of the world, and even to-day he protects me and often saves me from entire destruction, when I am attacked by enemies. This king loves me, for my father's sake; my father belonged to his court and was a most faithful servant.

"One day the king made me a present; a very precious present it was. Though it is neither gold nor silver, nothing of pecuniary value, yet still it is of the greatest blessing. It is the simple, spiritual food you spoke about, the Bible; not in extract, but, as you call it, by the pound. The king told me that if I should use it pure, unadulterated, it would give me everlasting happiness. I promised to do so. But alas! I often neglected the king's command, and ate the food of my neighbor, and came to trouble; until the king got tired of my conduct and drove me from the land. Again he had compassion with me and let me return. After I was home again I never went after other meals to leave Bible entirely out, but I adulterated the Bible. I mixed and seasoned it with what people call traditions. That article does not grow, but it is manufactured. I also mixed with it ordinances, to give it strength.

"In short, I so prepared Bible that it tasted no more like Bible, but it became a hash, called Talmud; no longer to be recognized as Bible. Many people disputed the propriety of using Bible at all, for there were always philosophers making spiritual food according to science, and they called Bible old fashioned food. But I never cared for their talk, as I received the Bible from that great, faithful king myself. Now, in consequence of my using that Talmud hash my constitution changed and I became bad. The king sent servants to exhort me but I maltreated and even killed the servants and did a great deal of mischief. The result was that the king drove me away from home; and so I am a wanderer ever since.

"My troubles were beyond imagination. People used me cruelly and tyranically; they mocked and scourged me, imprisoned and burned me; they tortured and plagued me. They opened my veins and drank my blood, yes the very blood of my heart. Any other living being would have died from the smallest part of my sufferings, but, wonderfully enough, I live, and shall live. Is not my existence supernatural? It is that very Bible, although I use but little of it, which cures me and keeps me alive. As long as there is a grain of Bible in me I cannot die, and the king promised me a glorious future.

"Now, my son, mark this: whenever you are tempted not to believe the supernatural power of the Bible, think of me. If there was no supernatural power in the Bible, my bones would long ago have rotted in an unknown grave. These very men of science and critics, who work to make Bible extract, would reject Bible altogether as old fashioned, as the world has done with many old fashioned things, but for the fact that a supernatural power holds our people to it, even if they do not use it, and do not follow the king's will. Look at me, and use the Bible. I testify to its genuineness, and my troubles, and the most wonderful preservation of my life, are the unanswerable evidence.

"Science has nothing to do with supernatural things. I, the supernatural man, have received the Bible direct from the king, and the world got it through my hands. I was the sole agent for that article. Use it, and think of me and the great king."

That living miracle, Wandering Jew, went his way; I noticed that his road is different from other men's roads. He seems to be led by something invisible, for such roads nobody but he can pass. He overcomes all obstacles and leaps over precipices, swims through rivers of blood, and crosses lakes and oceans. He is a marvelous man. Who can reject the Bible after looking at Wandering Jew? And everybody sees that wonderful man, every one knows him; his way is marked in the annals of history ever since history began its record.

CHAPTER VI.

THE NEW TESTAMENT.

"A new heart also will I give you, and a new spirit will I put within you, and I will take away the stony heart out of your flesh, and I will give you a heart of flesh. And I will put my spirit within you and cause you to walk in my statutes, and ye shall keep my judgments, and do them." Ez. xxxvi: 26, 27.

It is obvious that Wandering Jew's history is the most forcible evidence in behalf of the Bible, but how could I really believe, as there is a law in the Bible, and that law is surrounded by Rabbis with their Talmud? Could I become an orthodox Jew again? I would not reject the Bible, nor would I really accept it on account of a law being no remedy for my heart. For if I did accept the law, with the Talmud or without it, I knew from experience that law does not make happy. If I even do believe the Bible, and take it as God's Word, I do not find the solution of the problem of life; my heart and soul suffer as before, notwithstanding the Bible. I was in perfect despair.

So I lived for a time without any hope of finding rest. I feared that I should become crazy, or commit suicide. Daily I became more restless, my passionate temper grew worse, my uneasiness increased. My sole aim was to get the question of religion out of my mind. But while I was hopeless, Providence had other plans for me.

By accident I happened to read the New Testament. I formerly had read it, but with the same spirit as I would read a novel. I admired Christ's character as a man. His teachings, mildness and sufferings tended to pacify my soul. I never thought of the possibility of my becoming converted. Who would think of such a thing? I considered myself too acute, too wise to believe such impossibilities. Indeed, I pitied a Christian for his belief, and despised a converted Jew beyond anything. A Jew thinks it is impossible for an intelligent man to believe Christianity, and suspects all intelligent Christians of not being sincere, especially the Christian ministers. It is commonly supposed that a Jew never confesses Christianity but for base motives, as he cannot possibly believe.

Neither was I directly prompted to believe. I did not even think of the Christian articles of belief. But the words and the life of Christ impressed me more deeply than ever before. Every word he said found its echo in my heart; in his life I saw the only way to be good, to be relieved of troubles, the misery of heart and soul. I was miserable, restless, I did not know why; consequently I could find no way of relief. In him I saw a perfect man; nothing can make him miserable; why? Because he is entirely given to God. Therefore I saw that my misery must be on account of my being so far away from God. My eyes were opened. I saw I was sinning, not on account of the law, not because I did not keep certain things, but on account of my life; my whole being, my inner part, my heart, my soul, my thoughts and my words, my motives and principles, my all, not being prompted by subjection to God, but by self. I found too much "I" about me. My conception of sin changed entirely. I saw that men do not only commit sins, but live them. I found that I could live a sin while doing nothing wrong. The sin comes out of my own *self*. Every thing I want, I desire, makes me miserable, for the want and the desire are of "self," while I ought to be subjected to the "All." Also the objects of the desires are perishable, and there is something eternal in man, which needs things eternal for its satisfaction. Depending on myself, my heart revolted on account of every unfulfilled desire, and I was restless, and a rebel against the source of all being, God. Now, the Bible is the word of God, and still could not help me out of my troubles, because it only told me what to do, and not what I should be. *My* deeds cannot satisfy me because they are *my* deeds, and, as I said, I felt that the sin is not so much in my doings as in my being, in the center of my heart. I am in enmity with God because I am "I," a separate individuality from the "All," which is God. And peace is only in the harmony with the "All," therefore in the subjection to God. The very consciousness of the earthly "self" is rebellion against God; therefore selfishness excludes love, for love is the something which makes all *One*. Thus the word "monotheism" is the best translated with "love." But Christ showed me how to get rid of sinful *self* by subjecting it to God. When I have offered myself entirely to Him nothing can trouble me any longer. If I go to the source of all being and learn to love Him and let His will be mine, then how can anything disturb my happiness, while I know that whatever befalls me, whatever *is*, is His will, as He is the source of everything. If I am satisfied with God, then I am satisfied with everything, for *He* is everything. There is an everlasting consolation, for the most lovely Christ suffered so much and still He is . . . . . He. There is an everlasting hope, which is God.

So by reading the New Testament my heart gradually changed. I not only found the way, but also the strength, to be better. The thought of God, the feeling of His presence, goodness and love, which anybody must perceive in contemplating Christ, gave me the strength to surrender everything for God. I partly lost my peevishness and hot temper. There was something to tame me. There came over me a mildness, through looking at the mildness of Christ. I became quieter, calmer. If anything happened to irritate me I thought of Christ; in any trouble and suffering I thought of his troubles and sufferings. The God of Israel, that revealed mysterious God of holiness, who dwelt in the Cherubim in the midst of a chosen people, became something more of a reality to me. I was the more enabled to believe in a God of miracles, since Christ was devoted and subjected to that God. The result of the perfect belief and subjection to that God, I saw, was a character like that of Christ; consequently I found that belief in the Bible can give perfection, and happiness,

and peace of soul. The belief of the Orthodox Jew
never kindled my heart to believe and to love; I even
despised the Jewish orthodoxy. I never found that the
Jewish orthodox belief could make the man better.
Thus I went astray and became a Reformer. But here I
saw that belief can make one something like Christ. I
could see a purpose in believing, namely, subjection to
and peace with God. I always believed in God, but the
life of Christ impressed me so as to engage my mind
seriously and incessantly with Him. I always believed with my mind; but Christ's example enabled
me to believe with my heart. I also received another, milder conception of God. God became the
object of my love. I found that I never could love God
before. Maimonides and all Jewish philosophers and
moralists say that a man must strive to love God; as to
love God is the highest measure of a religious life.
Their precept for attaining that measure is to be a perfect Talmudist, and especially to keep everything of the
rabbinical codex without fail; and then they say it is
necessary to be a great philosoper and to *comprehend*
God's mysteries. In short, they say it is necessary to be
very highly learned in order to love God. Learning is
the way of perfection. I had kept the codex and had
learned a little. Yet neither the keeping of the law nor
the little learning ever brought my heart nearer to the
God of Israel, nor did it enable me to become better
and govern my passions, or to love God. But now I felt
that I could love God. Christ's life taught me how to
do every thing which I could not do before. All I had

to do was to imitate Christ, and he drew me by his example. I never thought yet of accepting the Christian belief, I had not the least idea of doing it; but, in place of pitying a Christian for his belief, I commenced to envy him for it. I found that he is happy to be born a Christian and able to believe.

All those with whom I was in daily intercourse noticed that a singular change had come over me. My mother remarked to me that she saw a help of God, as I seemed to become a better and quieter man. I never noticed so much of my change as others did.

Deep sighs came out of my breast, but they were no longer the sighs of misery, but of contrition. I longed and yearned, but I knew that it was for my Creator. God engaged now not only my mind, but also my heart. I pressed nearer to Him in love.

At the same time, I found it strange that Christ was so much misunderstood in Israel. As I realized that Christ was the holiest man, the one nearest to God of all men who ever lived; as his whole aim and life was to do the will of his Father in heaven, and his Father in heaven is the God of Israel, why do Israel consider him as the enemy of their religion? While I found Him to be the purest being, my orthodox people look upon him and his church as the source of spiritual uncleanness. Since he teaches such a subjection to the one God of Israel and draws to Him by love, and imbues the heart of his disciples with such a love for that God, how is it that his disciples are of the Gentiles, and Israel is without that principle of Christ which seemed to me the only way to God? I could no longer doubt that true Christians must be a good deal happier and nearer to God than a man can be with every shape of Judaism. Christianity teaches God, and I, with all my people, always considered it to be the world, the flesh, with a few dogmas. I saw that Christ's doctrine is necessary for man's happiness, and how is it that Christ is not considered our greatest, dearest prophet? The Jews are undoubtedly a chosen people, but I always thought, and so every single Jew thinks, that everything is not right in Israel. Every Jew complains about the Jews, and finds fault with them. The very fact that Christ is so misunderstood by the Jews, and considered unclean, is a proof that the Jews must be wrong in the matter of religion.

How is it possible that a man should influence the world so much, and destroy so many religions of the heathen, without any supernatural power? Why do all the civilized world accept Christ's religion, and through that the Jewish Bible, while the Jews refuse Christianity, and, as they say, on account of that very Bible, and still do not live in accordance with it? How is it possible that the writers of the New Testament should not have pure motives when they taught such elevating morals?

Such questions arose in my mind and caused me very much thought without any result; but I daily got stronger in my convictions that I cannot be good and happy, that I cannot find peace and rest of soul, without Christ and his teachings, for he is the only one leading to God. It is very natural, also, that the farther I felt myself from God, and the deeper I was convinced of my sinfulness, the more admiration, thankfulness and love I felt for the one who showed me the way and led me to God by his own life and sufferings. Moreover, as my reason could not find the solution of the above questions, I had to give myself entirely up to that One who can make me happy. - So I thought no more, but felt. I cared no more to know anything. I despised my own reason. For after I saw, that with all his thinking, with all modern discoveries, and with all the joys of earth, a man could be so very miserable, and in an entirely self-denying life, like Christ's, there was such a delight, such a perfection, such an ineffable loveliness and happiness, what good could my reason afford me then? My reason always told me that Christianity was idolatry; but how could I believe that an idolatrous religion could draw to the one God of Israel so much? I could no longer doubt that if one is a true Christian he surely fears and loves the God of Israel more than any Israelite in the world was able to do. Now, since I saw that the object of Christianity was the fear and love of God, and I had more belief in the Bible and less confidence in reason, I began to doubt whether it was not a mistake to consider Christianity idolatry. I knew many passages of Scripture which the Christians cite in evidence of Christianity; but as I was sure Christianity must be idolatry, any answer of the Jews and other unbelievers satisfied me. I even used to say that some passages must mean Christ, but if a prophet teaches Christianity I do not believe him either; for I considered Christianity to be idolatry. But now these Scripture passages caused me many a pang. A year before I had already preached in the synagogue that many Gentiles were better than the Jews. How near then was the thought to me that the Jews might be mistaken, and ought to accept Christianity. How painful are such thoughts to a Jew, who has all his life despised a converted Jew more than anything. At the same time I did not as yet see how Christianity was not idolatry. As I said, I did not want to think any more, but resolved to imitate Christ. Until one day, tired and weak, looking for spiritual and bodily rest, and thinking of my worldly and spiritual troubles, I looked up to God and, after a deep sigh, said involuntarily, "Jesus Christ, my Redeemer." I was astonished at myself. I felt as if I was coming out of myself, and becoming another man. For a moment I feared that I was out of my reason, but was still more astonished at the great delight the words gave me. They were sweet to my mouth, a balm to my heart, and light to my eyes. It was to me an entirely giving up of myself and believing God, without regard to mind or understanding. I was satisfied that Christ was my Redeemer, no matter if I understood it or not. I surrendered the arms of rationalism before God, and in that I felt that my spiritual troubles were taken from me, for I cast myself entirely upon God. It is no little sacrifice for a Jew, especially a minister and a rationalist, to accept Christianity, even in his own heart; the belief in the cross is a cross for the body and mind, it is the deepest humiliation before God, it is sorely self-denying

I repeated the words, "Jesus Christ, my Redeemer,"

many a time, for they gave me much delight. A voice in my heart asked me whether I wanted to be an idolater; I had only the answer that it could not be idolatry, as I knew, and consequently God knows, that I only meant to do the will of the One God of Abraham, and that is all Christianity wants me to do. I also thought of the Scripture passages which predict Christ, and saw that there was no necessity to accept queer interpretations when the simple meaning of Scripture so perfectly agrees with what I felt and knew was true, and leading to God. Indeed, I knew that I now really believed the Old Testament and saw that it was a gift of God; now I understood its aim. I also felt that I really did love God as a Father, in a way I never could before.

I never realized what the aim of religion was until I felt that I was reconciled to God through the belief in Christ. Now I understood that it was worth having a religion, and that its aim to reconcile to God is a reality. I felt it, I saw it. It appeared to me now as the only aim of the Old Testament; and my joy at finding that aim was beyond description. I could perceive, now, how David found such a delight in loving God. As I found that Christ was true, I also found my sins were covered in his love; I felt less of my selfishness in loving his selflessness. There is a pardon unto eternal life in loving his life. In finding that in his life lies the life of the world, I consequently also realized that I had been under the sentence of death before. Thus a culprit pardoned under the gallows cannot feel such a joy, for he was about to lose only the short life of this world. And this assurance of being pardoned seems to me to be a *supernatural* power influencing the heart. It is a feeling of safety which no reasoning can give or disturb. And as this feeling of safety and joy was a thing I never anticipated, it made me exceedingly amazed. It is really wonderful. I perceived an assurance of the grace and love of God, and realized the truth of religion, as if God had spoken to me in words.

The thought of being redeemed by the grace of God, and by a way which I always used to consider folly and even idolatry, engaged my mind all the time for many weeks. All nature seemed to me changed and covered with a veil of poetry. Sun, moon and stars seemed to notice me and to look at me with smiling glances, rejoicing in sympathy over my redemption. The heavens seemed to be lowered and coming nearer to me; the wind and the water seemed to speak to me, whispering love. None can imagine that happiness save one who has experienced it; everything looked loving and lovely.

I shall not dwell on other Christian experiences, for which may the Lord keep my heart always thankful. The struggles of my heart before God gave me the courage to confess Christ publicly. What I sacrificed, suffered and still suffer, I shall not undertake to describe. The Jews do not believe it and the Christians cannot imagine it. I had to ruin myself concerning this world. I made my name a subject of hatred and contempt. The grief I caused my mother and nearest relatives is harder than death for me.

My attachment and hope for Israel as a nation is

stronger than anybody can believe; God knows how willingly I would die for His people and suffer everything for their felicity. It is truly not a little thing to leave a circle of dear friends, and to go among strangers, to be a subject of indifference and even suspicion. I stand alone in the world, and am subjected to all sorts of abuses and derision. Oh! I am alone, alone, forsaken and shunned by men; I am alone! "Fear not the reproach of men, neither be afraid of their revilings." Is. li: 7. I have lost nothing, after all; for this world I shall overcome; it is not worth grieving for. And of religion there is none with my people. Jewish orthodoxy is ridiculous and the reform an arrogant wickedness. Would the Jews only not misunderstand Christianity they would surely accept it. One who would do the will of God and reads the Bible, will soon find out who sent Christ into the world. Christ said, "My doctrine is not mine, but his that sent me. If any man will do his will, he shall know of the doctrine, whether it be of God or whether I speak of myself." John vii: 17.

In his mind a man can never be converted; if the heart does not search the truth and yearn to God and change entirely, then he will surely never see the truth. "Verily, verily, I say unto thee, except a man be born again, he cannot enter into the kingdom of God." John iii: 3.

From what I have stated, it is obvious that I was not converted because I found out that Christianity was in agreement with my reason, but because I discovered my own weakness, and felt that my only strength is in belief. My heart was restless with my reasoning and found rest in believing. My soul languished; it yearned for something I knew not myself. In Christ I found living water for my thirst, living water in the wilderness, and I could not refuse it. I accepted it without asking the mind's counsel. Could a man in a wilderness, when he is near perishing with thirst, think much when water is offered to him? I found the world cold, empty and dark, and the only light is with the God of Israel, to whom Jesus Christ is the only way. I embraced Jesus Christ's religion for the sake of the God of the Israelites, who is the God of Jesus; for no other reason. I accepted the belief when I could no longer resist. My heart believed before my mind could, until thinking and a close examination of Scripture satisfied the mind of the truth of Christianity, as I shall try to show in the following chapters.

CHAPTER VII.

HUMAN DEPRAVITY.

"The imagination of man's heart is evil from his youth." GEN. viii: 21.

In relating my experience in the last four chapters, I have spoken of the sufferings of the human heart, Judaism and Christianity subjectively, that is, according to my own experience. It is my intention now to treat the same topics objectively, and more extensively.

It is an indisputable fact that every human heart yearns after a something unknown, after a happiness which seems to be unattainable. There is a certain ideal aiming with every man, of which he has no clear definition. There is a consciousness of a relationship with the universe, with the unbounded "All," a kind of moral magnetism, attracting every soul, and in which the consciousness of its own individuality seems to be weakened. After certain sublime perceptions, men often feel something like a desire to embrace all the universe. We may also call it an insatiable desire to love, without finding the object for it, for we see that even the most tender and pure mutual human love does not satisfy that desire; on the contrary, increases it. This yearning, or desire to love, is always awakened by contemplating the beauty and wisdom which are manifested in creation. A beautiful landscape seen by moonlight, a deep glance into the starry heavens, often elicits sighs of longing. Also in man's bereavements, when he is troubled and forsaken, his ideal longing is awakened, and his heart is opened and made more susceptible of that hidden and covered love. Every man pondering and meditating upon this finds himself dissatisfied, even unhappy, for he finds out that he wants something he cannot obtain.

Nor can it be denied that man's own conscience is his perpetual accuser. Who is satisfied with himself? Who can examine his own heart without finding reason for complaint and sighs? Who can say, "I am innocent"? Where is the man who has no reason to be sorry for some of his thoughts, feelings and actions? We often even try to be good, and it is of no avail.

The consequence is a fear of death, for who can die perfectly satisfied with his own life, without pangs of conscience for the past, without fearing what is to come? Who has to anticipate only good fruit from what he has planted, and not to fear the poisonous fruits of his bad seeds? Even if some say, "I do not know what is to come, and therefore do not trouble myself about it," still he *is* afraid and *does* trouble himself about the future when he feels it approaching. Man feels that he is immortal, he anticipates something after death. If his head denies it, his heart still feels it. An immortal being slumbers in every human breast. What would conscience be if there was no future? The fact that man has a conscience is a sufficient proof that he perceives his responsibility for his bad deeds in a future life. Conscience is only an anticipation, by feeling, that a judgment is to come. If there was no future and judgment, then conscience would be only a foolish spleen, which we ought to resist.

What we have said about man is enough to make us conclude that he is born to be unhappy; but we shall find other sources of human unhappiness, and that through his weakness his unhappiness increases to misery. "No man dies having half of his desires fulfilled," is a true proverb of the Talmud. There is not only the ideal longing disturbing the happiness of the heart, but the everlasting, insatiable desire for earthly things and lusts causes the deepest misery. Indeed, the carnal wishes cause far more trouble, while they disturb the peace of conscience.

Men chase after carnal pleasures, after riches, honor, and sensual charms. To reach these things they even do many things wrong. Conscience pierces them, for they know their wrong. Who does not love the truth? but who is perfectly truthful? If one finds the other untruthful he despises him, and forgets his own untruthfulness. The wrong of another provokes you; are you yourselves perfectly just?

The soul says, Do no wrong; the flesh wants its lust; man listens to the flesh, and the poor soul speaks with the voice of conscience.

Soul and body demand meat and drink; man responds

to the body, but the soul is left hungry and thirsty. "What they love" both claim; body receives its desires, and poor soul is forsaken; alone she sits in a corner of the heart, and sheds hot tears, which burn like live coals, and kindle a fire in the breast, and man understands no more his soul's wish; he does not recognize the voice of his dearest. It pants, and boils, and rages, and burns; man knows not what he wants. Driven by a restless heart he runs into the wilderness, that we call world. Here he expects to find cooling and rest in the world's goods. He is rich, he has enjoyed life. Has he found rest? Is he happy? The heart is hollow, the fire has increased, and the desire is stronger after living water; but he misunderstands his restlessness and runs still farther into the world. In place of cooling water for a languishing soul he takes more fiery drinks. And he is never, never satisfied. The more he has, the more he wants.

So years of enjoyment pass and leave no satisfaction, but a hollow, raging heart, and a soul with stains and spots. Past enjoyments are like a past intoxication, leaving nothing but misery. The dishonest hand digs its fingers deep into its own heart, when taking goods unjustly; in speaking falsehood one breathes a stinking fog which cleaves to the soul; sensual intoxication causes an everlasting spiritual headache. Every thing springing from carnal motives wounds man's spirit. The joy of the body is the sorrow of the soul, the uneasiness of the heart. The insatiable flesh leaves the soul languishing.

Man, feeling his misery, and not knowing how to

remove it, tries to cover, to hide it. He thinks of his own imagined or real merits and acquirements, and becomes conceited. Then he wants others to think and speak of them as he does, and is vain. The more lie the more vanity; the more inward dirt the more desire for outward shine. So he not only says lies, but acts and lives them.

Now comes the consequence of relying on vanities. The world's goods are not equally divided. Riches, strength and beauty, fame and honor, even gifts like brain and talents, science and arts are possessions, and unequally divided. Some gifts are acquired in the world, and some are given by nature. The learned man is not a better man on account of his learning or ability. The doctor is not justified before God more than the laborer. As to the man's real "I" every one is alike, every thing is given to them. Therefore, in his individuality each one considers himself as good as the other. Man's brain and talent and wisdom leave him at the hour of death, as well as his riches and beauty. So the one who relies on perishable gifts has reason to be jealous and to envy the other. Why should I not be so rich, so honored, so famous, so smart as the other? The school children already envy and hate the best scholar; the little merchant envies and hates the bigger one. The men of learning exhibit more jealousy and hatred the more learned and the better known they become. Ambition, envy and hatred prevail among the famous statesmen, and have been the cause of many wars.

Fame, an immortal name, is the highest attainment.

But the immortal name cannot make you happy, as it is with perishable creatures. It is an honor to be spoken well of by men; are these men less miserable than you are? Can things perishable give everlasting satisfaction? Therefore the rich, the honored and famous men are as miserable as the poor, the despised and the unknown. All around us are whitened sepulchers.

If what I have said about men is true (and I do not believe a man who is honest with himself will try to dispute it), then we see that men are weak and do not listen to the voice of their soul until they know no more what their soul wants. It is obvious, then, that the cause of human misery is the flesh, and as no one can resist it entirely, therefore no one has a perfectly clear conscience, and therefore death is a terror to mankind. Of the object of man's unknown longing and love we shall speak again below.

The human weakness is termed, in the religious language, "human depravity," man's moral disease. The power of the flesh, which causes it, is personified and called "Satan." Men are weak, and the more they go after the flesh the less they can resist it; so the religious man says, "men are sinners." Some Jewish Reformers, not denying the existence of such experiences as we have described, say *this* is religion: Man's perception of affinity with the "All," his ideal longing and anticipation of a future, and his conscience, are the religion given by God. They say this is the law God wrote with his own finger in every human breast; this is revelation. Thus they deny every other revelation. So I used to say myself, and expressed it through the "Deborah." This is the principal doctrine of the radical Reformers. Truly the above described experiences of the human heart are the proof that man needs a religion, that he has a propensity for it. Man's conscience and ideal longing are caused by the voice of his soul, and show that he is susceptible of everything good, and yearns after it without attaining it. This is the symptom of the moral disease. If we take this to be the religion, then we take the sickness for the medicine, for the cure itself. For if this were all the religion God gave, so that He gave it with the human nature, and men are born with their religion, then it ought to reconcile us with God, and give us a feeling of safety and felicity in place of terror; it ought to cause joy instead of misery. What, religion a gift of God, to make man miserable? If that is religion, then the animal is happier without any.

Rationalists say, men were no sinners, there is no human depravity. Religion is pretended to be the medicine for a spiritually sick mankind; but if one claims not to be sick, then he wants no medicine. God, they say, could not have made man to be bad; everything which *is* is good, consequently men are good because they *are*. They see mankind improving, progressing in every respect; so they say mankind in its youth needed a religion, now as it is advanced and ripened to manhood the religion becomes superfluous. How, ask they, can mankind after it has reached its maturity have the same religion which it had in its infancy? Shall the man believe the same thing the infant did? Nobody denies that mankind progresses. The human race must undoubtedly be considered ripe now, if compared to what it was in early ages The human race has really advanced and changed. But religion is not given to mankind as a collective body, but to every one as an individual. As mankind we are advanced, as single men we have surely not advanced concerning our individual weakness, sinning and responsibility before God. Every one has his conscience individually, and is also responsible to God for *himself*, and so he was five thousand years ago. The relationship between God and man has not changed. We perhaps have some civilized weakness, refined sins, and sublime wickedness, but they are just as much the cause of the soul's misery as the weakness and sins and wickedness of the old barbarians; on the contrary, the refined man may consider himself more responsible. As God is immutable, so his relationship with men can not be changed. How can we deny human misery? I have given a little picture of the heart's struggles; who can dispute it? And it is a picture of our hearts as they are now, in spite of civilization. Look at your heart; look at the world around, weak and sick. What do men run after now? After things which make them miserable. The trouble is not only that we cannot reach our desires, but that what we do reach does not make us happy; and still we run after more. Who was ever satisfied with what he had reached? Who became happy on acccount of the fulfillment of the lasciviousness of his heart? There we see that the very fulfilled wish is the cause of our misery, exactly the same as it was since mankind exists. Where is the progress, then? You say you are not sick when you faint. You claim to have courage, while you tremble. You say you are full of health, when every one of your members is rotten. You laugh at the doctrine of human depravity; and try to prove by philosophy that men are good, but your own heart feels its own misery. If even your head has proved that men are good, if even you see it logically clear, will that help to remove the heart's misery? When you lie with a broken leg, and the doctor comes, and in place of curing you, proves that your leg is perfectly in order, according to the science of anatomy: the doctor may be highly learned, and his treatise about your leg may be admired by all the universities of the globe, and every doctor may say he was right; but still you are tormented by pain, your leg swells, and you cannot stand up. So, whenever you deny your spiritual trouble, are you able then to stand straight and look up to God? Do you expect to be justified before your everlasting Father by your deeds?

Laugh at hell, it is within you. Mock at Satan, while he ruins you. Say, I am comfortable, when the fire consumes your life. Deny the Devil, who tortures you right here. Hell, and fire, and Satan and his devils give you a foretaste on earth. Sin is a burning spark which will blaze up and increase to a flaming fire. That emptiness of your heart will become a solitude of terror; that coldness increase to a gnashing of teeth: every sting of conscience grows into a furious, poisonous snake.

If here on earth, where your individuality, your "I," is composed of flesh and soul, and you hardly perceive the existence of your soul, still you can conceive that your soul is suffering—here, where you live under the intoxication of the flesh; what will it be when that sleep which we call death has removed your intoxication, when you are undressed of the perishable garment, and left by your company, and your soul stands naked, and sober, and alone, before the object of your unknown love, before the light, and life, and joy of the world; before that pure love, that living truth, before the Almighty God? How will it be with you then? Will you look with pride at that yellow dirt which we call gold? Will you then use your smartness and subtlety? Will you then be proud of your nationality? Will the ripened mankind, with its civilization and culture; will the progress of the age, the science of the learned; will wisdom and beauty and power and influence reconcile you with that great, sublime and glorious simple truth, which is, God your Maker?

Your life sticks to you, and there is the hell with its tortures. You can see it from here; it is the natural consequence of your life, of your "human depravity," at which you laughed. The belief in human depravity and the resultant hell, is therefore reasonable, rational.

But as we must also believe, with the philosopher, that everything God made is good; for as God, the source of everything is absolutely good, everything coming out from Him must be good; so I believe that God had not made man to be a sinner, but originally he must have been created able to keep the balance between soul and body. Still, we see man bad, and we must conclude that with the free will which was given to him, he fell. So the fall into sin is not only credible, but logically it must have happened.

The Bible relates a fall into sin on the part of Adam and Eve, on account of which they lost Paradise. Judaism and Christianity derive from that occurrence the corruption of the race of Adam and Eve, the cause of the depravity.

Some reformed Jews maintain that the doctrine of the fall of mankind, originating with Adam and Eve, by eating the forbidden fruit, is an exclusive Christian doctrine. But the Talmud, Midrash, and all the Rabbinical literature are full of the same teachings, exactly like that of the Christians. "Chet Adam" and "Suhamah shal Nachash" are common expressions with the Rabbis. We also find in the Rabbinical literature that they expected the correction of Adam's sin, and a return to the former state of innocence, by the coming of the Messiah. I am entirely without books, and can cite nothing, but I only allude to the Chaldaic translations of the Pentateuch (Thargumim) of Gen. iii: 15 ; where they interpret to that effect. The Bible also affirms that no man is without sin. But Reformers believe only those parts of the Bible which suit them. Even the Jewish philosophers of the Middle Ages hold that doctrine, notwithstanding they have sometimes been rational where they ought to have, been believing, as I said in my first chapter, because that doctrine is essential to the truth of religion, and is a divine truth.

It is immaterial what the Reformers say, but genuine Judaism teaches that on account of this world being vain, and mankind weak, God in his infinite love and mercy has revealed himself to mankind through Israel. As men, on account of their flesh, no longer know the right way of life, as they no longer understand the voice of their souls, God gave the law that they may know his will and do it according to what he shows them in his word. At the same time, the prophets based their hope upon a future. Besides the many promises of glory and salvation through a king of the house of David, a servant of God, there was also promised a new covenant, a renewing of the human heart, as I shall show below in the passages of Scripture I am to cite. The Talmud also bases all hope for Israel and mankind on the coming of the Messiah, when the law would no longer be necessary, and should become void. They teach "Mizwoth Beteloth leathid labo." "The commandments shall be void in the future."

From what we have said in this chapter we see that mankind is miserable on account of being subjected to the powers of the flesh, and therefore in enmity with its spirit, with God. Consequently, every man must fear death; for his conscience makes him anticipate a judgment. Thus man wants a religion, for his soul seeks a reconciliation, an atonement with God. Atonement is, therefore, the purpose of religion; and we surely need not embrace any religion for secular purposes. Thus if religion shall answer its purpose, namely, to make atonement with God, it must also be given by Him.

Thus far we see that our own hearts feel the necessity of a religion. But in connection with this our reason reminds us of our frailty and the greatness of God. We see a providence of God in history and in our own life. We see his wisdom manifested in guiding mankind as well as our own selves, while we perceive our own blindness in seeing that the greatest men are only instruments in the hands of an all-wise Providence. How wonderful, how incomprehensible are the ways of Providence! How much wisdom, how intense a love, are visible in its guidance of mankind and also of every individual man, from the cradle to the grave. What is man's wisdom compared with that of Providence? What are our best contrived plans to that one wonderful plan of history, extending from the birthday of mankind to this present age? Must we not bow our heads in humility? Where is our wisdom, our strength, our glory? And what a wonderful part has Providence assigned to that one book, the Bible, to play in that history! And this Bible offers us a religion.

We have also seen already that the Jewish Bible has sure evidences of its divine origin, and Judaism claims to be the religion according to the Bible. It remains now to examine whether Judaism is according to that Bible, and then whether it answers the purpose of Religion, namely, whether it gives reconciliation with God by bringing us nearer to him, by pacifying our conscience and giving of moral strength. This we shall do in the next chapter.

CHAPTER VIII.

JUDAISM.

"For the children of Israel shall abide many days without a king, and without a prince, and without a sacrifice, and without a monument, and without ephod and theraphim." Hosea iii: 4.

In speaking of the condition of our souls, and our responsibility before God, in the last chapter, we have moved in exclusively rational spheres; that is, we have seen our weakness according to the conception of our reason, and the perception of our heart, without any dogma to be believed. We only believe in human depravity because we feel it, we see it; and hence we perceive our desire, our propensity for a religion. Thus the belief in God, immortality of the soul and judgment, that is, that man has to stand the consequences of this life in a future world, is supposed to be in the heart of every human being, which is not too much hardened. For we have the revelations of nature, history, heart and conscience testifying to the truth of this belief. But in entering the grounds of the Jewish Bible, in order to find God's remedy for our disease, we must begin to *believe* what we do not perceive. If human reason could *understand* God's way in giving a religion to reconcile us to him then it could also *contrive* it itself, and there would be no necessity for

God's religion; man could make his own religion if it were not beyond the reach of his spirit and power. But we only look for a religion because we find ourselves too weak, our reason and moral power inadequate to make us good, or to reconcile us to God after we were bad. We therefore look for something supernatural. Our disease we comprehend; a remedy for it is not to be discovered by our reason, on account of our blindness and weakness. The same is true of diseases of the body; every man feels his pain but must believe the doctor for the cure. It is not necessary that the patient shall understand medicine; if he only knows what ails him and finds the doctor who deserves his confidence, then he believes. Should the patient understand medicine, there would be no need for the doctor. All the patient needs is the doctor's testimonials, or reputation for learnng and ability, in order that he may trust him and take his incomprehensible medicines.

Thus the first condition of Judaism is to believe that the Bible was given by God. The Bible is not comprehensible, therefore it must be believed. In the Bible God appears different from what he did in his revelations to our heart and reason. The Divinity which we conceive in nature, that God of reason, is rather revealed as an impersonal God. But as man has the propensity to pray, as he seeks help from God, therefore we have a kind of perception that God is a free, independent, personal Being. The God of the Bible is a wonderful God; He speaks in words, gives a special law, writes on tables of stone, appears to our reason to be partial in choosing one people, changes the laws of nature to work miracles, and has angels as messengers. Thus not only God, but also every spiritual power becomes personified, and the spirit of bad influences appears as a malicious Satan. [Zech. iii; Job i.] The God of the Bible, his ways and laws, are by no means in accordance with reason. In short, with the Bible we receive a world of mysteries, even absurdities and contrarieties, as I shall show below. I only allude now to Ezek. iv.

But how can we believe such unreasonable things, such mysteries and contradictions? Because we say they are God's mysteries, and therefore seem to be contradictions because we cannot understand him on account of his being above our reason. For we have seen above, that history, especially the marvelous history of Israel, proves that the miracles must be true; and therefore we believe the Bible, on account of the miracles. These miracles happened in the presence of all that nation whose very existence is an everlasting miracle; and one generation testifies to another of their truth. These miracles were also of such a nature that they could not be disputed; for instance, the division of the Red Sea, and the giving of the manna. For about fifteen centuries the Israelitish nation also had prophets, through whom God's revelation was continued, and who also worked miracles, in accordance with Moses' promise that they should also have prophets in his place. The first miracles by which God introduced himself as a God who works supernatural things, as the real Lord of creation, were performed in presence of all the nation; but with the latter prophets and their miracles there was no longer a necessity for such a general publicity. The latter ages already had what was necessary to belief. All the nation was a witness to the genuineness of God's revelations, and nothing but hardness of heart could make any one disbelieve or disobey. To dispute God's miracles by Moses, was disputing history. Besides, God's supernatural presence was always visible in the fate of the nation : they were great and happy as long as they followed the way and believed, and became oppressed and miserable when they disobeyed. Also, everything that happened to them was predicted before it happened; even their fate, their dispersion and most marvelous preservation up to this day are predicted, and furnish conclusive evidence. No reasonable man, after looking at the facts of history, can doubt any longer the existence of a real supernatural revelation, to that exceedingly wonderful nation; moreover, their book of revelation has conquered all the civilized world and still excercises that sublime power which we see, and which is also according to its own predictions.

Thus the belief in the Bible is founded upon supernatural miracles, not upon reason. As I said in the first chapter, the God of Moses is not the God of philosophy. Again, if Israel's history, with its miracles and the power of the Bible, prove its being the book of God, we must not only be glad that we have a book from God which we may believe, but we are also compelled to believe. For if God in his infinite mercy has revealed himself for our benefit, it becomes our most binding, and most sacred duty to bow our heads and believe and obey him. Shall God have spoken in vain ?

So far, that is, concerning the belief in the Bible,

the Jews are undoubtedly right. The question is now, only, whether Judaism does not misunderstand the Bible; whether they acquire the necessary atonement in accordance with that Bible; whether their religion is the remedy for the soul's disease. Seeking help for the soul, Judaism points to the law. It teaches that the only way to do God's will is to keep the law. We are bad, but God gave us commandments in order that we should acquire merits by keeping them. Through keeping of the law we become righteous, and we must therefore work out our righteousness. There is no radical cure for the disease, no medicine to change our spiritual constitution, so that the disease should be removed, no giving of another than a natural direction to our life. The law leaves us sick, but prescibes a great number of medicines and a strict diet. Every minute you must take a commandment, not for a cure, but that the sickness may not kill you. But as it must be supposed that you will fail in your diet, since men are weak, therefore an extra medicine is prescibed for you. The sacrifice of an animal and the sprinkling of its blood will cleanse you from your sin. As a general relapse is supposed to take place every day, there are daily sacrifices prescribed, also some extra for the Sabbath, new moons and holidays. A special cleansing from all sins by the services of the High Priest is promised for the day of atonement once a year. According to the prescription of the Bible, the sacrifices are necessary for the forgiveness of sins, for there is no atonement promised without them. And as we found that men *are* sinners, therefore the main power of the law must be in sacrifices, and it is of no avail without them. We have, thus, good reason to think that the law has lost its power by losing the integrity with the sacrifices, for there have been no sacrifices during eighteen centuries. According to our reason God can surely forgive sins without the sprinkled blood, even now, but according to that, there never was any necessity to give the command to bring sacrifices. The sacrifices are, from the beginning, wholly against our reason; but God said they were necessary, and if they were necessary then, why should they not be so now? Truly, they are incomprehensible; we cannot possibly see why God wants the blood of an animal in order to forgive our sins; but, as I said before, the God of the Bible is not according to reason, but above it. As soon as we accept the Bible we only judge according to its teachings, for we must believe it. We judge no longer whether God's command is in agreement with our reason, but whether we live according to his command; and he says, decidedly, that the sacrifices are necessary for atonement. Especially the services of the High Priest on the day of atonement seem to be the most valuable part of all the Mosaic law. For Moses says, explicitly, that the sins should be forgiven on that day. We read, Levit. xvi: 30, " For on that day *he* shall make an atonement for you, to cleanse you, that ye may be clean from all your sins before the Lord." In reading the whole chapter, we can not doubt that the word "*he*" alludes to the High Priest, who, by his services, makes atonement before the Lord. Jewish commentators also interpret it to this effect. It was also the only day in which *only* the High Priest could enter the Sanctum Sanctorum, where the Lord dwelt between the Cherubim. It was the highest service in the year, and his object was to make atonement. The work of this day seems thus to be the main object of the law. There we can see that God's law is not only incomprehensible, but also intended for atonement, which can any way be the only object of religion. It is utterly absurd to believe with some, that the law was only given for worldly purposes, as the old Saducecans believed. For concerning this world we find that the heathen enjoyed it better than the chosen people. If the eternal God reveals himself it must be for eternal purposes. Reason suffices for this world's affairs.

We have said that because we yield to the power of the flesh we feel that we are bad and the pangs of conscience tell us that we are in enmity with God, and therefore we seek a religion in order to find reconciliation. Now we have the law, does the law make us better? I cannot say that the law, because it tells me what to do and what to omit, does me any good, for in seeking for a religion I must necessarily have known what is bad, else I should have no pangs of conscience. That very conscience which makes me look for a religion, must have told me first what is bad. Consequently, I do not look for a religion in order to be taught what is right or wrong, but to give me a way to keep the right and to make atonement for my wrong. For instance, my conscience tells me that I am not truthful. If I did not know that untruthfulness is wrong, my conscience would be quiet. I want a religion to give me strength to live according to my conscience, and to make atonement for my untruthfulness, which sets me at enmity with God.

The law tells me what my conscience told me long ago, that I must be truthful. Now I am worse off than ever: my conscience wounds me more because the sin is stronger. God in his revelation, in his law, said also that I must be truthful, and I am not! The voice of revelation becomes the voice of condemnation; for the law says it more explicitly, that I am a sinner, hence the law sounds like a curse. And not only this; the law says I must eat no pork, no oysters, etc. Fearful! Not only that I am a sinner on account of my old sins, I have temptations and sins now of which I never knew before. I could eat anything before without sinning. Now I, one who cannot live according to the law of conscience; I who was too weak to carry that burden, have a still heavier burden. There is no inducement for me, then, to accept the law, but the sacrifices through which atonement is promised. Else the law leads to sin, and is a curse.

Now, the Jews also teach human depravity, as I said in the chapter treating it; they admit that we are sinners, but claim that the righteousness of the law justifies. They admit the weakness, that we cannot keep the law; and especially teach, that, before the destruction of the temple we had sacrifices to make atonement for us. They also admit that the day of atonement is the holiest day in the year, and that its services were the holiest and most precious services for Israel. Since the destruction of the temple the Rabbis lament very bitterly the loss of the sacrifices. The great value they placed upon them is expressed in the many prayers for their restoration, as we find in the prayer-book. We can hardly find a prayer, but it expresses a burning desire for the restoration of the sacrifices. It is heart-rending to read their description of the services in the prayers for the day of atonement; they were inexhaustible in describing it. The loss of the promise of the forgiveness of sins caused them the most insupportable sorrow, and many hot tears. Indeed, they had good reason to lament and to weep. Any one who has the least sympathy with God's chosen and dispersed people, can find tears for the fearful loss of such privileges as my people had. Tears blind the eyes of the writer of these lines. Flow, my tears, without ceasing. May your fountain never dry up. May my eyes shed blood and my heart break for my people's loss, for the loss of such a visible glory. It is related in the Mishnah that a certain red thread in the sanctuary always turned white after the services of the day of atonement, as an answer from the sin-forgiving, Most Merciful God of Israel, that he had cleansed his people from all their sins. What a privilege! It is also stated that they felt great joy in their hearts. Perhaps it was something like that sweet joy Christians often perceive in their hearts. To-day the reformed Israelites laugh at such things, and so I did once. They think it was superstition for a man to be troubled about his sins, and foolish to think of the future. A greatly learned Rabbi, Nachman Krochmal, explains, or rather perverts, this historical passage of the Mishnah so as to teach that the whitening of the thread was no miracle, but a kind of mechanism. But according to the meaning of the Mishnah it is related as something wonderful. Krochmal's perversion is, besides, absurd of itself, and needs no contradiction.

Such interpretations of miracles to make people believe they were natural occurrences, and all those reformed ideas, are not Judaism, but deviations from it. Only those teachings can be considered as Judaism which are in accordance with the Talmud. Nobody ever tried to treat anything else as such until this century. And, as I said, the Rabbis stand on the platform of belief. Nobody can accuse them of not believing, but of perverting the Bible. So they do with the doctrine of the sacrifices and the day of atonement.

In order to give their disciples consolation in the loss of their privileges, they say that the earnest reading of Scriptural and Talmudical passages which describe the ordinances of the Scriptures, will be accepted before the Lord, like the blood of the animal. And they pervert the above cited verse of Levit. xvi: 30, where Moses says, "On that day *he* shall make atonement," which means the *priest* shall make the atonement, by teaching that the "*DAY*" makes atonement. The day cleanses from sin. It is true, they say that the day cleanses only upon the condition of repentance and reformation. But what an anti-biblical, almost heathenish doctrine that is! To say that a certain day had the power of atonement before God! Where is the biblical authority for that teaching? Where is the "*Thus saith the Lord*" for such a doctrine? I will believe everything God said, even if it should cost my life. But I must have a "Koh amar Adonai," "*Thus saith the Lord*," for it. We can often find that the Rabbis were not embarrassed how to pervert the Bible.

They were very inventive, and seemed to have no scruple in interpreting passages against the most obvious meaning, as we shall see in the next chapter.

But truly, we can see that the sacrifices can not be replaced by reading the law appointing them, nor is the atonement which the Lord promised and which was to be attained by the high priest's service attainable now through the power of a *day*, or through the works and goodness of man.

If anything is calculated to be imposingly solemn, to draw the heart into contrition; if the Jew has any time when, being entirely withdrawn from this world, he can devote himself exclusively to God's service, then it must be the day of atonement. Notwithstanding some corruptions of the Synagogue, as the praying in Hebrew, which they do not understand, and other corruptions of which I do not wish to speak, it seems as if the world ceased to exist; there is nothing for the real Jew on that day but a Synagogue. The strictest abstinence from everything is observed. To take one drop of water, to wear shoes, even to wash the face, is forbidden by the Rabbis for twenty-four hours — from evening unto evening. (*The Bible only commands to afflict your souls or yourselves, and says nothing about eating or drinking, and gives no description of the manner of affliction.*) And all that time of twenty-four hours of fasting is devoted to reading and singing hymns, praying, and making confessions; some, even watch all night, reading psalms. But all this service is of no effect for the heart. The Jew's heart finds no consolation; he perceives not the atonement in himself. He has no joy of God; he does not feel reconciled to his Creator; does not stand near him after the "*atoning day.*" After this wonderful day, which, according to the Talmud, makes atonement, the Jew naturally feels very tired, worn out, and very hungry. He also experiences some satisfaction that the fast is over. The burden of fasting is taken, but not the one of sins. Then, he often feels very low from the effect of the fast. The glorious day of atonement is no more a day of atonement but a fast. A fast of no avail.

God's people know nothing of that indescribable, blessed experience of joy in God, which is the assurance of atonement and reconciliation with Him, an experience which gives such a quiet conscience, such a sweet rest of heart, such a refreshment to the soul, such a calmness, and peace, and love, and hope. They know nothing of it, and if you tell them of such experiences, they say you are insane, and laugh you to scorn.

Woe to God's chosen people, without a sacrifice, without an atonement, without the mediating High Priest! Woe, a thousand times woe! Have they no tears in heaven? Does Abraham not weep? Rachel does! I wonder that the stars do not shed tears, that the sun does not cease to shine, that the earth does not stop in her course, that the silent moon does not speak, that all nature does not suspend work, mourning for the misfortune of the people of their Creator. Does Sinai keep silent? Do the waters of the Red Sea, which retired once in reverence before my people, do they not boil and rage? Does Jordan yet run towards his destination? Israel, Israel, my dear Israel, my Israel! Where art thou? Where is thy atonement, thy hope, thy precious promise?

Where is the nation like Israel on the day of atonement? In every corner of the earth they stand up like one man; from every country their shouting ascends. They pray for atonement! Oh, it is as if all the creation ought to join them in prayer; stones ought to cry and mountains pray for atonement.

But the Lord said: "And I shall surely hide my face in that day. "Deuter. xxxi: 18. As I said before, we can see that the day makes no atonement, notwithstanding the teaching of the Talmud.

The Rabbis of to-day, who try to show that Judaism was an entirely comprehensible religion; that everything Judaism teaches was according to philosophy (and there are even so-called orthodox Rabbis who hold that doctrine), preach that the only way to receive atonement is to repent and be good. The day, they say, cleanses only in the sense that it is set apart for retirement from the world, and examination of one's own heart. But this is not only anti-biblical, it is also against the meaning of the Talmud. It is altogether against the principle of religion, which is, that atonement must come from God. It leaves again the man to himself. If man's repentance and personal goodness are sufficient to give him atonement; if he is able to be good enough in the eyes of God, then religion becomes superfluous. And why did God promise atonement through the High Priest's service? The Talmud held to the principle of Religion; its authors considered a supernatural way of atonement necessary. They knew that the High Priest's services were ordered for atonement, but simply perverted the Bible so as to teach that the day had the power. The

Talmud had no intention to make religion comprehensible. Indeed, the Talmud is not against belief, but, on the contrary, wants its disciples to believe too much.

It is not to be wondered at, that the Rabbi of the Reform lately put forth the curious doctrine that God does not forgive sins according to Judaism, and that the doctrine of atonement is entirely a Christian invention, and that another Rabbi proclaimed that he does not believe in a personal God. Such doctrines are the logical result of refusing to believe in supernatural revelations. If God did not literally speak, and there is no supernatural way of reconciliation, how can we expect an atonement? There is more logic with these Rabbis than with those who deny revelation and still believe in the day of atonement. The inconsistency of the former is only in the fact that they do not resign their position as Rabbis, for they have nothing to do with religion. The human propensity for religion, which they take to be the religion, and which is nothing but the human misery, that human misery man can cultivate without synagogues and Rabbis. The impersonal God needs no service, he is a dead God. He does not even deserve the name God. Surely he was not the God of Moses. I cannot be astonished at a reformed Jew when he denies the existence of a personal God, for I had such pantheistic temptations myself.

Let us return to the doctrine of the sacrifices. According to Scripture and Talmud they were necessary for the forgiveness of sins, thus they preserve the integrity of the law. If I fail to keep a commandment I am enabled to make it right by the sacrifices; but if I have no sacrifice, by what can I replace it? as the rabbinical doctrines of reading the ordinances and of the atoning day have no Biblical foundation. The Jews claim they were innocent in not bringing the sacrifices, as the destruction of the sanctuary was not directly caused by them, and its rebuilding was beyond their power. But, if God, in his infinite mercy and wisdom, has revealed himself on earth, and told us to bring sacrifices, then they were necessary according to His wisdom. Is it to be supposed that he would have allowed the sanctuary to be destroyed, or, at least, that he would not have given the opportunity and the command for its rebuilding, if he wanted it to be rebuilt again? Especially as we find that he did so after the destruction of the first temple. And as God left us without sacrifices, which obviously were to integrate the law, is it not rather to be supposed that they are no longer necessary, for the reason that they only pointed to a certain thing which was to come, and were only to teach the principle of God's way of atonement? As we find the law of no avail without sacrifices, we must necessarily examine if the Bible has not other aim besides the law. We must see if there is no other atonement offered besides the sacrifices of animals. For, shall God have spoken in vain, because the sanctuary is destroyed? Is the word of God useless because the law is void? May not that law have been a preparation for freedom without a law? Every father and teacher has laws and rules for the children, to teach them obedience, but when the child grows up to be a man, he is free of these laws and rules. But still the laws were, from the beginning, only calculated to teach him as a child in order that he might be free when he became a man. We must any way say that the aim of the law could not have been to give a way of atonement for Israel only. The God of Israel is the God of mankind; thus he chose Israel to be the instrument to give a religion to the world. Now, the law and the sacrifices were given to Israel alone, and it is not to be expected that the law should be accepted by the nations, that God should reveal himself again to every nation and tell them to keep the law he gave to Israel. Israel is chosen, and the Bible, the word of God, cannot be revoked; so the nations' help can only be expected in the revelations to Israel. Consequently, the very law and sacrifices *must* have pointed to and prepared a religion for the world. Moreover, as we have seen above that the law is not a radical cure for man's spiritual disease, therefore Israel itself had to expect a development of its religion, a full cure of the disease, and a delivery from the burden of the law. And so they did expect it. We cannot say that the law and the sacrifices were only binding for a certain time, for the Bible does not teach so; nor can we suppose that the sacrifices are necessary now, else the Lord would have given the opportunity to bring them. But we must say that law and sacrifices were preparing a building which is finished, and they exist in the building under a different form.

For instance, a man gives orders to carry bricks and lumber and other materials, in order to build a house. He only wants the materials brought as long as they are needed for a house. As soon as the house is finished no materials are necessary, and he wants none to be brought. Has his order been in vain? Are the materials useless? No; the materials brought are in the house, they exist, and are there used as they were intended. The man's order is not revoked, but fulfilled. May not this be the case with the law? It was a work for a house which is finished now, and it is understood of itself that no more materials are needed, for the necessary materials *are* in the house. The law is fulfilled.

The great Jewish teacher, Maimonides, teaches that the law is still in force, but the sacrifices were only a temporal institution. The sacrifices of animals, says he, were only tolerated by Moses. Because the heathen were in the habit of sacrificing wild animals and their children, therefore Moses, fearing that the Israelites would wish to do like the heathen, only permitted that they should bring their offerings of clean animals before the Lord. He considers it only a necessity for the time. Maimonides, trying to find reasons for God's commandments, made many blunders, but none like this. The Reformers accept this doctrine of Maimonides and apply the principle to the whole law, saying it was for the time. They go with Maimonides when it suits their purpose, they even believe the Bible, sometimes, when they can pervert it and bring it in accordance with their made-up religion, or even with pantheism.

Maimonides' doctrine that the sacrifices were only given temporarily has not only no biblical foundation but is even plainly against the Bible. He had no more authority to affirm that the sacrifices were for a temporary purpose than to say all the law was only temporary. It is true that the prophets and the psalmist placed more value in obeying God than in sacrifices, and considered it better not to sacrifice than to do it in disobedience. We may learn by this, that the main object of the sacrifices must have been as a symbol, pointing to the subjection to God, and that our main object in sacrificing must be humiliation before God while believing Him; that we ought to bring a nobler, inward sacrifice, the one of our heart, our life, our all. *No* sacrifice is of any value except the heart is sacrificed before its Maker. This is what the prophets teach. But there is no shade of a reason to suppose the sacrifices abolished when all the law is binding. We have seen, before, that the sacrifices could only be in order to integrate the law, and Maimonides himself wrote the first codex of the rabbinical law. And, again, where is the object, the aim of the religion, if it offers no atonement. What a profanation of the sanctuary this implies; for the law said, "For I will appear in the cloud upon the cover." (In the English version, "upon the mercy-seat.") Lev. xvi: 2. The Lord promised to dwell in the sanctuary, and allows only the High Priest to enter into the Holy of Holies on the day of atonement when He promises to forgive the sins after the High Priest makes the atonement by sacrifices; but, according to Maimonides, the sanctuary must have been valueless. For where is the value of the sanctuary when the sacrifices are nothing? Also the promise that the Lord shall appear there must have been a deception. If Moses had considered the sacrifices absolutely wrong of themselves, he would rather have strictly forbidden and not tolerated them, in order that the Israelites might not learn to walk the way of the heathen. This would have looked more like Moses. Moses was not diffident; he was very strict, especially when it touched heathenism. All the air of holiness with which the Bible surrounds the sanctuary; all the assurances of God's dwelling in it; all those particular ordinances for its construction, or the forms of utensils to be used in it; all those inestimable promises of the forgiveness of sins through the sacrifices; all the sanctification of the tribe of Levi, and especially the children of Aaron, were nothing but mockery; and the awe and reverence which the children of Israel perceived for their sanctuary, were the most ridiculous foolishness, and ought to provoke our contempt in place of respect, if Maimonides' opinion were right.

Moreover, we find that the principle of sacrifices was by no means heathenish. Abel, the son of Adam, already sacrificed animals, and the Lord had respect unto Abel and his offering. Noah, coming out of the ark, sacrificed animals, and the Bible says, "And the Lord smelled a sweet savor," etc. Gen. viii: 21. There was no necessity for Abel and Noah to sacrifice, lest they should fall into the way of the heathen. And what can the Lord's smelling of a sweet savor mean, if not a mystery? There you can also see that the Bible can either contain sacred mysteries, or else it is the absurdest book according to our reason. For the Lord's smelling is not according to rationalism. The Patriarchs also sacrificed. It must have been according to the sublime will of God, then.

The language of the Bible is, moreover, decidedly plain, that God commanded to bring sacrifices, and promised to forgive sins through them. We read,

Lev. i: 4, "And he shall put his hand upon the head of the burnt offering. And it shall be accepted for him."

Lev. i: 2-7, "Speak unto the children of Israel saying, if a soul shall sin through ignorance against any of the commandments of the Lord, etc. . . . . . If the priest that is anointed do sin, etc. . . . . And he shall bring the bullock unto the door of the tabernacle *before the Lord*, and shall lay his hand upon the bullock's head, etc. . . . . And the priest shall dip his finger in the blood, and sprinkle of the blood seven times *before the Lord*, before the veil of the sanctuary. And the priest shall put some of the blood upon the horns of the altar of sweet incense *before the Lord, which is in the tabernacle of the congregation*, etc. . . . . "

Ibid, 20, "And the priest shall make an atonement for them, and it shall be forgiven them."

Ibid, ix: 7, "And Moses said unto Aaron, Go unto the altar and offer thy sin offering and thy burnt offering, and make an atonement for thyself and for the people, and offer the offering of the people, and make the atonement for them, as the Lord commanded."

Ibid, 24, "And there came a fire out from before the Lord and consumed upon the altar the burnt offering and the fat: which, when all the people saw, they shouted and fell on their faces."

No; dear reader, allow me to ask, is Moses, with his Bible a lie, a humbug? or did God command the sacrifices to be brought, and did the fire from the Lord really come out to devour them? In many places, Moses also adds, that the sacrifices shall be a sweet savor unto the Lord. Anybody reading Leviticus will soon find that the Bible is in real earnest about the sacrifices. I have cited, before, that the Lord promised a general forgiving of sins on the day of atonement. In reading all the 16th chapter of Leviticus, we find how explicitly that promise was given.

Maimonides also teaches that Moses has forbidden to eat blood and commanded to sprinkle it on the altar only because the heathen used to worship their imaginary devils by drinking blood. They used to kill animals in the wilderness where they expected to meet the devil. Nothing can be more against the plainest teaching of Scripture. Moses teaches, in the name of the living God, that blood cleanses from sin. Notwithstanding it is incomprehensible, we must believe it if we claim to be Jews who believe the Bible, and do not say that Moses was an imposter. For we read:

Levi. xvii: 11, 12. "For the life of the flesh is in the blood: and I have given it to you upon the altar to make an atonement for your souls: for it is the blood that maketh an atonement for the soul. Therefore I said unto the children of Israel, no soul of you shall eat blood."

Could the Bible speak plainer concerning the blood? And we find similar passages at other places.

Concerning preventing the children of Israel from sacrificing in the desert places like the heathen, where they might expect to meet the devils, the Lord gave the ordinance that as long as the Israelites were in the camp in the wilderness they shall kill no animal but before the door of the tabernacle: as we read in

Lev. xvii: " And the Lord spake unto Moses, saying: Speak unto Aaron, and unto his sons, and unto all the children of Israel, and say unto them : this is the thing which the Lord hath commanded, saying: What man soever there be of the house of Israel that killeth an ox, or lamb, or goat, in the camp, or that killeth it out of the camp, and bringeth it not unto the door of the tabernacle of the congregation, to offer an offering unto the Lord before the tabernacle of the Lord, blood shall be imputed unto that man; he hath shed blood; and that man shall be cut off from among his people, to the end that the children of Israel may bring their sacrifices, which they offer in the open field, even that they may bring them unto the Lord, unto the door of the tabernacle of the congregation, unto the priest, and offer them for peace offerings unto the Lord. And the priest shall sprinkle the blood upon the altar of the Lord, at the door of the tabernacle of the congregation, and burn the fat for a sweet savor unto the Lord. *And they shall no more offer the sacrifices unto devils*, after whom they have gone a whoring."

This passage declares, plainly, that in order to avoid the offering unto the devils, they have to bring before the tabernacle every animal which they even killed for the use of the meat. No part of the meat was burnt upon the altar, and it was only a peace offering (Shelamim). They were forbidden to kill animals in the wilderness, even for their own use, on account of the temptation to offer to the devils. Later, they were allowed to kill all they wanted to eat, at any place after they arrived in Canaan. [See Deuter. xii.] This ordinance is only for the camp, to avoid the sacrificing unto devils. Anybody conversant with the Talmud knows the distinction; that the killing of the animals for private use (Bassar thaavah) was allowed in Canaan at any place; but a real sacrifice had altogether another object, that of atonement or thanksgiving, and was only allowed to be sacrificed in the sanctuary. Rabbi Akiba (in Chulin) interprets the passage of Lev. xvii to a different effect, but his perversion cannot be accepted by any commentator who goes after the plain meaning of Scripture. Now, we see plainly that the heathen sacrificing to devils caused a special ordinance, and we cannot possibly say that this was the cause of all the ordinances for the sacrifices.

In short, we see that Maimonides is, respecting the sacrifices and the blood, plainly against the Bible, and we must believe the Bible in spite of all the philosophers of earth. And, according to that Bible, God commanded the sprinkling of the blood as a necessity, and afterwards by destroying the sanctuary, he made the execution of his command an impossibility, and consequently, the law of no effect. God did not revoke the law by a special revelation, but left it as it is, indicating that the law is always true but so fulfilled, and the work of it becomes superfluous, as we find in the example with the building I mentioned above, and which will be clearly explained in the course of this book. Still, the Jews claim that the law, even to-day, without the sacrifices, is the only way of justification before God. Let us, therefore, for the sake of argument, leave out the question of sacrifices, and examine, in the following chapter, whether the Jewish law is according to Moses, and what it affords us by keeping it. Let us see whether we can find in the Jewish religion, as it is, what we desire to find in a religion; reconciliation with God in bringing us nearer to Him, in giving strength against our weakness, peace for our conscience, and a hope for the future, the remedy for our spiritual disease.

CHAPTER IX.

THE RABBINICAL LAW.

" For with stammering lips and another tongue will he speak to this people. To whom he said, This is the rest wherewith ye may cause the weary to rest ; and this is the refreshing ; yet they would not hear. But the word of the Lord was unto them ; precept upon precept ; line upon line ; here a little and there a little." ISA. xxviii: 10 to 12.

I have said, before, that the Bible and the law are not according to reason, but still we may, and even must, believe it because it is the word of the Author of our reason; a fact to which history testifies. Consequently, we do not give up our reason in believing, but, on the contrary, reason compels us to believe what God says, without comprehending it; reason makes unreasonable things credible by the proof of the miracles. The *mind* believes what it does not understand. This is true concerning the Bible, and it is thus for our reason to determine whether what we believe is according to the Bible. But in believing the Rabbinical law we must give up reason altogether; we must believe the Rabbis, who have no miracles to testify for them. Also their interpretations of Scripture are entirely against reason. They do not teach according to the reasonable meaning of the Scripture, often obviously against it. For an illustration I shall only mention here some of their ordinances.

Moses has forbidden to *work* on the Sabbath day. The Rabbis, without any Biblical authority, count up thirty-nine principal works, and from these principals they derive offsprings of works without number. It would be too tedious for the reader to have their method of making up these many works explained here, nor can I devote this little book to such a purpose; but any sensible man must be tempted to think that they were perfectly insane in using such a logic as they did. They also forbid many things as ordinances of their own.

The reader knows, from what I have stated in my experience, that conscience gave me pangs for carrying a handkerchief. I was taught to consider it a sin, because the Bible forbids to carry a *load* on the Sabbath. It is forbidden to put on a plaster when anybody suffers; also almost everything necessary for healing purposes, unless life is in danger. Suffering is no excuse; only when life is in danger you may break the law. If your house is on fire, you must allow the house to be burned, else you commit a crime; if you see something burning in your house, and know that all the house will be in flames if you let it burn, you are not permitted to put it out; this would be a principal work, and you would deserve to be stoned. Nor are you allowed to save your movable property, except such clothing as you can put on. You must not comb your hair on the Sabbath, because you will tear out some hair through combing, and there is no difference between tearing a hair from the head and reaping wheat from the field; both are the same kind of work, plucking, or reaping. It is true, say they, that, for instance, in plucking the hair, you do a work which you did not intend, it is a work which you do not want, of itself, you only mean to have your hair combed (melacha sheenah zericha legupha); but as you know that you cannot comb the hair without tearing, you know you cannot accomplish the work without having some hair plucked out. Consequently, it is just as bad as if you should go and commit that fearful sin of plucking a hair intentionally. And this they very wisely compare to one who says, "I shall cut off the head without killing," while you know that cutting off the head surely must kill. (Pessik reshah veloh yamuth.) Also, you cannot wipe your hair if it is even wet, because in wiping you press the water from it, and pressing wine, for instance, is surely a work. You must not play any musical instrument, because a string or something else of the instrument may break, and you may forget yourself and repair it, which is a work. You must not swim on the Sabbath, because if you do swim you might get a notion to manufacture an instrument for swimming. You must surely not write, no matter how pressing a necessity it is, even for religious purposes, or even if you do it with the greatest ease; for writing, of itself, is a principal work. But doing mercantile business they consider not forbidden according to law; the sages have forbidden it only because in doing business you might be tempted to forget yourself so much as to write. On the same principle you are warned not to read by candle-light on the Sabbath evening (which is rightly Friday evening, for the Biblical day surely commences with the previous evening, and nobody can dispute that the *Biblical Sabbath* is the seventh day), if you do read at the candle-light you might forget and trim the candle. It is related that such a horrible disaster happened to one of the saints in reading on Friday evening; but it is supposed that the Lord had forgiven him. If an apple falls of itself from the tree on the Sabbath you must not eat it, nor the egg which a hen laid on that day.

The most amusing part of these laws is, the principles they set forth, and the logic by which these principles are combined, especially the manner of deriving everything from the Bible, which would be too much to be given here. So far I have cited a very few of the Sabbath laws, but the Sabbath laws are only a small part of the rabbinical codex. Everything in human life is surrounded by laws. I will therefore give you some specimens of laws of another character. For instance, the Jew is not only forbidden to eat milk or butter, together with meat, but he must not even use the same utensil in which he used one for the other, and must also wait six hours after eating meat before he may take milk. Now, the reader who is conversant with the Old Testament, and knows not the Talmud, will ask, Why is it forbidden? The Rabbis say it is forbidden in the Pentateuch. Listen, and I will show you an original explanation of the Pentateuch.

Moses said three times, " Thou shalt not seethe a

kid in his mother's milk." Any sensible man knows that if one says, thou shalt not seethe, he means not that thou shouldst not eat, and if he repeats it *three times* not to "*seethe*," then he certainly means nothing else but seething. The more he repeats the same word the less he is apt to mean anything else. A repetition of the same word surely emphasises it. But the Rabbis say, because this command is found three times in Scripture, one means not to seethe, the second, not to eat, and the third, not to enjoy the use of milk and meat in any other way. You must not even sell it and have the benefit of the money. If, by accident, a little butter falls into your meat soup, and that soup contains not sixty times as much as the quantity of butter which fell into it, so the butter could be considered dissolved and lost, then you are forbidden to use this soup or the utensil in which it was when the sad accident happened. Reader, what do you think of that logic? Now, Moses was only speaking of a kid in the milk of his mother; how do you come to forbid me to eat a piece of meat from an old ox imported from Texas, with the butter of some young cow of a farmer in Illinois? But they say that they know it by tradition, that by "kid" Moses meant all kinds of meat, and by "the milk of its mother," any kind of milk. And the Jew must believe this, without any reason. They admit, though, that poultry is not included in the term "kid," for experience shows that kids do not fly. Still, they forbid to eat butter with your chicken, for the very sound reason that if you eat chicken with butter to-day, you might go and commit that dreadful crime of eating meat with butter to-morrow, and then the law would be shattered in pieces. They also say that Moses had commanded only to wait one hour between eating meat and milk, but they made it six hours. How do you like that? Now, there are many Reformers who do not believe that God divided the Red Sea, or spoke on Sinai, and keep their business open on Sabbath, but still, in their houses they keep that holy law, and have two different sets of kitchen and table furniture for the use of meat and milk. By this they think to be Jews according to religion.

Let us admit that Moses left some oral teachings and principles for the leaders of the nation, concerning the manner of executing certain laws not sufficiently explained in his book. The teachers of the nation must also have had authority to legislate according to the time, in agreement with the spirit of the Bible, for not everything is written in the Bible. Moses gives authority to the priest and judge and elders of the time. [Deut. xvii, and other places.] We must even admit that traditions are of some value and authority, as every nation, every judge, must respect the use and custom of the country where no special laws exist adapted to the case. I even think that, necessarily, Moses must have orally taught some divine mysteries, which were not adapted to publication, and there must have been some gnostic doctrines and rules for the understanding of many passages of Scripture, as I shall mention it below. But if we are to believe any authority, doctrine, tradition, or mystery, it must be according to the Bible, in agreement with its spirit, not obviously against it. Is it possible that Moses meant to forbid the eating of meat and milk, when he explicitly forbids only the seething of the kid in its mother's milk? and his repetitions emphatically exclude any extension of his prohibition. There we see that the rabbinical law was against the distinct law of Moses. We see that the Rabbis misused their authority, and invented things which they passed for traditions.

The reader who is conversant with the New Testament knows that they commanded certain washings of hands without the least authority. But they also prescribed certain blessings to be said at the washing. Before regular meals the Jew must wash his hands and say, "Praised be Thou, Lord our God, King of the world, who has sanctified us and commanded us to wash our hands." Where has the Lord commanded that? Is it not blasphemy to say such a blessing? They say, that whoever does not keep that law, deserves death. They even declare that he will become poor; though I know that many Jews who keep not that law still die very rich.

So far the reader may think that the Rabbis only made heavy burdens without authority, but that at least they were conscientious not to break the law of Moses. This, however, is not the case; for where it suited them they openly broke the law. For instance: they have excluded the woman from such laws which are commanded for certain times only. It is commanded to sit in booths seven days, in commemoration that the Lord made booths of clouds for the children of Israel when they were in the wilderness. Why should the women be excluded from this duty? Have the women no souls? Were the clouds not for them also? But the Rabbis teach that because this command is only for certain seven days in the year, therefore women need not observe it. And so are many commandments, only for a certain time. I wish the woman-suffrage ladies had lived in the time of the Talmudists, and had given them some of their lectures.

Moses commanded that on the four corners of the garment every Israelite must have tassels, or, as some falsely translate, "fringes." He also said that they should be made to the " *covering* with which thou *coverest* thyself." It follows, therefore, no doubt, that quilts and blankets must have those tassels (Zizith). There is also the reason for this commandment given. The Bible says, "that ye may look upon it and remember all the commandments of the Lord and do them." Num. xv: 39. The tassels are intended to remind of God and his law. The Rabbis teach that because it says, " that ye may look upon them and remember," and people do not usually see well at night, therefore the commandment of having tassels is only valid in day-time; consequently it falls under the category of commandments which depend on a certain time, namely, day, and not night; thus women are excluded.

On the days of Passover no leaven must be found or seen in the house of an Israelite, according to God's law. But the Rabbis know how to avoid this. They say that if you make a sham sale of your leaven to a Gentile, and receive one cent of him on account of your sale; if you even do know that this Gentile has no idea of buying it, that he is worth nothing, knows nothing about the leaven sold, only does it to please you, and signs your Hebrew contract, so that this sham sale is a perfect mockery; still you deceive God with it. Men know that it is your leaven, the contract is only used to avoid God's law; but God must be expected not to know it. Also, when you have a farm, the animals must rest on the Sabbath, and you are not allowed to let your workmen work your field; but you make a sham sale. You know that no one would take the farm on account of such sale, but you tell God that you sold it, and how can he find it out?

I believe I have given the reader examples enough of the rabbinical codex, so that any body can see what sort of a *Mosaic law* the Rabbis teach. I by no means feel inclined to quote much of the Talmud and codex; yet a great number of its laws have no better Biblical foundation than those I have cited. Even the law for killing the animals after the Jewish custom, which of itself is an innocent, perhaps a commendable institution (Shechitah), is devoid of any Biblical reason. Moses never commanded it. Some Rabbis in the Talmud are even of opinion that in the wilderness the Jews used to kill their animals in a different way (Bassar nechirah). There is even a Mishnah (in "Maasser sheni") which makes one think that the Jewish method of killing the animals by cutting the throat only, was introduced by John Hyrkanus, the Maccabean. According to that Mishnah it is anyway clear, that either they used to stun the animal or to kill it by piercing, (it depends on the meaning of the ambiguous word "*nokphin,*" which means either to knock, to blow, or to pierce,) until the time of the said John. This is certain, that there is no shade of a reason to think that Moses commanded to kill by cutting the throat. The way by which the Rabbis tried to prove this a Mosaic command is perfectly absurd, as are almost all their interpretations.

We thus see that Judaism, as it is, is nothing but a blind belief against reason. It degenerated into Rabbinism, and is not only very far from keeping the law of God, but the rabbinical law is often against Moses; it is a perfect insanity, carried into Judaism, that the words of Moses may be fulfilled: "The Lord shall smite thee with madness and blindness." Deuter. xxviii: 28. Such is the blindness which befell my poor people of God.

We have seen, before, that the first foundation of Judaism is the belief of the mind. This *could* not have been the aim of the Bible, however. Man's depravity lies in his heart, so that the religion must be for the heart, to break and bend it, to turn it to the things of the Spirit. Consequently, the belief of the mind was only necessary in order to convince the heart; the mind must be used as the instrument of the heart. It is only a channel. The mind is perishable, is the flesh, is not the *man*. The mind's belief is the *preparatory* religion for the heart. So all the law is preparatory, a visible religion, a service of symbols, a visible service, a visible priest as mediator. As the visible things are of the flesh they could only be shadows, symbols of the things of the Spirit. Now, the misapprehension of the Rabbis was, taking the shadow for the real thing. They did not look after the aim; they mistook the way of religion for the religion itself. Thus they took the law for the religion, while the law never was intended to be the religion. They stopped with the religion of the mind, and went no farther. So they had a religion of the mind, of the flesh only; a visible religion which required an everlasting work. If there is no work there is no religion. Thus I said in the beginning of the last chapter, the law does not cure radically; it is only a medicine which is to be perpetually taken, for the disease remains. You are spiritually wounded and have to carry the plasters with your wounds all your life long. Are you a better, a spiritually healthier man because you keep the law? No, you only have to keep it because you are sick. If you break it, and you do break it, you are still worse for the responsibility the law puts upon you. As the law is no remedy for your human depravity, it pacifies not the yearning, languishing soul; it removes not your weakness; it gives you no reconciliation and atonement; it pacifies not your conscience; death is still more fearful, for you have not fulfilled the requirements of the law. Why do you believe the law, then? Because your *mind* makes you believe that the law is from God, on account of the miracles. Thus Judaism is a *belief of the mind* only; besides that, the Talmud is against it, namely, a belief in spite of common sense.

The belief of the mind is like that of a sick man entrusting the doctor with the care of his body because he has heard that the doctor is able to cure him. The mind trusts on account of the doctor's reputation. As soon as the medicine evinces the doctor's skill by its good effect, then the patient's heart also gets confidence; he then believes with his heart, he feels safe under the doctor's care. Should the medicine not have the desired effect, and he only has the doctor's assurance that after a long time he will be cured, he can only continue the medicine on account of a *blind belief of the mind*. This is exactly the case with believing the law. If you did not think that you were spiritually sick you would want no religion. But you feel sick, and fear the consequences, and take the medicine, and you believe the law, for you consider it to be able to cure you. You only know the law by reputation and trust, without seeing the effect. The doctor's ability is not proved by your own case; you perceive no improvement. But what can you do when your mind sees that the Bible must be from God? Your mind thus believes blindly until death. There can be no love for keeping the law as long as only the mind believes. The law is a *schoolmaster*, it only teaches to believe.

After finding that Judaism remained to be the religion of the mind, and took the law for religion, we can easily trace up the historical way by which it degenerated into Rabbinism. A law which leaves the heart unaffected had to degenerate. A law cannot be written for every circumstance of life; every lawyer and judge has to decide by analogy from one case to the other, and so the Rabbis had to do. Much was necessarily left to their arbitrariness. As long as they kept to the simplicity of the Bible, and did not depend on their own wisdom, and legislated in accordance with the Biblical spirit, in humility and subjection to God, so long they were executing the law in His name, so long they steered towards the aim of the religion. But not everybody could study the law, not everybody has the brain for it; knowledge and, in some respects, shrewdness are necessary for the lawyer and judge. Thus, the best-brained men became the Rabbis, and consequently, the authority. In consequence of this, their first sin was in leaving the spirit of contrition and meekness which David and the prophets breathe, and turning to sophistry and haughtiness. Knowledge of the law and shrewdness were the highest in estimation. It is considered by the Talmud as about the highest state of wisdom to be able to prove, by one hundred and fifty sophistical reasons, that a thing which was really legally unclean could still be considered clean according to the law. This beats the Grecian Sophist, and the Jewish Sophist was more dangerous, as he taught with the dignity of the divine teacher. The blind, erring Jewish Rabbi, with his much brain and vast amount of legal knowledge and traditions, almost always believed in his own authority. What was the authority? The brain, the learning of men, not the Spirit of God. The head alone was working in religion, it went on without the heart, until it wandered into a spiritual wilderness. Things went so far that the Rabbis ceased to teach God and His word, but themselves and their sophistry and absurd perversions of Scripture. And as the prophet said, "Precept upon precept, line upon line here a little and there a little," so they made law upon law, ordinance upon ordinance. The people were sinning and they gave them an ordinance to observe, thinking this would please the Lord. "Here a little, there a little," a little saying with the lips, a little doing in keeping a command. But the Lord wants all of you, your heart, your life; the center of your heart you must give Him, even when you do nothing. The law should only be the way for the heart to go and cling to God; to remind you and teach you to believe Him, and to show you how to tame your wild heart. The religion must be intended for the heart; the heart draws the whole man. In the heart God reveals to you that you have atonement; the heart wants to be reconciled with Him. You must *live* religion, think it, feel it, not only do it. Thus Judaism ceased to be a religion in the real sense and object of the word. What they called religion could even no longer be the religion of all, for it takes much brain and an everlasting study to know the rabbinical law before you can keep it. Thus religion became a monopoly; the learned men were the only religious people, and the common man had to look up to them, not only as the learned but also as the pious ones. Learning became identical with piety. The man of the country, who even had no school, was fearfully neglected, despised, and hated by the society of the learned. In some respects the common man was even considered unclean. Those who learned formed a kind of society (Chaberim), and extra laws were made to be observed in communicating with the countryman. A sort of an aristocracy sprung into life. It was an aristocracy of learning; but, nevertheless, the most heartless, pernicious and wicked one which ever ruined a nation. The term "countryman" (*Am-haarez*) became identical with "ignoramus," so that even to-day the word "*Am-haarez*" is used in the common jargon of the Jews, signifying the ignoramus in matters of law and religion, while the Jews, generally, not understanding the Hebrew, do not even know that they really say *countryman* in place of *ignoramus*. "The (*am-haarez*) country-man cannot be pious," is a proverb of the Fathers, and means the unlearned. Some of the sages, I believe it is the great Rabbi Akibah, says, "It is lawful to tear an ignoramus like a fish, even on the day of atonement." He did surely not mean it literally, but expressed only his enthusiasm for learning and law, and his hatred of the poor, neglected man of the country, who had no school. "An unlearned," or "countryman, is like unto an ass," is another human proverb of the "*sages*" (?). There are a great many such brutal expressions in the Talmud. They also teach that a learned man must nurture hatred, and take revenge like a serpent (nokem venoter kenachash). The consequence was, that the countryman hated the Rabbi in return, as Rabbi Akibah, who did not commence to study until his advanced age, testifies of his awful hatred for the learned people in the time of his own ignorance. Indeed, it was impossible for the common man to be anything else than a sinner, as the Rabbis made more law than they could keep, and themselves were carrying out haughtiness and hatred to excess.

This, my dear reader, was the spirit of the authorities of my people, when they rejected Jesus of Nazareth, not to speak of the hypocrites who devoured widows' houses, against which the Talmud also warns. I have only shown you a very little of the character of the *good* Rabbi according to the Talmud. They asked the single-hearted man who followed Christ, whether he saw the authorities believing. Every thing must go after human authority. The human authority outgrew that of God. They could not believe that anything good was coming out from Galilee, from the country. They were punished by their own sins, by their self-dependence and haughtiness.

I have already said that man's knowledge and wisdom are not identical with his "I," but are inward possessions, as money is an outward one. Brain and knowledge are the most precious gifts, if used in the right way, in subjection to and in the service of their Giver. But they are also the source of many evils when misused. They are the greatest source of temptations to vanity and conceit, to ambition, jealousy and hatred. These vices may look in the eyes of man more spiritualized. The man of learning meets with more forbearance for his vices; his ambition is surely considered excusable. But how many things may appear even righteous in our own eyes, yet are wickedness in the sight of our Omniscient Father! If you depend on your wisdom you depend on your "*self*" even more than the man of money. The owner is always subjected to the danger of losing his property, which is not the case with the learned. Some men of certain learning believe even that they are nearer to God, and holier men because they are learned. Many of them are the most jealous, selfish people, with an obnoxious, aristocratic air. They often wear a sweet face and make a show of meekness and humility, but they may be proud of their humility. And the learned man is surely more responsible. Man's depending on himself is the center of sin, and makes him look for nothing else but perishable gifts; as the "*self*" with its learning and wisdom are perishable. Very often the man of self believes in God and looks to Him for every thing he wants. But what does he want? Not the removal of his self-dependence, he wants not God Himself, to be dissolved in the Divine humility, purity, sweetness, love and truth. He wishes an addition to his selfishness; he prays for nothing but outward things. He dishonors God, he sins in praying, his belief becomes a source of sin, he is a pious sinner. Many an affliction is sent by our loving Father, intended as our best blessing; the pious sinner misses such precious blessings. Shining glory is all he wants. It is immaterial whether one wants to shine with money, brain, or even with religion. Religious wickedness and shine is surely the most abominable of all.

My people Israel's wickedness is a religious one. For these nineteen centuries learning shines, human authority leads. "*I*," nothing but "*I*." The mind and the shine. Israel with his Rabbis looked for a Messiah who was promised. But the Messiah of the mind is the one of the flesh. They expected nothing else but a mighty

King, who should beat the armies of the world, and sit upon a throne of gold, making others work for his people. They pray for a Messiah and God answers by many afflictions, by many fearful, gaping wounds; but, alas! of no avail. Come into the circles of Orthodox Jews to-day, and you will find Rabbinism the same as it was eighteen centuries ago. Sophistry and subtlety are the spirit of learning, the subtle head is the authority. The fruit of the authorities is an endless number of ceremonies. The people are experienced in keeping them now, but still the unlearned is fearfully despised unless he is rich. Every thing is founded on a blind belief. Necessarily every one must break the law more or less, and the very pious ones endure fastings and everlasting mouth-prayers, but they never hear the voice of God whispering in their hearts, "I have forgiven" (Salachthi).

All their religion consists in forms; do this, do that. Here a little, there a little; nothing else but doing. Even praying becomes a form for certain hours. Prayer as a communication with God, as the free utterance of the spirit between man and God, the closet prayer, is unknown in Israel. The prayer-book is every thing, and this is written in Hebrew, thus intelligible for the learned ones only. They pray with the lips. For the holidays, there is also a good deal of so-called poetry (Piut Machsor) to be said, which sounds more like a travesty than poetry. The language of the most of that so-called poetry is not to be considered a bad language, it is *no* language, but a bombast of rhymes and quibbles. The poet forms words and expressions after his own method

He does not pray, but shows his mastership in torturing the language. The best Hebraist has to give special study to some of this poetry in order to decipher it, and when he has succeeded he often finds it to be a part of the Talmudical law in rhymes. The great poet wanted to show his knowledge of the Talmud, as well as his mastership in manufacturing language. Some very pious Jews read this kind of poetry with such earnest, long faces, frequently looking up to heaven, and even shedding tears, without understanding one sentence of what they say. One may even be tempted to think that sometimes the poet himself did not understand what he wrote. I have spoken in the last chapter of the solemnity of the service of the day of atonement. The beginning of the service of this day, on the previous evening, is intended to be the most solemn hour of it; but the initiatory piece read, and called, *"Kol Niddre,"* may fill the heart of a civilized man, who understands it, with horror instead of devotion. At first the piece is written in the Chaldaic language, which sounds, to almost every one of the audience, like Chinese. And the following is about the substance of what it says:

"All the vows, pledges, oaths and obligations, which we shall vow, or give, or swear, or take upon ourselves from this to the next day of atonement, shall be null, naught, void and zero. Our vow shall be no vow, our swearing no swearing," etc.

Must not every sensible man be astonished that a people can say such words in their most sacred hour of the year, and *that* before the living God! But it is a fact. And not only the orthodox Jews say it, we can find

many congregations in this country, who claim to be
Reformers all the year, but when the *atoning-day*
comes they are afraid, and cling to all kinds of superstition, and would not banish that horrible piece from their
synagogue. The fact is, they do not know what it
means; it is Chaldaic, and being used to hear it from
their childhood, sung with a moving melody, they think
it was a moving prayer. Thus they perfectly defile their
most holy day by such a fearful sham prayer. The
Talmudical reasons for the saying of the *Kol Niddre* will
not interest the reader. There is surely no reason in
their reasons. It is, however, not so bad in its meaning
as it seems. It is only intended to declare oaths and
vows void when they are made under the impression of
error, when one swears falsely through a mistake. But
certainly this is not explained in the piece. According
to the literal meaning of the piece, anybody is apt to
think that the religious Jews do not consider an oath
binding, which is not the case. On the contrary, the
real orthodox Jew has great respect for an oath, and is
not to be considered apt to break one. An oath is very
sacred with the Jewish orthodoxy. (That is, an oath
before a Rabbi or any court of justice.) There have
been even orthodox authorities who protested against the
saying of this abominable piece (like R. Iizchack bar
Shesheth), but to no effect. The spirit of error prevailed.
This will illustrate sufficiently how the spirit of the synagogue has also degenerated. Some Jews to-day say, " I do
not believe in such things as Kol Niddre, and this is not
essential to Judaism. This is all true, but I only cite it

to show how a spirit of error has come over the synagogue. Supposing *all* the Jews would give up Kol Niddre to-day, it would still be a historical fact that they were in error and off from the way of religion. Such errors I only cite to show the result of a religion of forms; these errors prove the obliquity of the Jewish spirit. God forbid that I should write anything out of antagonistic feeling. I feel nothing but love and pity for my people, but you cannot show the truth till you have pointed out the error. If the Jewish religion were according to the will of God the Jewish heart could not become so petrified as to cling to form and to *pray* Kolniddre. Why did the spirit of the synagogue degenerate into what it is? The spirit of prayer, as seen in Hannah, David, Elias, Hezekiah, Habakkuk and Daniel, is entirely banished from Israel. A rabbinical codex points out the words to be used in praying.

The Jewish heart yearns, perhaps more than any other, for that unknown aim. As an average, God's people have heart and conscience. The fear of death is beyond description; the only hope is founded on the fact of being a son of Israel and Abraham. The heart is left hollow, but the people believe what the Rabbis have written; they believe with their minds. They believe the Rabbis so much, that they do not even read the Bible; if one studies it is the Talmudical literature. Bible study is considered a theme too trifling, as it takes no subtlety to understand it. The shining glory of learning is the rabbinical lore. All they usually read of the Scripture is the passage of the Pentateuch which has to be read on the Sabbath. There are a very few who, for the sake of the study of the classic Hebrew, study the Bible, but a man can be a Rabbi of reputation without having ever read all the prophets.

As regards the Jews themselves, I believe I have good reason to be proud of being a Jew. It means something to be a son of Abraham. Notwithstanding their oppressed condition, a great number of them have distinguished themselves in every branch of arts and science. In proportion to the number of souls, they are more numerously represented in the high schools and universities of Europe than any other nationality. The American Jews are an exception. They are generally more tender-hearted than the other people. Their blood is proved to be the purest on earth by the fact that notwithstanding their being without real religion, still they are not addicted to low vices and crimes. When do you hear of a Jewish murder? When do you see one a drunkard, or a burglar? They have also retained a pure belief in the One God; alas! the belief can only be one of the head, which does not govern the life. Notwithstanding the dreadful rabbinical law, there are a great many excellent and sublime moral teachings scattered all over the rabbinical literature. The people of God are not devoid of the best moral teachings (if moral teaching alone could make the man good). They teach the fear of the Lord, but as the prophet said, "And their fear towards me is taught by the precept of men." Isa. xxix : 13.

Now, my dear reader, supposing one believes the

Rabbis, as the humble writer of these pages once did, supposing he keeps every single law of their code; can the law satisfy? Can Judaism in any shape pacify the heart? Can a soul find rest and peace at the bosom of the old Rabbi? Has the Talmud any balm for the human wounds? Is the aim after which the heart yearns, for which mankind sighs, to be realized in a synagogue? Does a ray from heaven ever break through the windows of a synagogue to fill an empty heart with a mild warmth? Can the man in despair find consolation there? Is there any hope for the sinking soul? Have they arms with which to meet that terrible foe called death? Where is the object of the religion, then? The soul languishes to starvation, yearns after a drop of living water in the great wilderness of this life, but the rock which gave living water to Israel's children is taken from them. And as long as it was with them, even Moses struck the rock, even Moses came in passion and worked to get living water. Israel strikes the rock, but God said, "Speak and trust, else thou canst not come into the land of rest."

In what manner Judaism influenced the private life of the Jews to give solace, peace and felicity for this life, I do not consider necessary to discuss here. Surely such religion can be of no good influence. Not to touch here the point of dogmatical atonement, there is a certain atonement which is to be seen in this world; it is the perception of the heart of being nearer to the living God, and to have life and action governed by this perception. It is the everlasting consciousness of having a religion, the strength to resist the power of the flesh by the religion, the peace of mind and heart, the holiness of life, which is the seal of atonement. This kind of atonement is not known in Israel. The religion of the most pious Orthodox does not exercise any influence over his social and business life. The religion does surely not improve the Jewish character. The Jew never tastes the sweetness of God, nor does he comprehend what atonement means, how it feels. They have not the least idea of it. The religion is, as I said, nothing but forms; do this, do that, " here a little, there a little."

We may therefore say, with Saul of Tarsus, that the Jews have a zeal for God, but not according to knowledge. They suffer much with their piety; that rabbinical codex is a heavy, ugly burden, but they mean to please God with it. They are erring zealots, or zealous errants. They deserve the sympathy of every devout man. The hand of the Lord is visible in their error. The originators of the Talmud could not have taught such a law without being blinded. People with hearts, such as the children of Israel have, would not have yielded themselves to such insanity as to consider it their holy religion, and to be able to die for it. It is nothing but a punishment of God to have such a religion. They have shed streams of blood for this so-called religion. Where do the broadest streams of martyr blood which wind their way through the annals of history originate, if not in the poor heart of Israel? God's curse through Moses and the prophets is fulfilled.

There is another comparatively small sect of Jews

dispersed in the East, called Karaites, who do not believe the Talmud, and ridicule its authority. They keep the law according to the dead letters. They are surely right in not accepting the authority of the Talmud, and show very successfully where the Rabbis are against the law in many places. Yet the principle of keeping the dead letter is still less of a religion than even the talmudical Judaism. For the execution of the law undoubtedly requires an authority for every generation, and the Rabbis, occupying the seat of Moses, had authority to legislate for their time only, in agreement with the spirit of the law, as I have said before. As long as the sanctuary existed the Jews were under the obligation to obey their teachers. The wrong of the Rabbis was in deviating from the spirit of the Bible, the wrong use they made of their authority. They degenerated and made too much of themselves. So long as the law was in force there was a visible sanctuary, and also, so to say, an invisible one in the authority which was given to the legislative body of the nation (Synhedria) to regulate the law according to the time there was a human authority necessary for the old dispensation. Both sanctuary and authority were necessary for the keeping of the law. No law can be in force without some human authority with it. With the fall of the nation, with the destruction of the temple, with the dispersion of the people, there the authority ceased with the law. The Lord destroyed everything necessary for the keeping of the law. With the *fulfillment* of the law its church, its head and the legislative authority became superfluous and were destroyed.

The Talmud bases all its authority upon the following passage in

Deut. xvii: 8: "If there arise a matter too hard for thee in judgment between blood and blood, between plea and plea, and between stroke and stroke, being matters of controversy within thy gates, then shalt thou arise and get thee up into the place which the Lord thy God shall choose. And thou shalt come unto the priests, the Levites, and unto the judge that shall be in those days, and enquire; and they shall shew thee the sentence of judgment. And thou shalt do according to the sentence which they of that place which the Lord shall choose shall shew thee; and thou shalt observe to do according to all that they inform thee. According to the sentence of the law which they shall teach thee, and according to the judgment which they shall tell thee thou shalt do; *thou shalt not decline from the sentence which they shall shew thee to the right nor to the left.*"

The last words of this citation, "thou shalt not decline from the sentence which they shall shew thee to the right nor to the left," are the foundation upon which the Talmud is built. Its authors say that every Israelite owes them obedience because it is forbidden to decline (*lav delo thassoor*). But we must not forget that in this very passage the authority is only given in connection with the place "*which the Lord thy God shall choose.*" As soon as the chosen place is destroyed there is no authority. Place, and sanctuary, and priest, and judge, and elder formed together the visible church of the visible law;

neither can exist without the other; each integrates the other. The Talmudists did not look upon it in this true way.

But even so long as the law was in force, and the Rabbis had authority, they were not allowed to put their ordinances down in writing, because it was only for the time; their ordinances could only have the durability of their authority, namely, their time. One generation could not prescribe for the other, for the coming generation had the same authority as the preceding. The very passage of Deuter. I have cited above, and upon which the Rabbis founded their authority, also forbids to make laws for coming generations, as far as the authority is given in connection with the time. Therefore it was considered like two laws; one *written*, for all the generations, the law of Moses, the other oral, for every single generation, which was not permitted to be written. (*Debarim shebaal peh e atha reshai leomron bekethab.*) But towards the end of the second century, as the nation became depressed and persecuted, the Rabbi saw the danger of losing the oral law with the loss of a legislative body at the head of the nation, and they were blinded to believe that the oral law of the different generations was binding as much as the law of Moses (not to speak of their not seeing the signs of the time, that the law was altogether without effect now, and that they had no authority whatever), they wrote their oral law down for the coming generations. Supposing the law was not abolished now, and consequently the leaders of the nation had the right to have their oral law, still then the Talmud would be of no authority, for it never had any, but as an oral law, *i. e.*, only a temporary authority. The writing of the Talmud was against the principle of oral law, as this ought to be changeable. Thus we find error upon error.

Returning to our Karaites, now, we may say that, notwithstanding our agreeing with them that the now written oral law, namely, the Talmud, is an imposition, for it is no oral law, still they err in denying the principle of the oral law, because the written law can not be sufficient with the dead letter, but has to have a head of the nation to apply the law in accordance with its spirit and with the time. In other words, the law can only be binding with an oral law, that is, with one of an authority of the chosen place, or not at all.

While not proposing to dwell here upon the many contentions between the Karaites and Talmudists, I must mention the one about the Jewish Calendar. The Karaites have not accepted the Jewish Calendar, and their holidays fall, most of the time, on different days. In examining their reasons, we shall find that the Karaites are perfectly right; for the acceptance of the Calendar on the part of the Rabbis, was not only without any Biblical authority, but against Scripture; as the Jewish holidays certainly do not fall on the days appointed by the law. The Karaites show, and anybody can see it, that the new moon's day of the Calendar often falls not at the time of the real new moon. Thus the holidays do not fall on the day of the month appointed by Moses. The day of atonement, for instance, which is the tenth day of the seventh month according to the Bible, falls sometimes on the ninth or eleventh day after each new moon. The appointment of the day for new moon or holiday was left by Moses to the authority of every generation of the nation, to be sanctified according to the time of the new moon. "These are the feasts of the Lord, holy convocations, which *ye shall proclaim in their seasons.*" Lev. xxiii: 4. Thus they had no more authority to accept a Calendar for the future generations than to impose the Talmud upon them; for the authority of every generation had to proclaim the new moon and holidays; it belongs to the oral law, moreover, as the Calendar, of itself, is not according to the law.

It seems that the most eminent Rabbis have accepted that Calendar, but with aversion. Several centuries after the destruction of the temple the Jews still had a kind of religious head in the Patriarch of Palestine, and with him some kind of a school of the most learned Rabbis, claiming to have the authority of the old Synhedria. These Rabbis called out the day of the new moon, and thus appointed the holidays. Those Israelites living too far from the seat of the Patriarch, not being able to know within a few days when the new moon was seen and sanctified, had to keep two days as holidays, because they did not know which was the right one. In the second century the Babylonian Samuel, who was an astronomer, made out a Calendar and offered it to the authorities in Palestine, but they refused to accept it. They paid no attention to the astronomical calculations, no matter how correct they might be, and acted rather

according to the law. But the patriarch Rabbi, Hillel
II., who lived in the fourth century, accepted the
Calendar, making it binding for Israel. The Jews,
trained to bow before the rabbinical authority, accepted the Calendar. Now they asked the Rabbis in
Palestine whether they might not abolish the keeping of
the second holiday, as they knew now which was the right
day. No sensible man could see any reason now for
keeping two days instead of the Biblical one any longer,
if the Calendar was right. Still they answered them from
Palestine, "Take heed to keep the customs of your
fathers." This makes it obvious that the Rabbis had
not full confidence in this Calendar, else they would not
have retained the keeping of two days. This Rabbi,
Hillel II., cannot have been a man after the heart of the
truly believing Jews. He showed unbelieving tenden-
cies in declaring that there was no Messiah for Israel;
the promises were fulfilled in King Hezekiah. I have
already said, in the second chapter of this book, that
most of the prophets lived after Hezekiah, and the Talmud also rejected emphatically this *quasi* infidelity of
Rabbi Hillel. I only cite it to show the spirit of the one
who introduced the Calendar. It is no place here to make
any historical researches about the usurpation, character
and time of Hillel II. But the fact that the Calendar
accepted by him was rejected before, and that the Rabbis retained the keeping of two days, as well as his expression about the Messiah, show plainly that the Calendar could not have been accepted without aversion
by those who were sincere Jewish believers. Now, see-

ing that the Karaites very successfully contest the Calendar, and show that the Jews do not even keep the Mosaic holidays, in the right time, thus we find that they cannot even keep their law.

The Lord shows that the law is abolished, as it is a thing absolutely impossible to keep it now. The Jews who mean to keep the law do not, cannot keep it. If the Calendar is wrong (which surely is the case even for other astronomical reasons as some have shown), there is even no authority now who could legally appoint the day for holidays; in case the Jews should wish to keep the legal time, who is the authority? We have seen that it is destroyed with the national independence. The Reformers have abolished the keeping of two days, not thinking of the fact that the Calendar is wrong. Thinking that I have cited sufficiently of characteristics of the Talmud, and of the Synagogue, which is possessed by the talmudical spirit, we shall close this chapter, leaving it to the unbiased reader to form his own opinion about Judaism as it is. I do not find it necessary to make any conclusive remarks. But after showing the corruptions which crept into the religion of the ancient people, I find myself obliged to speak again of the reform which claims to remove them. Justice requires me to devote the next chapter to the Jewish reform, its cause and error, before we can speak of the divine reform, of a divine religion.

CHAPTER X.

CAUSE AND ERROR OF THE REFORM.

"Behold, the word of the Lord is unto them a reproach ; they have no delight in it." JER. vi: 10.

After what we saw of the corruptions of Judaism in the last chapter, we can surely not blame those Jews of this century who demanded a reform: The cause of every reform is always to be found in the history of previous corruptions. So we find the cause of the Jewish reform in the chapter of the rabbinical law. In this century, the dawning of the coming bright day of true liberty, so soon as the air of freedom has touched the oppressed people, so soon as some of their leaders had entered the temple of free science and heard logic in universities, their discovery of the Talmudical error was only a natural consequence. They saw no effect of the Jewish religion upon the heart of the believer; they even claimed that an orthodox Jew, who sticks to all possible formalities of orthodoxy, is usually not so good a man as the unbeliever. They found that a religion of forms is useless, ridiculous. They saw that there is no real religion in orthodoxy; they found the most of the talmudical logic an absurdity. They also rightly contested the authority of the old Rabbis to prescribe laws and ordinances for them. Not looking at the fact that the authority of the teachers of the oral law depends on the place God had chosen as the capital of the nation, as we have seen before; forgetting that authority in religious matters cannot be taken by men of themselves but must be given to them by God, as was the old Jewish authority, a divine ordination, they claimed the authority of the time, according to the principle of the oral law. They cast the ugly burden called rabbinical codex from their necks. They made themselves free of the Talmud. As we agree with the orthodoxy concerning the true foundation of the religion, the divine origin of the Bible and its doctrines, so does the reform agree with us in seeing the structure of darkness and error which the Rabbis erected upon the sacred ground of truth. But the misfortune is, that while giving up the Talmud they did not abandon its spirit of self-dependence, of haughty human authority in matters of God. The spirit of meekness, of obedience to God, did not occupy the heart which freed itself from the pressure of the Talmud. Not finding the aim of the Bible, knowing of religion only the *belief* of the mind, they simply changed it to a *disbelief* of it. The difference is, that the Talmud did only erroneously pervert the Bible; the Reform, seeing no effect, does wantonly reject it, and in such an illogical manner that they expose themselves to the most absurd inconsistency, as I have shown in the second chapter.

Giving up belief in everything which seems to be against reason, not admitting that there is anything above it and therefore incomprehensible, they depend on themselves, and their reason has made them unreasonable. Seeing the uselessness of a religion of forms for a belief of the mind, they chose unbelief; instead of casting their hearts into the dust before the living God of Israel, who chose them to testify to his wonderful ways by their own existence.

If the *belief* of the mind has no effect, they concluded that the *unbelief* will have; but the true conclusion is: if the belief of *the mind* has no effect, then that of the *heart* must have it. At the same time they saw the marvelous history of their people, and the great influence of the Bible, so that they could not openly reject it, and they claimed that the Bible is a book according to reason, and its doctrines regarding Divinity were the same as those of the philosophers. Thus the Jewish religion is a perfectly reasonable religion. But as the law is not according to reason they reject it, and only claim to keep such parts of it as are reasonable; and the result is, they keep nothing. And, as much of the Bible is not to be comprehended by reason, they do not believe those parts of it. They thus fell into the inconsistencies I have described. They think that, with giving up the Talmud and casting the Bible after their own pattern, they make Judaism a rational religion. But, looking at the signs of the times, we must ask, If the Reformers were right, why did Israel suffer under the curse of having a Talmud? Why did the only religion which had the true principle of God fall into such a degradation? And if Israel has the true religion why has it to endure such matchless sufferings? Israel always suffers. Free in the civilized parts of the world, they suffer in Roumania, Persia, Morocco, and in many other countries. They never suffered all over the earth at one time, but the nation always suffers, according to prediction. Why does Providence allow this? The Reformers say that the Jews, sufferings are to be attributed to the wickedness of the persecutors, and thus refuse to take any lesson from it. Truly, no honest man can see in it anything else than the most abominable, atrocious wickedness and heartlessness. But the question is, Why did the all-ruling Providence subject them to such cruel wickedness? The wickedness of the persecutors can only be considered instrumental to the wrath of the God of justice. But, besides this, the main question is, whether the God of the Bible is really the God of the rationalists? whether the Monotheism of Moses is the same as reason teaches, so that the Reformers are entitled to say they believe in the God of Israel? We will therefore cite a few Biblical passages, in order to examine whether one can claim that he believes the Bible and still say he only believes what he can understand; whether Judaism is possible without belief. We read:

> Gen. iii: 8, "And they heard the voice of the Lord God walking in the garden in the cool of the day: and Adam and his wife hid themselves from the presence of the Lord God amongst the trees of the garden."

Is that comprehensible? Is it, or not, according to the other teachings of the Bible, that God is omnipresent? Who can hide himself from God?

Gen. vi: 6, "And it repented the Lord that he had made man on the earth, and *it grieved him at his heart.*"

That was after he saw that everything he made was very good. And is God's grieving at his heart comprehensible? We are, in other places in the Bible, assured that God is not man to repent. The plainest contradiction.

Gen. xi: 5, "And the Lord *came down* to see the city and the tower, which the children of men builded.

Must God go down in order to see?

Gen. xxxii: 24 to 30, "And Jacob was left alone; and there wrestled a man with him until the breaking of the day. And when he saw that he prevailed not against him, he touched the hollow of his thigh; and the hollow of Jacob's thigh was out of joint, as he wrestled with him. And he said, Let me go, for the day breaketh. And he said, I will not let thee go except thou bless me. And he said unto him, What is thy name? And he said, Jacob. And he said, Thy name shall be called no more Jacob, but Israel: for as a prince hast thou power with God and with men, and hast prevailed. And Jacob asked him, and said, Tell me, I pray thee, thy name. And he said, Wherefore is it that thou dost ask after my name? And he blessed him there. And Jacob called the name of the place Peniel: for I have seen God face to face, and my life is preserved.

Let us look at this passage a little nearer. A man comes, wrestles, is beaten, hurts Jacob, changes his name, would not tell his own, blesses him, and finally it turns out to be the living God. You cannot say it was a vision, or a dream, for poor Jacob halted after it. Can a sensible man deny that the Bible has incomprehensible mysteries? According to reason it would be most absurd; you cannot even make poetry of it.

Read further: "And as he passed over Pennel the sun rose upon him, and he halted upon his thigh. Therefore the children of Israel eat not of the sinew which shrank, which is upon the hollow of the thigh unto this day, because he touched the hollow of Jacob's thigh in the sinew that shrank." (Gid hanasheh).

We see the children of Israel do not eat that part of the animal until to-day, during these many centuries. And there was never any doubt in Israel about the authenticity of this passage as an historical fact. Is Judaism, is the Bible rational? There is a thing which suffers no kind of interpretation, but must be taken as a mysterious fact, unless we refuse to believe the Bible, and forfeit the right to claim to be Jews in our religion. In that case the Bible would be the most foolish book in existence.

Ex. vi: 3, "And I appeared to Abraham, Isaac and Jacob by the name of Shadday; but by my name Jehovah was I not known to them."

Is this not like a mysticism? What difference does it make under what name God appears? What does it mean, God's having names, and appearing by different ones?

Before the Israelites left Egypt, the Lord commanded every house to kill a lamb and sprinkle the blood upon the door-posts; and says:

Ex. xii: 13, "And the blood shall be to you for a sign, upon the houses where ye are: and when I see the blood, I will pass over you."

Did not God know where the Israelites lived without the blood? We further read:

Ex. xxiv: 9 to 11, "Then went up Moses and Aaron, Nadab, and Abihu, and seventy of the elders of Israel; and they saw the God of Israel: and there was under his feet as it were a paved work of a sapphire stone, (or, like the work of white sapphire) and as it were the body of heaven in his clearness. And upon the nobles of the children of Israel he laid not his hand: also they ‘saw God, and did eat and drink."

But we read, further, in Ex. xxxiii: 20, "And he said, Thou canst not see my face: for there shall no man see me, and live. And the Lord said, Behold, there is a place by me, and thou shalt stand upon a rock: and it shall come to pass, while my glory passeth by, that I will put thee in a cleft of the rock, and will cover thee with my hand while I pass by: and I will take away mine hand, and thou shalt see my back parts; but my face shall not be seen."

Can these passages be defended by reason? No man can see God and live; but Moses and Aaron, with the elders, saw God, and did eat and drink; and saw what was under his feet. And again, Moses is placed in a cleft of the rock, and the Lord puts his hand on him until he passes by, and then lets him see his back. In another place it says again that God spake to Moses "face to face" as a man speaks to his friend. The invisible, glorious God of Israel is seen! Are there no mysteries? A great number of similar passages are found in the Bible. In the thirteenth chapter of Judges we read that, when the angel of God comes to announce to Manoah's wife the birth of Samson, he appears like a man, *his name is wonderful*, and the woman says, afterwards, she saw God.

No one can be considered a Jew without belief in the revelations of Sinai, where God went down on the mountain and spoke, "I am the Lord thy God." The tables of the covenant are said to have been written by the finger of God. In short, notwithstanding that the Bible teaches that God is omnipresent, invisible, spiritual, still he appears not as the God of philosophy, but a wonderful God, with such marvelous revelations, which must be taken literally. As these revelations are the foundation of the Israelitish belief, as the Bible cannot be considered true without these revelations, consequently the God of Israel is not the God of philosophy. Is God to be called the God of Israel if the Biblical revelations were not true? Why is he the God of Israel? If the Bible, which originated with the Jewish people, and which this people always believed, is not true, then the Jews were idolaters; for they believed not in the one God, as even some Grecian philosophers have taught. They believed that God dwelt between Cherubim which their own hands had made. They believed that he spake and wrote. If what the Jews believed is not true, then that chosen people were idolaters, and the Reformers, who do not believe such incomprehensible things to be true, but consider the above cited Biblical passages to be either lies or poetry, then these Reformers, with some other Deists, are the only monotheists. Consequently, the Reformers have no shade of a reason to claim that they believe in the God of Israel. Or, if we say that the Reformers are right in their interpretations of Scripture, then the Jews were wrong. Thus a Reformer ought to abandon the name of Jew, to be ashamed of the glorious name "Israelite," for it means an idolater. For, they cannot deny the fact that Israel always believed that the revelations were literally true. And so they do believe to-day, with the exception of those in Germany and America who call themselves Reformers, and think that they spiritualize the Bible by their interpretations. Say the Bible is true in the sense of the Reform, then the Israelites were idolaters through their misapprehension of it, just as the Jew affirms to-day that the Christians were idolaters while misunderstanding or misinterpreting the Bible. If the Bible is not history, still it is a fact that Israel considers it as such. And God has chosen an idolatrous people; for God, as represented in the Bible, is not the true God, according to philosophy. According to the Reform interpretations, that is, if *their* God of Moses is the God of the philosophers, (and the revelations and miracles are only either Mosaic tricks, or lies, or poetry,) then the God of the Orthodox Jew is not the one of the Reformer. The God of the Reformer is not the God of Israel. Israel's

God is the mysterious God of holiness, the wonderful God of miracles, with all the qualities of the God of philosophy.

I have said, before this, that most of the passages relating supernatural occurrences are written in such a language that they cannot be interpreted any other way than in the plainest literal meaning of the words. Read the passages above cited, and show me how they can bear any other interpretation. One can only say, and many Reformers do say, that Moses and the prophets only taught according to their time; they say the Jews were not ripe yet for the full truth, that is the God of rationalism or pantheism, therefore Moses had to make them believe that he worked miracles, and to give them such a law and such low doctrines of the divinity, as if God will be one who speaks and writes. Well, if this is admitted, you say then, we live in an enlightened century and have purer ideas; but if Judaism was not ripe, not pure, then you must give up Judaism as an old-fashioned religion, like the Grecian mythology; and, pray do not claim that you reform it. When the Grecians gave up their idols and accepted Christianity they did not claim that they reformed their old religion. They said that their fathers were blind, and they must accept another religion. The Reformers declare, in every synagogue, that their fathers were also blind, and still they claim to keep the Jewish religion. The Jews always believed the Bible, without those sublime reformed explanations. You say that our fathers were not ripe and you are; then you are no Jews.

I believe that the Jews must have had some mysteries orally taught to some select ones by Moses and the prophets about such Biblical passages as I have cited above. These mysteries are called "Kabalah" (which word signifies tradition). Like the traditions of the oral law, this Kabalah became degenerated with the deviation of the nation from the spirit of the Bible. Just as a few of the Talmudical traditions must have been genuine, so there is to be found some divine truth in that gnostic science, Kabalah. There are many truths scattered all over the rabbinical and kabalistic literature, remains of the better times of the nation, but it is hard to discern now which are genuine. Scientific researches prove the very great age of the Kabalah, but the above cited passages prove that this science must be as old as the Scriptures (the very words of these pages are mystical) if it is not true that they had some traditions from Abraham, or, as they claim, even from Adam. Alas! Israel's knowledge and secrets are adulterated and not to be trusted.

Now, this Kabalah is accepted by all the orthodox Jews, and its doctrines of the divinity must be considered the plainest idolatry, according to rationalism.

Now we see that the God of the Reformers is not the mysterious God of Israel. Refusing to believe mysteries, and still bound to the Bible by their history and race-pride, they impute to it their own rationalism, and dare to assert that the Bible only teaches things according to reason. All the value of the Bible, say they, lies in the doctrine of the unity of God, and some moral comprehensible teachings. And to this they attribute the great influence of the Bible. The fact is that we can find more moral and sublime doctrines according to reason in the teachings of the old heathen. Did not Confucius, Zoroaster, Socrates, Plato and a great many other heathen teach a sublime moral? Still their Books do not conquer the world. Was not Solon a wise lawgiver, and were not Demosthenes and Cicero eloquent speakers? But the world reads Moses and Isaiah. What is the cause of this phenomenon, if reason is the only mediator between man and God, as the Reformers maintain? Then again, the world did not accept the Bible with the rational interpretations, but with the plain belief, and it is the belief which has exercised such a wonderful influence. And not only are there contradictions and seeming absurdities in the Bible, but even some things against our ideas of morality and humanity. For instance, the manner of taking vengeance upon Midian and Amalek, or the commandment to kill *every soul* of the people of Canaan; was it not cruel? Gentile infidels say that the God of Israel was a cruel God; they are at least consistent; if the Reformers refuse to *believe*, then they ought to join those infidels, in order not to be so foolishly inconsistent. The believer does not claim that it was not cruel, but he *trusts* the God of Israel, who is the love itself, as regards the justice of His command. There is no logical possibility of accepting the Bible without *belief*. Without belief they are without the God of Israel.

A Reform Rabbi, hearing of my conversion, wrote me a letter admonishing me not to forsake the God of Israel and fall so low as to take part in the Christian idolatry. I replied that I believe in Israel's God more than ever, but also in His Messiah. To this he responded that Israel has given up such a belief as the coming of a Messiah. My dear Rabbi, if the Biblical promises of a Messiah, which I shall cite below, are not true, then where is the God of Israel? If you do not believe the Bible regarding the Messiah, why must I believe your doctrine of the divinity? If the Bible is not true, then I need not to be better than Socrates. Even idolatry is no sin if the Bible is not true, since men like Socrates worshiped idols. Why is one part of the Bible true and the other not? You will say, our time has progressed; but I can not see any progress, when all the Christians are idolaters. You will say, it is against reason to be a Christian; but you are not reasonable in claiming to be an adherent to the Bible and still refusing to believe its promises regarding the Messiah. I believe in equal rights.

The fact is, that not being able to reconcile their rationalism with the Jewish history, the Reformers can not avoid being inconsistent. Thus their rational platform has caused their irrationality. They had a right cause for a reform, but their error grew from leaving the platform of religion, which is belief. Without belief the Jewish religion cannot possibly be reformed, but destroyed. And so it is with them. Through the Talmud the Jews lost the aim of a religion. The Talmud made religion a mass of forms; those being found useless, there is nothing left. If the Reformers had commenced with a zeal for God, if they had kept the Biblical platform, then they would deserve sympathy. But, brought up in the Talmudical school, knowing only the religion of the mind, they retained the Talmudical spirit of depending on the mind, on themselves. They saw the old error of the rabbinical belief, and they thought to remove it by giving up all belief. But the Rabbis' error was not caused by belief, but by the peculiar Talmudical haughtiness and self-assumption through which they missed the aim of the belief. Thus the reform has not removed the real cause of the evil. The cause of it they retained. It is the same spirit with both parties. It is, after all, no difference whether the Word of God is perverted or rejected, as long as the true aim of religion is not realized in its use. Before a man can see the aim of religion he must first be humbled in his heart, so as to feel his own depravity, the joylessness and hopelessness of his life; he must see that there is no satisfaction in perishable things, because of the immortal thing in man. He must feel that he belongs, not to the "All" as long as he goes after the "self." He must feel how far he is from true monotheism, which is the spirit of love poured over the "all," and making all one; from the real source of love, which is God. The religious expression for this is, "Man must be under the conviction of sin, before he can find reconciliation." The Reformers never reached the aim of religion; for their starting-point was not humility, but national pride and dependence on knowledge. One does not look after comfort before he feels his sorrow. What is the effect of their reform? A low materialism, under the name of a new Judaism. They have nothing but the carnal human mind for their guidance. They claim to be progressive, while they have made a long retrogression, and are now thirty-five centuries backwards in the time of Egyptian darkness, when the world had nothing of the Bible. There were philosophers and rationalists also in Egypt, but the greatest fortune the world ever received, and the greatest progress it ever made, was in the reception of the Bible. Still the Reformers consider themselves progressive. They have no religion, no spiritual comfort, no hope, indeed no God. Nothing but miserable materialism; the cold, hollow, insatiable flesh, the carnal "self." The reform Synagogue actually ridicules all religion.

The reform is rather adapted to deaden every religious propensity of the human heart, if this were possible. But as the need of religion is natural with the heart, and the reform really teaches against it, so we may conclude that it provides a way from Judaism to the truth. For, as the propensity for religion is natural with every man, the Jews could only be kept from seeking the true religion by the rabbinical pseudo-religion; they had something to cling to if it even is a shade. But now the reform is fulfilling a mission in showing to the Jewish nation, first, that their religion is false; while, as they offer nothing else for it, they can only blind the people with their inconsistency, though not for a long time. The people will soon be aware of the ridiculousness of such reform. They will find that there is something else necessary besides rationalism, that there is something worth believing, and that the God of Israel did not leave mankind without help and comfort. Those who believe not the Bible now, because they see no aim in it, will easily believe as soon as they find the aim, the object which it contemplates. The spiritual nature of man will drive him to find a religion. Religion is a natural necessity, for men are most miserable without it. Thus the reform, in destroying the false religion will cause men to search for the true one.

The Lord's ways are marvelous. He uses his enemies as instruments for his work. Israel's history is a chain of miracles, and this absurd reform will prove to be the greatest miracle in leading God's people to be reconciled to Him. "Canst thou by searching find out God? canst thou find out the Almighty unto perfection? It is as high as heaven, what canst thou do? deeper than hell, what canst thou know?" Job xi: 7, 8.

How wonderful, how ineffably wonderful are the ways of Providence! The people whose history is the Bible's unanswerable evidence, who own the Book of God, have left it; those who saw the great light walk in darkness. Those who saw Sinai in its shining glory grope after the guidance of the Talmud; those who were sheltered by the wings of God and led by His pillars of cloud and flame, are without refuge, and run after a shade called Reform. The very people whose life, whose very existence is God's witness, who sealed the truth of His word by their blood, shut their ears against His voice. The voice of Israel's blood cries from the ground; it is as if the numberless graves of his numberless martyrs would

open and the shadows of the dead would rise and
ascend, their hands pointing to the Bible. The blood of
the heroic Maccabeans cries, their shadows hover over
the destitute Jerusalem, whose ruins speak, and they
testify to the truth of the Bible. From the blood of the
murdered sucklings under Nebuchadnezzar and Titus;
through all the ages of darkness and of Spanish pyres,
until the last drop of Jewish blood which saturated Roumanian ground, every drop boils and cries, "Bible!"
"Bible!"

The voice of Israel's blood touches the ears of the
Gentiles, and convinces their hearts, but Israel's ears are
stopped; his heart is hardened; the words of the prophet
are fulfilled; "lest they see with their eyes, and hear
with their ears, and understand with their heart, and
convert, and be healed." Is. vi: 10. Israel's unbelief is
one of the miracles of his miraculous history. Who has
the heart to pray like Daniel? Who can make confession for Israel's sins like the beloved Daniel, so that the
voice shall ascend and reach the throne of the God of
love? Who can lament like Jeremiah? Who can pray,
lament? Pray, lament, take no rest; pray, be not silent
for the walls of Zion; pray, weep, let a flood of tears
come over the earth to destroy every word written by
man; the Bible shall never be destroyed. It will move
over the burning waters of tears like the ark in the
deluge. Pray and weep for the ashes of Zion, melt the
snow of Lebanon's venerable summit with your tears,
until David's silent harp shall again give its tunes; until
his crown shall again shine in Jerusalem; until Israel's

eyes shall be opened to see his true glory. Israel's misfortune is that it never sees the aim, the glory of its religion. The men of the Talmud, the Pharisees believed, but remained satisfied with a belief of the mind. The Pharisees were right in their belief; they had the authority, also, as I have shown above. "Salvation comes from the Jews." They had the right belief of the mind, but they did not find the aim of it, for there was too much "self." Thus those of their time who had more of a secular education, seeing no aim in the Phariseean religion, became like the Saducees, who were nothing but materialists. In this century we see the same thing in another form. The real principle of the Saducees and the Reformers is materialism, "I." Reformed Rabbis! Show me the effect of your so-called religion. What do you accomplish? Look at your flocks; does religion, God, anything which is ideal, govern them? Show me, all ye Reformers, all of you, show me one single soul you have turned from low materialism to even infidel idealism? Show me one man of you who lives in the real fear of the God of our fathers; one man, I would like to see, who is entitled to say that he is religious. What consolation have you for life; what hope for death?

Indeed, we only need to read the Bible to see rabbinism and reform refuted. The Bible refutes them of itself. Now, after forcing evidences for the truth of the Bible, as well as the falsehood of Judaism in any shape, we must conclude that there must be another religion, according to the Bible. For, if the Bible is truly the word of God, there must be a true religion to be gained from it, as God could not have spoken in vain. As soon as we know that the Bible is God's word, then every soul which seeks true comfort, which yearns for God, must look to it for help. Thus the fact that Judaism is false, proves that the other religion, which is founded upon the Bible, must be true, for God's word must have established a true religion. As Christianity is the other religion which claims to have a Biblical foundation, it remains our duty to examine whether it proves to be what it claims, and whether it does offer the living water after which our souls languish, the balm for the wounded heart; reconciliation with God. But before we treat this question, we shall first examine the Christian doctrine of the Trinity; for, as followers of the Bible, our first principle must be monotheism, the belief in *One* God.

CHAPTER XI.

TRINITY.

"Hear, O Israel, Jehovah our God, Jehovah ONE." Deut. vi: 4.

Far above our comprehension, too high for the conception of our reason, it has pleased our All-wise Father to choose three different ways by which He reveals Himself to man, and speaks "I am." Through three different revelations we know that He is, even while we can not comprehend *what* He is.

Looking at the infinite power which is manifested in nature, from the grain of sand and drop of water, to the vast oceans and gigantic mountains; from the microscopic worm to the unicorn and whale, what a wisdom is visible in the life of the endless varieties of all that breathes on earth, or inhabits the waters. Every creature speaks with the psalmist, "O Lord, how manifold are thy works! In wisdom hast thou made them all." Ps. cix : 24.

The silver-sprinkled blue firmament, the gold-faced moon, the light-diffusing sun, all these silently whirling, shining heavenly bodies, driven by the law of gravitation, what a wisdom is manifested in their harmonious dance, what a spirit of harmony and love is poured over these heavens! "Lift up your eyes on high, and behold who hath created these." Is. xi : 26. They all testify to their First Cause ; they sing the praise of their Creator. "The heavens declare the glory of God, and the firmament showeth his handywork." Ps. xix : 1. Hear the howling storm, the roaring billows of the sea, the rustling of the cascade, the voice of the thunder; they are the echo of His voice. The murmuring of the forest trees, with the charm of the song of their birds, the whispering of the quiet waters of the ponds and rivers, the sweet rays of the lovely moon pouring over a resting nature, the silver-eyed, sweet evening star, the rosy beams of evening-fall, like kisses of the departing sun to land and sea ; they all tell of the love and loveliness of our God ; they all solicit our devotion to the love-expending Creator. The infinite power and wisdom which we find in nature proves the existence of its Creator. Nature sheds a spirit of devotion over souls susceptible of the love of God. The harmony of nature opens your heart. Your breast expands, you stretch your arms, you bow your head before the infinite greatness of the Almighty God. This is the first of God's revelations, *God in nature*.

When, again, you cast the eye of the spirit backwards, over the past centuries of history, you follow the steps of mankind, you see nations spring up, grow, rise high to command the world, and then decay, perish, to make room for others. You see men lifted up to greatness and honor, they rule nations with their word, govern people by their will, and then fall into the dust and disappear. You often see these great men and nations steering towards their destruction when they imagine themselves climbing towards the summit of their fame; they prepare their fall while working for their greatness; they lay the foundation of their ruin while triumphing in success and victory; and you find them to be nothing but instruments in the hands of a higher wisdom. You finally find that the different rises and falls of all these men and nations, these seemingly unplanned changes of building and destruction, are combined to lead mankind under *one* plan forward to a point of destination. You perceive that mankind, as a race, is led like a child from the cradle through the different phases of age, and you conclude that there is an All-wise Father to lead them. You see an unutterable wisdom, an all-loving providence ruling the fate of men and nations, leading them after its own one plan. You find *one* wisdom, *one* spirit, *one* plan pervading all history. The loving Father has watched over mankind's cradle, has taught its lessons, managed its affairs and supplied its wants. An incomprehensible wisdom has made use of all the events of human history, kept them under control to apply them to the very highest good of humanity. Here again you have a revelation of God. You see God in history. But this second revelation is of an entirely different character from the first. The God of history appears not like the God of nature. The manner of revelation is different; it does not seem to be the same person. In the God of nature you saw the Almighty Creator, the giver of all; here you see the all-wise Father, the manager and ruler of everything. The devotion you perceive in your heart is also of a different character; you feel a kind of a yearning to the God of nature, and a reverence before the God of history. Here you feel awe, you drop your arms, you lift up your head toward heaven and exclaim, "Thou art the Lord who callest the generations from the beginning." Thus the two revelations of the One God make Him appear as two different persons, and cause two different kinds of devotion, while you know that the God of nature is also the God of history.

When, finally, we consider the manner of revelation in the Bible, here God appears as an entirely different person. The God of nature changes nature's laws; the God of history chooses, redeems and preserves one people against history's laws. We see the God of Israel, the God of Sinai, the God of miracles, the Lord of hosts, the Holy One of Israel and His Redeemer. The God of the Bible is the only one you can fear and love. What a difference in the manifestation! Thus, my reader, we see that it pleased the Lord to appear in three different characters, like three different persons. The God of nature, of history, and of the Bible is but one God.

These three different ways of revelation we may use as an illustration for the doctrine of the Trinity. I have only shown the three different ways of God's revelation in order to illustrate how the Christians believe in one God in a Trinity. Do you, reader, believe in three Gods because you see his three different revelations? Why shall the Christian be accused of believing in more than one God, while the unity of God is the principal doctrine of Christianity? The Christian believes that there is but one God; but that the *manner* of God's existence is as a Trinity. The doctrine of the Trinity does not touch the question of quantity, but of quality. The Christian says not, there are three Gods, or three is one, but only one God, whose manner of existence, or mode of revelation, is triune. Thus Trinity touches only the question of the substance of the Godhead, a thing which no man can understand, whether he believes in a Trinity or not. The philosopher who proves that there is a God, admits that nothing can be comprehended of his substance, his essence; the believer believes the same thing, that there is a God whose manner of being, substance or essence cannot be known; but he believes it is as a Trinity, a something he cannot comprehend. Thus the Christian stands on the same platform with the philosopher, but he believes something about God's manner of existence. Surely it is incomprehensible; but the manner of God's existence is also incomprehensible to the philosophers. Is it not perfect obstinacy to maintain that the Christian believes in three Gods when every Christian says he believes but in one? A man must know what he believes. Should a man who does not believe in one God desire to join a Christian church the minister and the congregation would surely refuse him, and most emphatically teach him that the first doctrine of Christianity is the belief in the Unity of God according to the Jewish Bible, which is the teacher whom the Christians follow. The Jewish Rabbi can teach nothing else touching the unity of God but what is in the Bible. And still it is charged upon the Christian that he believes in more than one God, on account of his belief in a Trinity, while the Christian does not claim himself to understand what the Trinity means. The writer of this, since he commenced to think, was taught to believe in only one omnipresent God. Not as what we consider one in number, but a unity which shares nothing with it, and has no comparison; a unity as far as unity can be a perfection, according as it is defined in the books of all the Jewish philosophers. To-day, I believe in Christianity, and am at the same time willing to die for my belief in this same only *one* God more than ever before. I was taught, and used to consider, that Christianity does not teach the belief in that one God; but I was only converted to Christianity because I felt that it draws me to that same *one* God. I would have died sooner than embrace Christianity if it had taught me to give up my belief in the one God of Israel; but, as I said, I felt drawn to Him more than in Judaism. I only embraced Christianity for the sake of the *one* God of Israel. The Jewish philosopher Bechaye, in his "Chobath Hallebaboth," did not teach anything else concerning the unity of God than the Christian philosophers do. Thus, concerning the unity of God, Jew and Christian have the same belief.

But, besides this, it is a fact, that the mystery of the Trinity in God's existence is a Jewish as well as a Christian doctrine, and every Jew believes in the plurality of the persons, as he believes in the Shechinah. Do the Jews not believe in the spirit of God, "Holy Ghost," or "Shechinah?" The second verse of the Bible says, "And the spirit of God hovered over the waters." That Spirit of God is one person of the Christian Trinity. Where God says, He will rest, the Chaldaic translation says, He will make his Shechinah rest. The spirit of God was called Shechinah, and is commonly believed among the Jews, and they pray that God should return the Shechinah to Zion. This Shechinah is not considered created, but something proceeding from God, and at the same time God but another person. The Christian believes in God, his Shechinah and his Word, on the very same principle. Now, if the Christian believes in three Gods, then the Jew believes in two. Has anybody ever charged it upon the Jews that they believed in two Gods? On what ground, then, can the Jew accuse the Christian of believing in three? The principle of the belief is the same. If the Christian believes one is three and three is one, then the Jew believes one is two and two is one. The Jew can give no definition of his belief in the Shechinah any more than the Christian can do it about the Trinity. The Talmud and all the Rabbinical literature consider the Shechinah identical with God, and at the same time they treat them as two persons. It is obvious that the belief in a unity of God with a plurality in persons is Jewish as well as Christian, the difference is only in the number. The doctrine is really a mystery and incomprehensible. Differently from his creatures and above their comprehension, God can be in three persons and still not *united*, but *One*. Concerning the incomprehensibility of the doctrine, it is no more incomprehensible or contradictory than the Biblical passages I have cited in the last chapter. The real fact is, that this question has nothing to do with monotheism.

I have hitherto spoken of a Jewish belief in a Shechinah, for this is the belief of every Jew; a fact which cannot be disputed. But we can find that even the belief in the Word was common with the Jews, and they really did believe in a Trinity. (I am not speaking yet of the fact that we find the Trinity in the Bible.) We find in the rabbinical literature often mentioned, God and his family, or family of above. The Midrash says that when God judges men he takes counsel with the angels; when he judges angels he counsels with the family of above. That expression, family of above, is very common in the rabbinical literature. (Familie shel maalah.) Jonathan's Chaldaic translation always treats the "Word of God" as a person (Memrah); and, I believe, also Onkelos, sometimes.

The Kabalah teaches the Trinity as plain as the Christians. In Sohar to Gen. i: 26, it almost teaches Christianity. The Sohar teaches of God the Father, a mother of above and a mother of below. ("Aba Elaah, Ima Elaah and Ima Delithatha," or "Shechinah Delela and Shechinah Delithatha.") This idea of a feminine gender in the Divinity, is not so absurd as it appears to be at the first look. They define the expression, "mother of above," as Philo defines his Logos. The Kabalists understand, in Mother, the power of conception in which everything exists, also they call it sometimes the architect of the building in creation. The word Shechinah is a feminine noun in the Hebrew language. There are numerous passages in the Sohar to the same effect, but not having any books I must cite all from memory. I do not mean to defend the antiquity of the Sohar itself; but its principles, that is, the Kabalistic principles, are surely very old. We find Kabalistic expressions all through the Talmud, and the Thargumim indicate that this knowledge cannot have been a novelty at their times. Besides what I have said in the last chapter, that a believing Hebrew scholar is compelled to see that some passages of Scripture indicate that there must have been some gnostic traditions with them. Frank and Jellinek have brought forward a good deal to prove the antiquity of the Kabalah. It is at least certain that the orthodox Jews believe it, no matter how old it is.

The "Sefer Yezirah," a little Kabalistic book whose antiquity is established beyond any doubt, commences: "*By three the world was created.*" There is a little Kabalistic prayer in every orthodox prayer-book, to be said before service, and adopted and said by every orthodox Jew. It reads as follows: "To the name of the Unity, of the Holy, praised be He, His Shechinah, through the hidden and unknown." (*Leshem Yichud*, etc.) Here we see plainly that the Jews pray to a Trinity even at this day. The Christian may say the same prayer in other words, namely: "To one God, the Father, His Shechinah (or Holy Ghost), through Jesus Christ." The difference is only that what is hidden and unknown to the Jew is, thank God, known to the Christian under the name of Jesus Christ. It is true this prayer is not very old;

it was prescribed by one of the ancestors of the writer of these pages, Rabbi Isaia Horowitz (Shelah), Rabbi, at Frankfort-on-the-Main. (All Israel goes after his authority.) This Rabbi did not make that prayer of his own mind, but according to his Kabalistic knowledge, in which he is a great authority, and is accepted in Israel.

We also find another Kabalistic prayer to be said at New Year after blowing the horn, to the effect that the Lord should accept the sound of the horn through Joshua, the prince of the countenance, and Metatron, the prince.

It is very remarkable how near the Kabbalists were to Christianity. And no real orthodox Jew will ever dare to doubt the Kabalah; it is accepted by all authorities. There is not the least doubt that Judaism teaches a Trinity, for they had some true traditions from the prophets. But still the Jews claim that the Christians are not monotheists, on account of their belief in the Trinity. The Jews and the so-called Rationalists monopolize monotheism.

Philo, known among the Jews as Philon Hayehudi, or Jedidjah the Alexandrian, who lived a little before Christ, believed in the Logos, the Son of God, who is the mediator between men and God; and teaches that men must cast themselves upon him entirely, for with his own morality only, man will be a sinner. In short, this Philo teaches all Christianity, with the exception of the incarnation, as he lived before Christ; but the doctrine of the Word and Mediator is as fully developed there as in Christianity. Still, Philo was a good, believing Jew, and without doubt a holy man, too. Some rationalists accuse the evangelists of plagiarism, saying that they used Philo's doctrines. As if Philo could have had a religion of his own. What Philo knew many holy and learned men in Israel must have known. The doctrines of Christianity are not new, but the real, pure Judaism. All that the apostles had to teach of new things, was concerning the person of the Messiah; that in *Him* hopes and expectations were fulfilled. The apostles may even have read Philo, or accidentally expressed the same thing, as they had the same Judaism with its doctrines. The same way any religious writer could be accused of plagiarism for writing ideas and doctrines in his book which have been expressed before. I think it would be hardly possible now to write much that should be actually new.

Although we have seen that the Jews believe in a duality and even in the Trinity, the principal question is not settled yet. For we must follow the Bible, not the Jews. The spirit of God is spoken of in the second verse of Genesis, as I cited above, but we also find the word of God treated as a person. We read in

> I Kings, xix: 9, 10, "And behold *the word of God* came to him, and said, What doest thou here, Elijah? And he said, I have been very jealous *for the Lord God of hosts*, for the children of Israel have forsaken *thy* covenant."

It is obvious that Elijah speaks here to the "Word" as a person, as he speaks *of* the Lord God at first in the third person and then in the second.

There we see plainly that the Bible treats the "Word" as a person, and I suppose there are more such passages to be found in Scripture.

It is further known that the word "God" (Elohim) is expressed in the plural in the Hebrew language. It is supposed by many Jews that it is an expression of Majesty; some of the commentators supposed that the reason was because the Hebrew language is older than the monotheistic belief and the expression was used by the polytheists, and remained in use even after the Hebrews believed in one God. According to my humble opinion it cannot be on account of majesty, because, why are the other names of God not expressed in the plural? Nor is it characteristic in the Hebrew to express majesty by using the plural pronoun; and if it is only a heathen expression, then surely Moses must have avoided it. The old Rabbis searched for other reasons, and did not accept the above; especially the Kabalists, and they do teach the plurality of persons, as I said before.

We also find verbs, adjectives and pronouns often (not always) expressed in the plural when they allude to God. But what is strange, sometimes there is plural and singular in the same sentence mixed.

Gen. i: 26, "And God said, Let *us* make man in *our* image, after *our* likeness." ·

Some say this was an expression of majesty. But the old Rabbis in Midrash did not feel satisfied with that; it is not natural in the Hebrew language, and they say that it alluded to the Family of above. (The Sohar teaches the Trinity on that very verse.)

Gen. xx: 13, "God *have* caused me to wander," says Abraham.

Gen. xxxv: 7, "The Elohim (God) *were* revealed to him there."

Joshua xxiv: 19, "To serve Jehovah for he *are* holy Elohim (Kedoshim).

II Samuel vii: 23, "Whom God *have* gone to redeem unto *himself*.

Ps. lviii: 12, "But there is Elohim *judges*.

Ps. cxlix: 2, "Israel shall rejoice in his *Makers*.

There are many other passages to be found with the same peculiarity. I only allude to these, since they furnish ample indications. But an explicit teaching of the doctrine of Trinity is found in

Gen. xviii: "(1) And Jehovah appeared unto Abraham in the plains of Mamre, and he sat at the tent door at the heat of the day. (2) And he lifted up his eyes and looked, and, lo, three men stood by him, etc. . . . (3) and said, my Lord, if now I have found favor in *thy* sight, pass not away, etc. . . . (4) Let a little water, I pray *you*, be fetched and wash *your* feet, and rest yourselves, etc. . . . (9) And *they* said unto him where is Sarah thy wife? And he said, Behold, in the tent. (10) And *he* said, I will certainly return unto thee, etc. . . . (13) And Jehovah said unto Abraham," etc.

I leave it to any impartial reader, whether of the Hebrew or of the translation, whether the meaning of this passage is not according to the Christian interpretation, that Jehovah appeared in three persons in human form. The first verse is obviously a general description of the revelation, and then comes the specification of it. In the conversation the three are sometimes addressed in the singular. In verse thirteen one assumes the name of Jehovah. Later we find two of them as angels in Sodom, and Jehovah still speaks to Abraham. This teaches plainly the doctrine of the Trinity. Jewish commentators, not able to dispute that the first verse is saying in general what the following verses describe (namely, that the three men were the revelation of Jehovah), still say that the three men, of whom two are afterwards called angels, were only angels, so that this was no revelation of God; for often, say they, angels are called Jehovah, since they represented Him. Rashbam cites from Ex. iii, where the Bible relates that an *angel* of God appeared to Moses in the bush, and *Jehovah* saw that he turns to see, and *Elohim* (God) calls to him. By this citation he tries to prove that angels were called Jehovah. We certainly find other passages where God appeared as an angel, for instance, to Hagar. Gen. vii: 13. But the very citation of Rashbam proves the opposite of his affirmation; for, in Ex. iii, the Lord says afterwards to Moses, "*I* am the God of thy father," and when Moses heard that it was God speaking to him, he hid his face; and later, that angel-God is called Jehovah, and tells his name, "I am" (or, "I shall be"). If this was not a revelation of God himself, then we must say that on Sinai only an angel spoke when he said, "I am Jehovah, thy God;" the same pronoun is used, "I" (Anochi). Any man reading the passages in Exodus, without being blinded by a spirit of obliquity, will see that it was a revelation of God himself, who at first appeared as an angel. It would be blasphemy, even idolatry, to call an angel, who is a creature himself, by the most holy name "Jehovah," while it is perfectly according to Scripture that the Lord appears as a creature. So he appeared to Jacob as a man, and so the two persons were angels in Sodom. The Lord appeared as a creature, but a creature can not assume the name of the living God of Israel. If in Gen. xviii and Ex. iii angels were only revealed, then we must conclude, on the same principle, that Jacob wrestled with a man only. It is, though, very intelligible why God is called angel at the beginning of the revelation, for as man can not see God as he is, the very vision is something created. God in the revelation is in a something created to be used as a mediator, for God is invisible. Thus the very citation of Rashbam proves that the three men of Abraham were the One living God, for we find God appearing as an angel, not the contrary. Aben Ezra hints that some derive the doctrine of the Trinity from the revelation to Abraham; but, says he, how can these three be the One indivisible, when we find two of them as angels in Sodom? I am sorry that Aben Ezra, the favorite commentator of my youth, had only such a childish answer. As if anybody would say that these three men were really three persons, sticking together without being able to separate themselves, or that these three persons were really God as He is. We do not understand God's being, and know nothing of his Trinity; even after he appeared as three men, we do not understand how he appeared as one, or as three men, or angels. We only see that in the revelation to Abraham the Lord teaches us that He exists in a

Trinity, and we believe it. If God can appear like three men, two of them can also go to Sodom, while no man can understand anything of the whole revelation.

We have seen now that the belief in a Trinity does not interfere with the belief in the one only God; that the Jews have the same belief, (at least in principle, for it cannot be disputed that they believe in the Shechinah,) and that we find this doctrine in the Old Testament. Neither can it be disputed that the New Testament teaches one God, and nothing can be considered Christianity that is not taught in the New Testament. Still, every Jew will cite Deut. vi: 4, "Hear, O Israel, Jehovah our God, Jehovah One," as an evidence against the doctrine of the Trinity. They forget that they believe in a Shechinah themselves, and, as I have shown, even in a Trinity; so we need no further refutation. But it occurs to me that this very verse may hint at the doctrine of the Trinity. Let us examine it a little nearer.

The Israelites have heard a voice from the living God on Sinai, saying, "*I* am Jehovah, thy God." This implies that there is but one God, for "I" means one. Moses, always in speaking of God, leaves no possibility of thinking that there was any more than *one*. In the song the children of Israel sang after crossing the Red Sea, they surely spoke of *one* God. Thus the verse, "Hear, O Israel," etc., appears to be superfluous. All the Bible breathes the doctrine of the unity of God. At the same time we find that when Jehovah (which is the proper name) assumes the title "God" (Elohim) it is expressed in the plural, (and also the pronouns and verbs are often singular and plural together, as I have shown before). Now, the language of the verse; Moses did not say that there is only one God, or one Jehovah,—not even that Jehovah *is* one (Jehovah echod *hu*), but "*Jehovah one.*" He also repeats the holy name in saying *Jehovah*, our God, *Jehovah* one. Why this repetition? The plain language would be, "Jehovah, our God, *is* one." Can any one show me such a singular construction in the Hebrew language as this verse is?

But we find that the Israelites had three different manners of revelation: one on Sinai, where they heard the voice of God; at other times they saw the glory of God in a cloud. The elders had some other vision, as we cited in the last chapter. So they have three different kinds of revelation. There can, besides, be no doubt that the children of Israel knew of the revelation to Abraham, in person of the three men; they must also have been instructed in the mystery of the existence of a Shechinah and a Word, at least those who were initiated in the holy mysteries. Now, after they had these three revelations, and some knew of the doctrine of the Trinity, Moses told them to be careful not to take the Holy Trinity for three Gods. And he says, "Hear, O Israel," which is equivalent to *hear with understanding*, Jehovah (1) (Elohenu), our God, (2) Jehovah (3)—*One*. Any believing man, who understands the Hebrew language, and pays attention to the *words* of those passages which treat of the most holy mysteries, will find that this, my suggestion, makes the verse more comprehensible. We can understand this verse better with the doctrine of the

Trinity than without it. And there are, surely, many hints of that kind in Moses. God's being mentioned by different names must mean something; there are often hints to holy mysteries given in one letter. I can not speak much of this here, for only Hebraists can understand it.

Now, people say the Christians are no monotheists, for they have not the monotheism of reason. But how does it happen that, notwithstanding they had so many great philosophers, the Grecians and Romans still worshiped idols; and since they accepted the belief in the Trinity they pray to the living God of Israel? The world accepted the spiritual God through the revelations, consequently it must believe in the unity according to revelation. Rationalism never brought one heathen to the one God. Those very rationalists who boast to-day of being the only true monotheists, and call the Christians polytheists, would kneel before an image now, if their fathers had not accepted the belief in the revelation. They would perhaps be barbarous yet, as their fathers were, before they accepted the belief in a Trinity.

Summing up what we have said in this chapter, we must say that it cannot be the doctrine of the Holy Trinity which causes the Israelites to reject Christianity, so long as they themselves believe in the Shechinah, even if the doctrine of the Word had not originated with Israel, as it really did. If their belief was against Judaism, then the Kabalists and the Targumim ought to be banished from the synagogue; while, in fact, they are accepted in all Israel. Besides, what we have seen that the Trinity is taught in the Old Testament, and the Orthodoxy is believing in the Shechinah to-day.

The stumbling block which leaves Israel without a religion, without hope, without the true life of the world, without God; that stone of stumbling of which the prophet wrote, "Sanctify the Lord of hosts himself, and let him be your fear, and let him be your dread. And he shall be for a sanctuary, and a stone of stumbling, and for a rock of offence to both houses of Israel," etc. Is. viii: 13, 14; this stumbling stone, which is at the same time a sanctuary, is nothing but God's revelation in Christ. In Him God is a sanctuary for some and a stone of stumbling for others. Without Him the above cited verse of Isaiah can not even be understood. We shall devote our following chapters to Christ and his religion. But before we examine Christianity dogmatically, to see whether it is the religion of the Bible, we will first contemplate Christ as he is perceived and comprehended by his followers.

CHAPTER XII.

CHRIST.

"Ye are my witnesses, saith the Lord, and MY SERVANT WHOM I HAVE CHOSEN that ye may know and believe me, and understand that I am he: before me there was no God formed, neither shall there be after me. I, *even* I am the Lord, and BESIDE ME THERE IS NO SAVIOUR." Isa. xliii: 10, 11.

"And he said, It is a light thing that thou shouldst be my servant to raise up the tribe of Jacob, and to restore the preserved of Israel: I will also give thee for a light to the Gentiles, that THOU MAYEST BE MY SALVATION unto the end of the earth." Ch. xlix: 6.

When the owner of the world, the Father of Mankind, introduced Himself to his chosen people through his servant Moses, he proved his authority by working public miracles. He struck the wicked Egyptians with their idols, the waters of a sea withdrew, leaving a dry path for the chosen, and returned to cover and to destroy the children of iniquity. Clouds visited the wilderness, a region never known to them before, in order to make shade and shelter; heavens rained food, wind brought birds in its wings, and a rock gave water for the redeemed. The earth shivered when glorified by the majesty of her Lord; the air quivered when magnified by His sublime voice. The heavens were surprised, sun and moon embarrassed, hosts of holy angels rejoiced, forests sang, rivers and seas shouted, mountains danced and melted like wax, when Sinai was enveloped with heavenly flames, covered with divine glory. Marvels are the testimonials for God's word. Numberless miracles, supported by the marvelous existence of the nation for whom they were performed, prove who sent Moses.

But silent and unnoticed, quiet and humble, appears Christ among his brethren. He strikes no enemy, he raises no staff. Peace is his way and his kingdom. Asked for a sign from heaven, he refuses it, and points to God's word, to Moses. Nature's change to testify to the Messiah fails to convince one who does not listen to the voice of the Lord of nature and yearns to do His will. And the Lord of nature had already testified of His Christ. God's word has not now to be introduced, but fulfilled. Christ must expect his followers to believe, for the law and the prophets were his forerunners; the law had taught to believe; it showed, it pointed to the way of God; the law was the school-master in teaching subjection and belief. The religion of Christ is not founded upon his own miracles; thus His belief is not of the mind. When Korah revolts against Moses, the latter appeals to the miracle which shall happen; when Christ is opposed he says, "Ye shall have no sign." Love is *his* sign, righteousness *his* wonder, and *his* spirit is a miracle. His truth speaks louder than the thunder of Sinai, and his life shines brighter than the lightnings. Those who were not convinced by such miracles turned from Christ after they were even fed by the miraculous bread coming from his hands.

Moses had to convince reason of the truth of things which appear to be against reason, by miracles. Christ wins the heart by his love, by his purity, and makes the incomprehensible thing perceptible to heart and soul by his life. He never worked a miracle in order to convince, to win a new disciple; his miracles were acts of benevolence, which at the same time testified to him, giving strength of faith to his followers. A man can never be converted to Christ on account of the miracles; for if one is not touched by Christ's life, if he does not enter into his spirit of *loving* to do the will of his father in heaven, if he does not see that there is no satisfaction in the things of earth, but there is with Him, if he does not believe *Him*, he will not believe His miracles. Those again who know Christ, easily believe his miracles. The miracles testified to Moses, and Christ testifies to his miracles, even if it is at the same time in another sense true that Christ's miracles attest to him, since it must be expected that the Christ should work miracles, still they are not the foundation of the belief. The miracles do not make the Christ, but the Christ makes the miracles. The Old Testament and His life form the rock upon which Christ's Church is founded.

Notwithstanding that Christ's religion has the strongest evidences to convince the mind of its truth, in no way inferior to those of the Old Testament, as we shall find below, still the conviction of the mind does not make a Christian. Because Christianity is not a religion of the mind, therefore are the historical evidences, the miracles, not sufficient. The definition and proof of this will be found in the following:

Israel was trodden down by the Roman empire, and still more by its own rulers, priests and teachers. Domestic discord consumed the marrow of the nation. The treacherous Idumean family of the Herods occupied a throne which was, in fact, a footstool of Rome. The humble man of the lower classes sighed under many burdens imposed upon him by his Pharisaic teachers, besides those of the foreign oppressor. Revolutions and seditions were common occurrences. Hypocrisy devoured widows' houses. The land of Judah represented a picture of sorrow and suffering. Still, Israel looked for a Messiah. A *Goël*, Redeemer, was promised to Israel, and they doubted not the truthfulness of their Bible. The word of God was believed, the miracles lived in the memory of the nation. (According to the Rabbinical literature they even had not yet ceased to happen.) They believed, they could not doubt; but as we have seen before, it was a belief of the mind. The belief turned not the heart in humility to God, but it filled it with pride and haughtiness. The Pharisee did not pray for mercy on account of a burdened conscience, but he gave thanks for his righteousness. There was nothing but an outward religion, which consisted in form, in doing, not in feeling. It was in fact no religion, but a law. I have given a picture of Rabbinism and need not dwell upon it now. We have seen how Judaism had degenerated through a spirit of haughtiness and self-dependence. This spirit shaped their expectations of the Messiah. They did not feel enslaved by sin and self, therefore they looked for no inward freedom; despising the Gentiles for being without the law, they waited not for the redemption of mankind. Since they only realized an outward, political oppression, they could not look for the redemption of the oppressor. They could not realize their departure from God, since they had so many laws, and this was all they considered to be religion. Thus they sighed and yearned for . . . . . wealth and power to oppress their oppressors. They hoped that the redeemer would lead Judah's armies to victory and prey. The belief of the mind has no other ambition but for fame and wealth; its wishes and hopes are carnal, its so-called religion is form, its love the flesh, worldly power.

The Pharisees fully believed in a future judgment, but also, that keeping the law is the sole means of justification; thus the Messiah is required to be the greatest lawyer, a sophist. They also found consolation in the belief that every born Israelite must reach heaven, and if he were a sinner against the law he only had to suffer purgatory, which, according to some tradition, lasts not longer than twelve months. (This is believed even at this day by every orthodox Jew.) Thus the cause of their haughtiness was not only in their legal knowledge and self-righteousness, but also in an excessive national pride. They believed, even that the Messiah would heal mankind of its depravity, which is caused by the fall of Adam and Eve. This doctrine is held by the Jewish orthodoxy, and so they interpret Gen. iii: 15. "*He* shall bruise thy head, and thou shalt bruise his heel," as alluding to Messiah's breaking Satan's influence. There are also passages which show that they expected the Messiah to be exalted above the angels, thus the nearest to God. I only allude here to Thargum Is. lii. But mainly and firstly he must give worldly glory to the Israelites.

This was the condition of Israel when the humble Jesus of Nazareth in Galilee suddenly appeared. He did not call to arms, nor did he have any treasures to distribute. Poor and lowly, he despised all honors, and sought only to turn the hearts of his hearers towards his Father in Heaven. His actions were prompted by love, his exclusive business was to do good, his meat to do his Father's will. His doctrine and manners were new and strange. He communicated with the lowest classes, with sinners, with such as knew themselves that they were sinners. He went to the most despised, who hardly dared to hope for mercy. He went to the "lost sheep." But he did not teach law, he broke the ordinances himself, and did not even respect the authority of the Rabbis. The character of his preaching was just the opposite to what was customary. There was no subtilty in his sermons. When learning and wealth were the highest thing in estimation he said, "Blessed are the poor in spirit, the mourners, the meek." The humble hearers breathed, their eyes were filled, and a voice in their own heart shouted, "Amen." He said, "Blessed are the pure in heart, for they shall see God." What is the greatness of the Rabbi, the philosopher, the rich man now? He promised no glory but that of heaven, he turned hearts into another direction, he had no legal measure for doing good. He only taught submission to God, patience, humility, love, unselfish love. He enjoined love like that of God, or universal love from which no one is excluded. " Love your enemies, bless them that curse you, pray for your persecutors." A heart in which the love of God is the center has no room for enmity, one who has no self has no enemy. He reduces all religion to that which comes from an humble, single heart. He tells of the poor woman who only casts a very little into the treasury, of the good Samaritan, of the praying sinner who dared not as much as to lift up his eyes to heaven, and of the poor Lazarus. He says, nothing makes impure but what comes from the heart. He never puts any value on much learning, but says, to whom much is given, of him much will be required. He requires the gifted man to *minister* with his gifts. All are equal with him. He never refuses a broken-hearted sinner, and censures not the sinner, but the hardness of his heart. He has forbearance, forgiveness and consolation for every one. He leaves the narrow platform of nationality and says, that from the far East and West they will sit down with Abraham, while the children of the kingdom shall be cast out. Teaching in the name of the God of Israel, sent to the lost sheep in Israel, he still advances humanity, not Judaism. His words find an echo in every heart. In listening to his words every heart melts, the world vanishes, in the midst of a roaring world we stand alone before God, and not terrified, but yearning for and loving Him. Heaven opens for our hope and consolation, eternity for our life, and we see the Father of mankind as the one who wipes away our tears. Is there any wounded heart for whom the words of Jesus are not a balm? Any man who could listen to them without emotion? The slumbering soul awakens at his voice, the restless finds rest and peace, the despairing consolation. Take all the inestimable treasures of man's literature, destroy all human wisdom which all generations have gathered, still mankind will be happy listening to *His* voice.

And yet, he teaches but very little with his words. He teaches with his life. Some of his sayings are even found in the rabbinical literature, (surely this literature was written long after Christ,) some are found with the old heathen; but the value and power of his doctrine lie not in the single sayings; together, as a system, they turn the heart of the hearer and lift it towards heaven.*

---

* Christ's words need not necessarily be original. His different doctrines must not be all new. He did not come to give a new law, but to make free of the old one by improving the heart and giving strength to the soul to do the will of God by virtue of love, not of law. The moral law existed, man knew what was wrong, else he would have had no conscience, but he is weak; there is a depravity that prevents his living according to his conscience, and therefore he is not at one with God. In the chapter about Judaism we have already treated this subject and shown that this causes our want of religion. The moral law exists always, on account of our depravity. If men were good there would be no law. If it was against human nature to lie or to steal, there could be no law not to lie and not to steal. Thus the law is on account of transgression. The law is the guide of consicence, conscience tells that we are behind the law. The law is the standard, and the will is the motive; when man's will is weak he still knows the standard, but cannot come up to it. Now the Bible promised a Messiah, who shall "*bruise the serpent's head*" and "*bear our iniquities.*" A ceremonial law was added to point to the need of a more entire submission to God, and on account of increased transgression to be a dam against

The value of his words lies in their combination into a perfect system, and because *He* teaches. He, the perfection, according to all true doctrines of all nationalities. He, with his ineffable loveliness teaches, or rather *enables* to be good. Indeed, we even have but very few of his sayings, just enough to interpret his life, to show his aim, but when his mouth is silent his life speaks, it speaks louder than the thunder, and still sweeter than musical tunes even from heavenly spheres. The Bible teaches in theory, by words; Christ, the aim of the Bible, its promise, fulfills it in· practice. The Bible tells God's way, Christ lives it, *is* it. Therefore the Bible tells what to do, and he shows how to be. The phrase, " Word of God," even in its common meaning, as applied to Scripture, may therefore be applied to him, as he speaks by his very life. He did not exaggerate when he said " I

---

the destroying power of iniquity, especially pointing to the Messiah, in view of our need of some mysterious supernatural propitiation for sins. Now when the Christ comes he must bring us to the standard of the law. He must make me what I could not be before; he must change and strengthen my will. He must quiet my con science by bringing my will to the standard. By this only he makes me free from my burden. Thus what the law taught, what conscience told me that I am not, this must be embodied in Christ. He must be such perfection that in him the law is fulfilled. He must be the expression of that which the conscience of mankind requires a man to be. And in addition to this, he must have the power of attraction, which the law does not possess, in order to enable me to live according to him. The law taught, but left me subject to my weak will; and he, the standard, according to the law, also strengthens my will. I could not *love* the law, but I can love him, therefore I have more strength. What duty *told* me to do love *inclines* me to do. By this he is the remedy for the depravity, he makes me free of a felt burden. Hence he must not be original in his doctrine, but he must express what the conscience of mankind felt before. Shall he make me free of a burden I never had? Therefore wise men who studied the wants of the human heart may have expressed Christ's sayings before, since the law existed before. Christ's originality is in his being, not in his saying.

am the way," even according to rationalism. He does not *preach* love, but he *is* love. He preaches not acquiescence in Providence, submission in privation, while surrounded by luxury and his hearers suffering starvation; He does not preach love and remain a stranger; but the *true shepherd*, united with his flock, *he* suffers above all. The *Prince of Peace* has no aristocracy. In short, seeking nothing for himself, he lived as an ideal of unselfishness, love, perfection and submission to God.

It is not my intention to write a life of Christ, nor is human language able to describe the beauty of his character. Rationlists who oppose Christianity, even the Jewish historians, Grætz and Jost, exhaust language in praising it. I only must remark here that the most striking feature of his life is his work to convert sinners to God by imbuing them with a love to his own person. His self-devotion spreads such an air of loveliness and holiness around him that it attracted hearts and made them melt before God. What reason, stern morality and diffident virtue could not accomplish, Jesus accomplishes by his love. Mary Magdalene, a sinner, debased and in despair, sees Jesus, the living love; she falls at his feet, she melts in tears, her heart breaks in contrition, she yearns for God. She weeps and loves, until her heart is submitted to God. Love changed her. The love to Jesus turned her heart to God. She is purified, for the love to him purifies, cleanses from sin. Love cleanses more than fire. " For strong as death is love," said King Solomon. Every desire and passion become overpowered, subdued by love. Everything is dead where real love speaks. And where the love of God has a voice, there sin is silenced, flesh loses its influence, hell and Satan have no power. This power to convert by love stands without a parallel in history. History counts many sages, many devoted martyrs; the Bible tells of many saints, and among all the children of Adam, Jesus stands matchless, with his converting love. Multitudes followed him, attracted by his love. Multitudes of sinners followed him in his walk with God. Sinners lived a life of saints since they found and loved Jesus. And still his life and influence belonged to the God of Israel. He took no self, he did not change, his life was devoted to God, to bringing sinners to God.

This Jesus claimed to be the expected Messiah, and worked most astonishing miracles. He claimed to be the King, but desired no throne, for he claimed no kingdom of this world. He desired nothing but that people should do the will of his Father in heaven.

We see that his spirit was wholly alien to the ruling spirit of the Pharisees. At first, his life was not in conformity to the dignity of a Rabbi; he went with publicans and sinners, he had no reverence for legal knowledge, he told the truth regardless of persons; he was in one sense what people would now call " unrefined." He also found all the value of religion in the heart, and broke the ordinances publicly. He taught no Judaism, but religion. He cared for no authority. Secondly, he offended the national feelings in telling that it was not sufficient to be a son of Abraham in order to go to heaven; every one is his brother who does the will of his Father in heaven.

He even had disciples among the Samaritans. His humility and universal love were utterly offensive to the Pharisees. Nothing in him was according to the expectations of the character of the Messiah. It seemed to them ridiculous that this Gallilean who had nothing, should claim to be the Messiah. Especially were his claims very strange; he made belief in him essential to salvation from judgment. He even spoke things of himself which were unreasonable. Notwithstanding his humility and utmost unselfishness, he claimed such things as were unheard-of. He made *everything* of himself. Finally he claimed to be the Son of God. As much as his disciples melted in his love, so did the majority despise and hate him, until they condemned and crucified him for blasphemy.

And since then his name has never ceased to attract men in love. There is as much an air of holiness and love surrounding his name as there was his person. His name draws and converts sinners to God. The belief in his name makes the civilized world worship the God of Israel. Jesus is not a name, but a principle; the principle of everything good. *He* is *religion*. Not his doctrine but himself; he is a doctrine, he is the foundation of his church. Jesus is not only the Christ, but Christianity. Many millions are called by his name, and he exercises the most blessed influences in the history of mankind. Notwithstanding all kinds of persecution his church grew and prospered, and the God of Abraham is the God of the Gentiles.

Still his church never ceased to meet opposition.

Ever since he claimed to be the Son of God the Jews have not ceased to consider it blasphemy, and his believers idolaters. Just as in the time of the Apostles, there are two classes of opposition; the Jews call it idolatry, and the Gentiles foolishness. If we want to defend Christianity to-day, we have to do it against a Jewish and against a rationalistic opposition. Against the former we have the Bible, against the latter history, and against both together the conclusive evidence of the experience of man's own heart. The biblical evidences we shall quote in the following chapters; we propose to treat here of the other evidences.

The strongest witness for Christ is his most firm opposer, the Jewish nation. Rationalists oppose Christianity for the reason that they refuse to believe in supernatural revelations; so they deny the divine origin of both Testaments. If they believed the Old they could surely not hesitate to accept the New. They admit that both agree, but neither, say they, is to be believed. Thus our evidence from "Wandering Jew," which is surely irrefutable, is also sufficient for Christianity. If the Old Testament is true, then rationalism has no foundation. Thus a Jew cannot cite Renan or Strauss against Christianity, for these writers are still more against Judaism. If a Rabbi is not a hypocrite, or inconsistent, and does really believe the Bible, as he claims, and as he ought to do, it will be a duty for him to write against rationalism as much as it is for any Christian. When Voltaire attacked the Bible the Jews wrote against him; to-day Jewish Rabbis cite Strauss and Renan against Christianity and still claim to be Jews. As I said, the evidences of the Old Testament are sufficient to refute the rationalists.

The next proof is, that Israel is punished; their punishment is perfectly unexampled, Israel's suffering is without an equal in history. This indicates that they bear the consequences of the crucifixion. Their spiritual suffering in having such a religion as the orthodox insanity, or the ridiculous, arrogant reform, notwithstanding their having the pure belief in the one God, is also a thing for which reason cannot account.

But the most direct proof for Christianity, is the fact that the Jews have never ceased to believe that Jesus worked miracles by the power of the unclean spirit. They consider his claim ridiculous, and his death deserved. Thus as this belief lives among all the orthodox Jews to-day, and agrees exactly with what is related about their belief in the New Testament, we have a strong evidence for the historical truth of that book. But besides this tradional belief, there are many passages in the Mishnah and Talmud, which prove that the Jews condemned Jesus for blasphemy, according to their law. These passages can only be found in some very old editions of the Talmud, for the governments prohibited their publication, which was a mistake, as they contain evidences for Christianity. Dr. Grætz cites some passages in his history of the Jews which force him to admit it to be an historical fact that the Jews condemned Jesus to crucifixion for blasphemy, on account of his claim to be the Son of God. Dr. Grætz, admiring the character of Jesus like a man without prejudice, still defends the condemnation for such a claim, and considers it the weak side of Jesus that on account of his success in drawing people and converting sinners, he finally became ambitious enough to make such a claim. At the same time, Dr. Grætz is not moved to believe that he also worked miracles. Now, I ask whether it is reasonable to suppose that the Jews would have condemned Jesus, or even noticed him. if he had not worked miracles. Could any one claim to be the Messiah *and the Son of God*, and at the same time be no conqueror, but an humble countryman, without working miracles? Multitudes followed him, some believed, the majority did not, in spite of the miracles. The Jews of that time were not yet reformed, and surely believed in supernatural things. Is it possible that he could excite such interest without miracles? Without them, the claim to be the Son of God would surely have provoked the laughter, not the condemnation of the Rabbis. Thus, if the Jewish literature proves that Christ claimed to be the Son of God, it also proves his miracles. But historians like Mr. Grætz, and others, refusing to believe miracles which history relates, manufacture parts of history of their own in order to have a history according to rationalism. But writing history does not make it such. History cannot be manufactured. The fact that Jesus was condemned on account of his claim, and was considered unclean, is a sufficient proof that his miracles are historical facts. Thus one can not defend the condemnation of Jesus from the rational platform, but he must try to do so from the platform of the Rabbis, the one of belief. If his condemnation is justified, then

Christ must have had a devil, as the Rabbis claimed; and if not, then Christ is the Son of God. History has neither Rabbis nor a Christ as they are represented by the rationalists. History has things which must be believed, and cannot be understood. Mr. Graetz, who is convinced of the historical fact of the claim, ought to admit the logical consequence of it, and confess that either Jesus had a devil or he proved his claims, and the Rabbis had a devil; there is no way between. We see that the Jews furnish most conclusive evidence for the miracles of both Testaments, consequently there is a religion given from God, and it becomes our dearest interest, and most sacred duty to accept it. One is true, Judaism or Christianity. We have seen what Judaism offers, we shall also see what Christianity affords. I have shown the method by which the Rabbis derive their authority from Scripture. I shall also show on what grounds Christ claims his authority from the Bible. There is no other way, a man must choose. Two antagonistic parties contesting about the origin of miracles, each exasperated against the other, both admitting the fact, and that the contest is only about the origin of it, we see that this fact has consequences in history which are marvelous of themselves. Shall we still deny that the miracles have happened, and ignore them in spite of the fact that our real life depends upon our right decision in the matter? The Jews and the Christians concur in stating the main facts, and providence has since spoken in history; shall we still ignore the fact of the miracles and not choose a religion? Is it possible that miracles never happened, with our evidences so clear? Reader, choose!

Some of those who reject the literal belief in any miracle, and take them to be legends, still find the miracles of Moses more imposing, more powerful, more public, and therefore consider these to be poetical expressions of historical facts, and those of the New Testament to be impositions. The amiable and great Jewish philosopher, Mendelsohn, refused to believe the miracles of the New, while he believed those of the Old Testament, on account of the latter's being performed more publicly. Also the humble writer of this, once not admitting the miracles to be facts, and still claiming to be an adherent of the Old Testament, like all the Reformers, expressed himself through the press, that the Old Testament relates *miracles of history*, while the New Testament only *histories of miracles*, which two kinds should be distinguished when we study *the history of the miraacles*. I came to this conclusion, because I seemed to perceive that the miracles of Moses were interwoven with the history of the whole nation. They are said to have happened for the benefit and in presence of *all* the people, while those of Christ were of a more private character. Thus, I said, the first were popular legends, born of the imagination of the people and their bards, and have some historical facts as a foundation; but the latter must be simply inventions. I followed in principle some of the unbelieving German Hebraists, without applying the same to the miracles of the New Testament, like some rationalists. As poetry I could not find the miracles of the New Testament poetically correct. I said, the first miracles had poetical truths which I missed in the others. I found no historical motive to justify the invention. Taking all miracles as an invention, I had reason to say so; indeed. Christ's miracles are of such a character that they would be a very low, even an absurd invention, notwithstanding the great scholar Strauss so deceives himself as to make myths of them. But I found that the miracles of Elijah and Elisha were of exactly the same character; they were wrought privately, to help some private persons; they cannot be considered as historical facts transfigured into miracles by an innocent imagination. I said, therefore, that Elijah and Elisha bear the character of New Testament prophets, and I would no longer consider them Israelitish prophets. They ought to belong to the New Testament, (because they did not suit the principle about miracles which I followed.) The fact is, as a Reformer, not being in earnest with anything concerning religion, only attached to the Old Testament by the tie of the sweet and powerful holy language, and race-pride, any thought occurring to my mind which could be used to refute the New Testament, I expressed with satisfaction, especially as I was applauded by every Reformer. But indeed, not all the miracles of the Pentateuch are of the same public, imposing, poetical character. For instance, God's wrestling with Jacob, which I have cited in the tenth chapter, would make the most absurd poetry; also Moses' first conversation with the Lord when he refused to go to Pharaoh, and the Lord's meeting him afterwards in the inn by the way, when he sought to kill him, until Zipporah circumscised her son; Ex. iv; what a sublime poetry that would make. And so are a great number of the miracles. And truly, Elijah's and Elisha's miracles and those of the New Testament are of one character. They were not performed in order to persuade, to convince, to make disciples; the miracles are only related with the history of the performers of them. Elijah and Elisha made a barrel of flour or a pot of oil inexhaustible, and revived dead children, not in order to prove that they were prophets, but to help the poor brokenhearted women. So Christ's miracles are more of a private character, mere acts of benevolence; they belong to the history of his life. Thus we may say that even Elijah himself was already in some respects a forerunner of Christ. As I had no real religion, since I gave up the belief of the mind, because seeing no effect of it, therefore I could not believe in Elijah and Elisha. (I must confess, though, that I had not a few pangs of conscience for ridiculing them, even in unbelief.) Only after Christ's life and love had touched my heart, I could easily believe in every prophecy; for the belief proved to be an effectual one. I could see that there is a God of the Bible, of Israel. I found the aim of the belief. I could believe in supernatural things since I felt that a supernatural power influenced my own heart. I found the God of revelation in my heart, and would believe Him. But since we find historical evidences for the miracles of the New Testament, then we must say that they are even more public than any of the Old, with the exception of those which happened when the Israelites were all in the camp. Thus it was only the circumstance that the Jews lived all over their land, which prevented Christ's miracles from being as public as those of Moses. And this publicity is not necessary, since the Jews testify to their performance even to this day. All distinctions as to the character of the different miracles are vain when we have evidence that they must have been actually performed. It is immaterial what character a miracle has, so long as it has the character of a miracle it testifies to God's supernatural religion. Therefore all the above cited objections are refuted by the historical evidence.

As touching the miracles in general, I said in the beginning that it is not my object to prove their natural possibility, nor do I believe any philosopher can do it. Some Germans, believing rationalists, so-called, tried to prove that the miracles agree with natural laws. They consider that it is possible for the human nature to ascend above that which we consider as human nature. They sublimate man above humanity and bring him so near to God by virtue of his own moral will, that he is enabled to work miracles. By this principle they define the doctrine of the divinity in Christ. This school, stands, according to my humble view, on the same platform with Maimonides, the inconsistent Aben Esra, and many Jewish philosophers, in thinking that they must believe and still understand everything. Man, according to these rationalists, is neither man as we know him, nor the man of the Bible. This doctrine can not possibly be reconciled with Judaism or Christianity. Revelation and miracles can only be caused by the sublime free grace of God, else they are either no revelations, or the revelation is not for us, who are common men. We should need the sublime power of a Moses, the prophets, and Christ, in order to derive any benefit from their revelations, if their revelations were only on account of their own sublime nature. Israel's being chosen must make us suppose that every single Israelite was a sublime man according to this system. If Christ's divinity was simply an exaltation of his own nature, then we ought to have Christs in every generation, at least prophets. As soon as we believe that there were prophets, we must believe that they only could be so by the free supernatural will of God. Anything we try to press into the laws of creation must be seen in creation now. It is logically impossible to *believe* the prophets if prophecy could be *understood*, it is still less possible to *believe* in Christ if his divinity has to be intelligible. This school is inconsistent, they believed, but the offspring was a system like that of Strauss and the Tuebingen school.

So soon as we have historical evidence that miracles have been performed, we must accept them without finding a reason. If they are reasonable, then they are no miracles.

Returning to the evidences, we have so far gained all of them from the Jews. Besides theirs, we have the following:

The character of Christ is the strongest proof that his claim must be true, when we see that it is historical. Contemplating his character, how can we mistrust him?

His character is admired more than that of any man by every one of his opposers. Atheists, Pantheists, Deists, and Rationalists unite in his praise as one unique in history, as a model of perfection. Strauss, Renan, and all who write against Christianity exhaust language in praising him. His character spreads out an odor of sweetness, beauty and love; how could he be an impostor? How can we unite his simple wisdom with the character of a dreamer, a lunatic even, who claimed to be the Son of God? And his character is such that it cannot even be the product of human imagination, as is also admitted by all unbelievers. It cannot be doubted that his *character* is historical. No one but the Jews who claim that he had a devil, ever contemplated his character without paying his tribute of admiration and love. And these Jews can only accuse him of blasphemy. Even enlightened Jews admit his supreme character. The great Jew, Spinoza, the hero of philosophy, and the Jewish historians praise his character not less than his devoted worshipers. Unitarians, who have detached themselves from the church, for whom the Bible is no authority, still build houses in which they claim to worship him. Now, must there not be something supernatural about him, that the Jews could accuse such a man of having a devil? Naturally, the Jews are more inclined to love everything that is good and noble, perhaps more than any other nation, and still concerning Christ they exhibited such a feeling that the world has always misunderstood the Jewish people on this account. Must there not be something supernatural about it? Must it not be a curse for misusing the divine religion they possessed that they are perfectly blinded concerning his character?

Next to his character is that of his Apostles.

What motive could the Apostles have to relate such impossibilities in connection with the sublime character of Jesus? Those men who followed their Master in living without self, who sought no glory of men, who even sacrificed their lives to their doctrines, who worked to convert men to God,—what object did they have to invent lies? Those men who breathe such a simple wisdom, could they not invent things more credible to adorn the name of their Master? Was it their only object to promulgate belief in *their* Master? then they could have accomplished this much more easily, without claiming for him the title of Son of God, born of a virgin. Why did they make it so difficult to believe, if their story was only an invention? The doctrine of the incarnation was surely an obstacle in their own way. How can the imagination of men produce a Son of God? How could Jews do it and preach the God of the Jews?

Besides, we have four gospels which could not have been written with collusion; for one could not have known of the others' writing, and they all concur in the main object; they present to us the same Christ, the same doctrines, the same religion. The very fact that they disagree in the specification of some miracles, proves that the one knew nothing of the others' writing, a thing which must be supposed if their hero and his miracles were only an invention. How could they agree in the main object if it was not true? Their little contradictions prove their innocence. That some misunderstandings and errors crept in is very natural. Take four honest eye-witnesses, to describe any occurrence, or battle, and you will usually find them disagreeing in some details, while their agreement in the main object will prove the truthfulness of each. This will be still more the case when they relate partly as eye-witnesses and partly what they heard. (Some contradictions may also arise from later copying, and the creeping in of some spurious passages.) Thus the Gospel contradictions are not only very far from being evidence against it, but they really testify to it. This is even admitted by rationalists. (See Renan.) We also find errors and some contradictions in the Old Testament. Providence has watched over the Bible to preserve pure for us all the historical and religious truths which are necessary for us to know, trifling details were left subject to the natural fate of other books. That Saul was only *one* year old at the beginning of his reign is surely an error in the Bible, which still does not affect the truth of Saul's history, or the moral we derive from it. And so we find other errors and contradictions, which still can not affect the divine truth of Scripture. It seems that Providence left stumbling blocks even in Scripture,

I do not mean to say that there is no distinctions to be made between the two Testaments. In one respect they form together one Bible, they are both given to us by the God of Israel; together they contain what is necessary for His religion. We see that the ancient people have no benefit of the Old Testament alone. But in another sense there are great distinctions to be made. The New breathes more the spirit of consolation, it contains everything in full. It is the open rose, while the Old is the bud of it. It was the fragrancy of the open rose which attracted the world, while the external change of the bud caused the error of its owners in thinking that it could not be the fruit of their bud, of which they expected a different harvest. Not cultivating the bud according to the will of the One who planted it, the misunderstanding was a natural result. The value of the New Testament is entirely spiritual. As the religion changed from a visible to a spiritual, so the book. The Old Testament has its spirit more hidden, but there is holiness in the words. It contains "*words*" of God, the New, so to say, His sentiments. The principle which distinguishes the two churches prevails all over, even in the books. We may compare the old dispensation to the body, while the New is the soul. So that we find a holiness in the very words of the Old Testament. The body died, and there is just enough left of it to testify to the spirit. We must know whose spirit it is. The Prophets uttered words which were *literally* spoken by the Holy Ghost. This is not the case with the Evangelists. We must not forget that even the words of Christ which we have, are not in the language he used. We have not a single one of his sermons in full. The Old Testament has a *holy* language; the New has not. The old church was given to a people chosen in the seed, it was a garden fenced in. Therefore the words were watched and counted even.

The New is opened to the world, free for everybody, a public garden; the owners are chosen spiritually. Therefore the New Testament was more subjected to corruption in the text. It is, though, obviously the hand of Providence which has kept the Book for us, preserving pure what was necessary, and leaving even the corruptions to be a testimony for that which is pure. The most reckless critics among the opposers of Christianity are compelled to admit that enough of the Evangelies is authentic to establish the fundamental doctrines of Christianity. Also the authenticity of the Apocalypse is admitted by the unbelievers. It is also admitted that some of the Gospels existed before the destruction of Jerusalem. In short rationalists can not deny that Jesus claimed to be the Son of God. Now, if the authenticity of the Testament is established, how can we doubt the credibility of its writers? For we surely find the most irrefutable evidence for the Evangelists in the fact that they exercise such an intense power in drawing men to God.

Besides the Evangelists, we find Paul, the man of the most self-denial after Christ. Paul, the Jew of the Jews, the terror of the church, the Pharisee of learning, this Paul agrees with the other Evangelists in the main doctrines. The most radical rationalists, like the Tuebingen school, after employing the most reckless criticism, admit that the first four Epistles of Paul were genuine. In the name of everything which is true, in the name of honor and humanity, I ask every reader, can you say that Paul, that suffering Paul, that man who was dead to himself, was *he* an imposter? He risked his life numberless times, suffered imprisonment, and even beatings, had a good many other things to suffer, (of which few can form so near an idea as the writer of these lines), and this Paul toiled laboriously for his own bread; was he an imposter? If Christ had no witness but Paul, I think it ought to be sufficient to move a heart of stone.* In short, we cannot take the New Testament to be an invention, for the character of Christ is too sublime, and the rest to which it relates would be too absurd for any human imagination to invent. It is psychologically impossible for the human imagination to create either such a Jesus or such miracles in connection with him. Especially when we consider these most sublime doctrines and the devotion to God which it teaches, and

---

* In former days Paul often caused me disturbance. I always admired him, and could never find an answer when a voice in my heart asked me, what will you do with Paul? I remember that just two years before I was converted, Paul engaged my mind very seriously, I tried hard to interpret Paul into my rational system without success. At the same time it never occurred to me that Christianity could possibly be true on account of that. I would rather have believed anything than in the possibility that I could ever be converted. I believe I would have killed myself if I had expected to live and be converted. I considered it the greatest disgrace. It is truly a disgrace, but not in the eyes of Israel's God. Yet a few months before I was converted, while I was unconsciously steering towards it very fast, I expressed to a Christian that a converted Jew can never be sincere. "Paul," was the laconic answer. It made my heart tremble, without knowing why. Many days the word " Paul," reverberated in my ears. I never could, nor shall I ever forget the impression of that moment. The last days before my conversion became completed, hardly an hour passed that I did not ask myself, " Was Paul a liar?" How wonderfully Providence united an endless number of trifling things to work out my conversion, without my having the least anticipation of it. What an endless number of incidents united to prepare my conversion, I cannot possibly describe them all. Once it was to convince the mind; another time the heart, and I was aware of nothing. Jewish brethren, I ask you: " Paul?"

the persecutions and martyrdom which those teachings entailed, it becomes impossible to believe that lies could produce such a devotion to God and such a morality. The presumption that what the New Testament *relates* was a lie cannot possibly be united with the fact that it *teaches* such sublime truths. The character of the book, and of its writers, especially that of the wonderful Paul, are sufficient witnesses for themselves. .

Besides Christ's miracles, which are related in the New Testament, we find the most stupendous miracle of history, in the fact that the Gentiles *believed*. This miracle can not be disputed, and therefore it testifies to the truth of the other miracles. The Gentiles, who knew nothing of the God of Israel, the proud Grecians and Romans, accepted the God of the Jews ; the inhabitants of the remote islands fell down to worship the God of Israel; Heathen sang David's psalms as soon as they heard the tidings of Jesus Christ. Is this not a stupendous miracle ? A few poor, unknown and despised Galileean Jews, hated and persected by their own people, mocked at by all the world, still established the Christian Church ! These men went into the distant regions of the world to tell their story; the Grecians called it foolishness and the Jews idolatry ; they told things against all logic and science, and the Grecians and Romans believed ! They believed without having our historical proofs. The Old Testament was no authority for them, the history of the Jewish people was not yet so marvelous for the eye of every observer. What made Gentiles give up their habits, their lusts and carnal joys if not truly a spirit from God ?

Shining gold has not bribed them, power and glory was not to be gained, everything was to be lost, nothing gained, and still they believed! They believed and turned their hearts to the God of Jacob in contrition and love. The very fact that the story which the Apostles related sounds so unreasonable and absurd makes the belief of it a marvel. Especially as they found believers among the different classes of society, among different nations and in different countries. If it is marvelous enough that they believed, it is still more so that they did it in spite of persecutions and even martyrdom. For not only were the first Christians not persuaded to believe by the sword, like the Mahommedans, but on the contrary, they even were persecuted. The sufferings of the first Christians were even severer than those of the Jews and Protestants in the time of the inquisition. If the Jews died for the religion of their fathers there is a psychological reason for it: it is the religion of their fathers. But Gentiles believed and became martyrs; it was only required of them to deny Christ with their mouth, and they instead suffered the hardest death which a most cruel oppressor could inflict upon them. And this for a religion just embraced and new of itself. Does this not testify that they were convinced by the power of God? The more unreasonable the belief was, the more proof it is that a supernatural power must have given strength of faith in order to die for it. It is no marvel that the christian religion had martyrs, martyrs do not prove the truth of a cause, since every cause has its martyrs. It is only a marvel that the young religion found its martyrs so rapidly. Gentiles died for a foreign religion. While Christianity was so much despised and so fearfully persecuted, Gentiles believed, endangered their lives and became martyrs. To believe and become a martyr was an every day occurrence.

And not only was Christianity *not* promulgated, and even *persecuted* by the sword, but it finally conquered the sword. In spite of all imaginable persecutions, in spite of the most cruel deaths which the believers suffered, the new, foreign religion grew and spread until it conquered its persecutors. It conquered the throne which persecuted it. It grew until the murderer Constantine, called "the Great," saw the necessity of accepting it. Christianity gained so much influence that the state had to court its friendship,

I must remark here that it was not beneficial to the true religion that the state was zealous to avail itself of the influence of the church. For this planted elements of the state into the ground of the church, so that men of the world represented the religion, and ambition took the seat which belonged to humility and devotion. It never could be Christ's church which stretched her hand to grasp a scepter, but the elements of the state, planted into the church. It went so far that even unmasqued infidels represented the church and made it the most dangerous enemy of religion. The consequence was that the church, which existed in the name of the loving Christ, this church which should represent humility and love, which should win by the spirit of love and holiness, this church persecuted and exercised the most cruel despotism, which was against Christ's spirit. An extreme anti-christian spirit in the church alone could create such an institution as the inquisition. This inquisiton, which the world considers the darkest spot in the history of Christianity, was far more antagonistic and dangerous to the Christian than to the Jewish religion, even though assuming the name of Christianity.

I must even say that to-day any aspirations of Christians towards civil power in order to promulgate Christian ideas by virtue of it, is opposed to the spirit of Christ. Christianity wants no law, no arms, but the spirit of love. Wherever and whenever men make efforts to use the force of law for religious ideas or institutions, they are surely not moved by the spirit of Christ, no matter how laudable their undertaking may be in itself. It may indeed be their sacred duty as men, but not as Christians, in the name of the religion. Christ desires no throne but that of the heart, and no submission but that of love. That alone is Christianity which is taught in the Bible, and there is no necessity to show that Christ teaches not to improve sinners or society by legal force. What is gained by forcing any one to a religious deed, since God only wants the heart, and looks upon the motive? Christianity has and wants no visible power. Legal force in the name of God can never be justified. Law is antagonistic to Christianity, because its aim is to lead mankind to a state where no law is needed. Law is narrowness; religion is broad, wide, endless; it is love. Law is necessary in the world only, because it has not the spirit of Christ. Law in religion is the spirit of Phariseeism. "Beware of the leaven of the Pharisees." Law is "*here a little, there a little.*" Christianity is a principle, monotheism. Whenever the force of law was used in the name of the religion it always had the opposite effect; it also created hypocrisy, and made "*the way of the truth evil spoken of,*" if it did no greater harm. "Not by might, nor by power, but by my spirit, says the Lord of Hosts."—Zach. iv : 6.

Returning to our topic, we find that neither law nor the sword promulgated Christianity, but quite the contrary. This is according to history, if we read it with an open eye, and do not misunderstand Christianity. Thus, as I said, the fact that the Gentiles believed, became martyrs, and that the religion spread so rapidly and extensively, is the most stupendous miracle, testifying that only the divine spirit could promulgate the religion, and the Apostles were only instruments in the hands of God. Civilized peoples could not have left their temples, their orators and philosophers, and yielded to the doctrine of poor Jews, if those had nothing but human reason and logic to persuade and convince of the truth of things naturally impossible. The very existence of the church is a marvel in itself, and testifies to its truth.

And what a sublime influence this religion exercised over the hearts of its true believers! How many millions of hearts it has purified and filled with consolation, hope and joy! How many sinking souls it has lifted up! Shall we mistrust the religion because it was misused? Shall we make the religion responsible for men who committed everything which is against the religion they claimed to defend? Is the religion false because there are hypocrites who claim to follow it, and sincere men who misunderstand it? We see men misuse everything which is great and noble. How many were oppressed, imprisoned, and murdered in the name of liberty? Shall we therefore be for despotism or anarchy? How many battles have been fought in the name of freedom.

So far we have evidence from history. To these we may add the predictions in the Old Testament which we will cite in the following chapters. The predictions which testify to Christ are probably the strongest argument for the Old Testament. For if its predictions are fulfilled then it must be of divine origin.

Now after having historical evidences for both Testaments there is no further necessity for writing against the so-called rationalists. They only assert that miracles never happened because they do not happen now.

It is perfectly irrational to suppose, with Renan, that Jesus was the sublimest being, and still dreamer enough to claim to be the Son of God, it would be lunacy. Renan's system is a contradiction in itself. Those who try to make a sort of political demagogue of him deserve no consideration; especially since they are sufficiently refuted by other rationalists. We have also seen that it is against history to suppose that he never claimed to be the Son of God, and Dr. Grætz also must admit that fact.

Some of the rationalists take Christ's miracles to be legends based upon facts. something similar to the prin--

ciple I used to follow in interpreting the miracles of the Old Testament. Dr. Strauss, whom rationalists consider a most impregnable tower of rationalism, after successfully refuting all other systems, takes the miracles to be a sort of tales, inventions of Christ's followers, and these tales he styles myths, without being able to find a real historical or allegorical motive for them; a thing which is necessary in order to show that they are myths. I have already said, and any really rational reader of the Bible will find it so, that we cannot possibly make anything else of the Bible but either a lie or history. The miracles of both Testaments cannot be so interpreted as to make poetry or myths of them. No human imagination could produce such fearful legends or myths. We only want to read the Bible in order to find Strauss refuted. The Bible of itself refutes reform as well as the so-called rationalism. The great Strauss sometimes even advances ideas which would be too simple for a child, He says, for instance, it was invented that Christ left his parents and was found in the temple, simply because the Emperor Augustus was found sleeping on the top of a house when looked for once in his childhood. It is related that Christ fed the multitudes by a miracle, because it is told so of Moses. Is it not easier to believe the miracles than these notions of Strauss? And there are a great number of such beautiful myths to be found in the works of the impregnable tower of rationalism.

According to any of the rational methods the Bible is an invention, and we must say, if an invention, it is also a foolish one; and still these foolish lies present to us such a perfect beauty as the character of Christ. And the world believed those absurd inventions. And these inventions promulgated the most lofty morals the world ever heard. Shall we believe Mr. Strauss because he displays rich stores of knowledge? Do his hypotheses, of which some are even absurd, receive any corroboration because he tries to find items of the ancient history and literature which resemble the facts related in the New Testament? As we have seen that Christ's claim and his miracles must be historical facts, I do not deem it necessary to treat upon the rational methods more at length. They try to show that Christianity is the natural result of Judaism and Paganism, and we must see the visible hand of God in the fact that it prevailed in spite of these antagonistic elements. 'They say it was an advance upon both, but if a lie how can a lie cause an advance?

It is true that we sometimes find ideas and tales among the Pagans which resemble very much the facts and the doctrines of both Testaments. The Jews knew this, and were not embarrassed about it. They were not only not moved to doubt their Bible on this account, but they even considered it a corroboration of its truth. It is mentioned in their literature, and can also be proved by that of the Grecians, that some of the ancient Grecian sages learned from the Prophets. The Jews have traditions that Plato or Aristotle learned from the Prophet Jeremiah. This, and most of their traditions are a union of truth and error. They are especially very weak in the point of chronology. Some later writers show that

Jeremiah must have taught Grecian sages, but surely not Plato or Aristotle, who lived considerable later. History indicates that some Hebrew, at least Semitic, elements were planted in Greece with its first settlers. Who can ascertain how much of divine truth the Phenecians carried into the world through their intimacy with the Israelites in the time of King Solomon? The rationalists can show what the old heathen believed, but not where they got their ideas, or how the truth degenerated with them. What mankind anticipated by feeling, so to speak, the prophetic spirit in mankind may also have been the cause of some old myth, which finally was found to point to the truth. That is to say, that some myths of the Pagans may even contain Christian truths and facts because it was a kind of prophetic spirit in mankind which predicted the truth. The religion which mankind needed was felt in their hearts, it was anticipated by feeling what they needed. God prepared the way for the religion. Many prophecies were introduced and enveloped in the myths of the Pagans; besides that, mankind had divine truths from their common ancestors which were afterwards corrupted and mixed up with their idolatrous belief. Hence we find something common in all ancient creeds, and also in the tales of their histories. Still, the Bible is pure and true. All the efforts of Mr. Strauss, and all his rich knowledge, is not sufficient even to show that *many* things of Scripture really resemble the Pagan tales, and he forces many heterogenious things to make them mutually resemble. After all, he only *asserts* that Christianity is the result of Judaism, Hellenism and Romanism, but he does *not* prove it, he only forces himself to do so. Nothing alters the fact that Jesus claimed to be the Son of God and worked miracles. History testifies to this, and the success and influence of the claim testify to its genuineness. Can the fact that the heathen had some myths which resemble some Christian facts alter anything in history?

The most consistent of all the so-called rationalists is the school to which Robert Taylor belonged. They teach that the whole Bible contains nothing but allegories, without any history. They do not try to manufacture history. The Patriarchs and the Prophets, David, all the Kings and Christ, say they, never existed in reality, but represent ideas and powers of nature, like the heroes and gods of the mythologies of the heathen. This school makes no distinction between common fiction, or mythology, and scripture. I wonder where the Jews come from, then! and what made the heathen of the first century mention Christ as a historical person? Still this school has the preference of the others as it is at least radical and logical in its madness. I love logic. Robert Taylor caused some excitement in England, and was considered original. But his ideas are very old. In the middle ages some Jewish preachers in France advanced similar doctrines, to the excitement and indignation of the Rabbis, who very promptly suppressed the movement. And these preachers were not even original. There were also adherents of this school to be found in the Vatican. The method of Mr. Strauss is in some respects an effort to reconcile these doctrines with history.

I must remark again that each of the above mentioned rational methods is directed against the Old as well as the New Testament. From the stand-point of Judaism no rational system can be used against Christianity. According to rationalism, the world must give up the Bible. They deny that any thing ever happened through supernatural causes. Will the world ever give up the Bible? Will the Jewish nation ever give up the Bible entirely? And what is the practical result of rationalism?

The fact is that the rationalists labor in principle under the same difficulty with the reformers. We have seen that some Jews, finding no effect, no aim of their religion consequently rejected all belief; but still being unable to find any reasonable solution for the problem of the marvelous history of their people, fell into the absurd inconsistency called reform. They claim to reconcile the marvel of their history, the marvelous and mysterious Holy Spirit of Scripture with what they call reason. They seek no solution of the problem of the miracles and influence of Christianity, for they simply ignore it. They see in Christianity nothing but foolishness, they would not even stop to think of the possibility of its being true, in spite of the fact that it governs the civilized world and has the greatest philosophers as its banner-bearers, in spite of the fact that it advances such sublime doctrines. Whatever good they must admit as springing from it they ascribe to what they call the spirit of Judaism in Christianity, so that *their* Judaism is the fountain of everything good. They are blind enough not to see that the

Jews and Judaism were always abhorred by the nations, and that the Gentiles never accepted anything from the Jewish doctrine but what is in connection with the name of Jesus Christ. The rationalists, though, know how to distinguish the spirit of Christianity and its influence from the post-biblical Judaism, as two extremes. They find the post-biblical Judaism a burning fire, which gives neither light nor warmth, while they are amazed by the beauty and the healing power of the rays which radiate from Christ. They do not ignore the influence and the marvels of Christianity. They admire, adore and exalt the sublime characters and doctrines of Christ and his followers. I have cited above three different kinds of evidence; the first is furnished by the Jewish nation, the second by the characters of Christ and his Apostles, the third by the church itself. Rationalists do not consider the first, but the two last; not willing to believe, they find psychological, and historic-philosophical problems, for which they must try to find a reasonable solution. The church is a fact; what caused it? They are not possessed by the blindness of my people, to say it was a lie, foolishness. They would not see its holiness, but they must admit its sublime ideas. They can reject the religion and go after reason only, but its existence causes an obstacle in their way, history compels them to recognize it as a something. They are embarrassed about what to make of Christ, his followers and church. The religion exists and its origin is the divine power of God, something supernatural: this they do not believe, and must seek to .

find the origin of Christianity in the human nature. They try to reduce the power of God to a common historical phenomenon. History relates miracles, so they must make a history of their own. It tells of a supernatural Jesus, and they try to create a Jesus of their own. Everything must have its natural, comprehensible cause, and if it has not, they make it, in order to reconcile history with rationalism. History furnishes the evidences I have cited, and they try to avoid them. The consequence is, that the rationalists must come in conflict with history, and with themselves, as the Reformers, in spite of all their knowledge and studies. They must make hypotheses which never can replace these facts which they refuse to believe.

They try to make of the Bible a something which is neither a lie nor the truth, and make a monster of it. At first they do not succeed, for their analogy is often so very far-fetched, their attempts to make poetry of some biblical narration are so forced, that they even sometimes become absurd, as I have shown in instances cited above. They cannot even find enough of apparently reasonable hypotheses to justify the presumption that the Bible could be anything but either a lie or a divine truth. But supposing they could show that there are reasonable motives for the miracles when represented as products of the imagination, even then, Christ and his Apostles would be liars, for they did not relate their stories in such a manner that we could suppose that they meant to promulgate their doctrines in the dress of their fables, but they made the *facts* which they related as the main point.

Paul, for instance, speaks too plainly, too prosaically, and asserts that he saw Jesus himself, therefore he must have been a liar, with all his poetry. Consequently, there is no solution of the problem of the existence of the church and its influence. They still have to ascribe the marvel of the existence of the church and its sublime doctrines and influence to the work of a lie. It is still unreasonable to believe that the Gentiles could believe a lie and become martyrs for it. The rationalists are just as inconsistent as the Reformers, for their system does not remove the salient difficulties which caused them to write a " Life of Jesus," the product of their imagination; the Jesus and the Apostles whom they created can not have been the authors of the miracles in history, any more than a Jesus and Apostles who were liars according to the Jews. If all the assertions of the rationalists were true, and there was no supernatural interference of God in history, even then, the problems of history remain problems. For if there is nothing supernatural, why does the Jewish nation live? Why did Christianity find martyrs so soon after its origination? Why does a lie conquer the world and prove to be such a blessing? *Their* Jesus remains a contradiction in himself. Besides this, the rationalists could never claim to answer the problem of the Jewish history and its testimony to Christ. For they never brought this into consideration. Thus the reform and rationalism are alike faulty in motive, and show the same result. Their motive is unbelief, which causes the problems, and the result is that they can find no solution. History cannot be understood when the most important link in the chain of its events, namely the supernatural divine interference, is not accepted. The problems exist not for the believer in true history, and reformers and rationalists have simply the history they make for themselves. Unbelief is not the result of rationalism, but rationalism is the result of unbelief. Messrs. Renan and Strauss did not come to their unbelief on account of their studies, but they prosecuted these studies because they did not believe. The same thing is the case with philosophers and naturalists who advance the lowest materialism. The knowledge of nature does not lead to deny God any more than that of history to deny his supernatural revelations. The more we learn of nature the more we are able to realize our weakness, blindness and impotence, and to see that there is a great God who surrounds us by his wisdom. We can easily discover that there is a something which we must believe, for we cannot understand everything. Is there nothing hid from the eye of these naturalists who preach the lowest materialism and ridicule everything ideal, especially religion? Is there no problem for them? And if they run the great machinery of the universe without a God, and claim to have no soul, but a phosphorus in the blood, who manages history for them? Even if history has laws which guide the evolutions, still how are the different occurrences picked up and combined for the general law, without a free will to manage? The spinning machine spins alone, but an intelligent manager must purchase the materials. Certainly, the great naturalists do not look at such a thing as the history of the Jews. All human knowledge and wisdom are not sufficient to understand the most conspicuous marvels in nature or history, still less will human wisdom be able to satisfy heart and soul, in order to make mankind happy. Science does not only not interfere with religion but it assists it. Happiness of the heart and freedom of the soul can only be given by God. He makes us free and happy by his supernatural way, for our nature is corrupted. To God alone we must look for happiness, life, and hope, and joy, and light, and truth. Believe, trust Him, lean on Him only.

As I said, knowledge is not the cause of unbelief, the real cause is a *misunderstanding of the belief*. All the evidences of history will fail to convert to Christianity, for they only convince the *mind*, and religion must be experienced in the *heart*. The evidences which convince the mind are only witnesses for the Christian that his religion is true, but they tell not what it really is, and a man must perceive this before he can believe. Reason fails to convert because if one believes, even with his mind, he is not a Christian yet, and does not even know what Christianity means. The belief of the mind is not religion.

Those Jews who were not drawn to God by a love to the person of Christ, whose *hearts* were not touched, could not believe in him. The passages in scripture and the miracles could not convince them; for the first they perverted, and the latter they ascribed to the power of the devil. So to-day, those whose hearts are not touched by Christ's spirit find belief impossible; the most irrefutable evidence of history can not convince them, and they pervert history by hypothesis as the Jews do the Bible. As some Jews left Judaism because they saw no effect from the religion of the mind, so some Gentiles leave Christianity since they only know the mind's belief, which leads them to misunderstand Christianity. They never knew its effect upon the heart. The belief of the mind is an objective one, the one of the heart is subjective. Or in other words believing that there is a God is not religion. He must be felt in the heart.

If Christianity, simply required belief of the mind, surely the promise of atonement through the belief would not only be an absurdity, but even an atrocious wrong, undermining every law of morality. We would have to consider a great number of drunkards and criminals as belonging to the Christian church. We could hardly say any one was a hypocrite, for many of those who devour widow's houses, many who are humble do-nothings on Sunday and "shrewed" the other six days, many who have no other object of life but to gather treasures of gold, are at the same time believers in their minds. For a man can believe that there is a God without this belief affecting his heart. But such a belief is not the Christianity which the New Testament teaches.

If the belief of the mind would make a Christian, then the man with little brain would have the most advantage, since he can easily believe anything. So the Jew supposes, and takes therefore every converted Jew, who was not brought up, or as they consider blinded, to believe the Christian dogmas, to be a base hypocrite. Moreover, the conceit that Judaism is entirely according to reason, is common among the Jews, while Christians do not even claim that their religion can be comprehended by reason. But it cannot be the weak mind that enables us to believe, since religion conquered the civilized world, and we find men like Descartes, Leibnitz, Kepler, Bacon, the pride of England, Sir Isaac Newton, Schelling, and a great many of the greatest philosophers among the banner-bearers of Christianity. We also find that the Christians erected universities, and cultivated sciences, while orthodox Judaism persecuted every student of science and studied nothing but the Talmund. They even persecuted Maimonides. The blind belief of the mind instinctively fears every scientific investigation. It is therefore obvious that it cannot be the weak mind, but a certain spirit which causes belief.

There are two ways of reading the New Testament; one with the mind, the other with the heart. The mind reads the histories of the miracles, the things which have *happened*; the heart reads the spirit, the things that *are* and ever shall be. The Jesus who lived more than eighteen centuries ago, who must bring his credentials from history, who was crucified, who meets with opposition, is the Jesus in whom some minds believe and some not. But the Jesus of the heart lives, and is seen and felt. If one once sees him he believes in him. This Jesus never finds any opposition. These multitudes gathered from the different parts of the globe, from many nations and tongues; behold these multitudes of Gentiles with folded hands, with hearts melting before the living God of Israel, and crying " Hossanah, Son of David;" they did not read the New Testament with their minds, but with their hearts. They know the Jesus of the heart. They did not become convinced, but overpowered, subdued by the love of God. They were not persuaded by ideas, but conquered; conquered not to slavery, but to freedom, not to work, but to love; conquered to love, by love. Jesus did not reason with Mary Magdalene. She only loved him, and therefore loved God. A religion which is acquired by love is the religion of the heart, the mind does not love. From the multitudes who followed him in Palestine to those who look up to him now, all have been converted to God by a love to his person. They believe him because they are brought to God in loving him. Atheists even admire Jesus' virtues, his unparalleled greatness in humility, highness when despised, majesty when condemned, and love when wounded. They admire his virtues, not him. The love of the abstract virtue is not a real love, a love that draws to the object; we love to be virtuous without a religion, else we would never have the pangs of conscience which made us look for a religion. We knew that we ought to be virtuous before, and as I said, we only want a religion because we are not such as we ought to be. As I remarked in the first note of this chapter, we must be brought to the standard by the religion. Therefore, I have no benefit from admiring abstract virtue, this does not turn me to God. But the love to his *person* converts. The flame of holiness which flashes from his person envelopes his followers, and makes them "sanctified to the Lord." His virtues abstracted are not new to us; the law teaches virtue: but the virtues personified in Christ bring nearer to the standard of the law. Therefore we see that even atheists may admire his virtues, but only those who love him are converted to God. Jesus is the Christ, not because he had amiable virtues, but because he was virtue itself; not because he taught good principles, but because he is the principle of everything which is good. This we see in the fact that those who accept his person, not his doctrines only, are turned to God, while admirers of his doctrines may at the same time be atheists. In him we are enabled to love God. It is the fact that the world vanishes in his love, and God becomes our only consolation, which testifies to his genuineness. Therefore I said that the most irrefutable evidence against all opposition is the experience of the heart. No one can deny that through Christ many turned to the God of Israel, and not through his doctrines, but through him. All the aim, the being of the person of Jesus, is the turning of men to God.

This is the most remarkable feature in Christ's life, that he converted men to God by imbuing them with a love to his person, that love is his instrument. The consequence is that he enables to be good, gives strength to the will and inclines the heart toward the things of the Spirit more than any doctrine or law could do. For in accepting the majesty which radiates from a cross, in making the poor and humble my King, and humility and simplicity my model, and above all in *loving* everything good *embodied* in his person, my heart becomes changed, I find a remedy against depravity. (*The fact is that there is a supernatural power which changes the heart, and improves the man, but I only speak of Christ's work according to what we perceive*). I was weak before because my heart was inclined to the things perishable. I loved them, while I knew that I ought to love the things eternal. I was depraved; now, the remedy is love. In loving Christ I realize in my heart more of the misery of the world. I must necessarily despise the world more since I love self-denial itself. I am better enabled to be virtuous because the virtue is *personified* in his person.* His love has a practical result. My will is changed, because I find more satisfaction in the spiritual things. Because I look for consolation where Christ looked for it. Because if I really love him I cannot act willfully against him, and it gives me satisfaction and joy to act according to his will.

It is therefore erroneous to think that Christ teaches resignation of the world, to chastise one's self without necessity. A man can chastise himself and be very far from God. But Christ imbues the heart with a love to

---

* This change of will is not a phrase, it does not exist in theory only, but in fact. Many have labored and sighed under the burden of vices, were overpowered by bad appetites which they could not resist, but were freed from their vices as soon as they were converted to Christ by a real love to his name. I testify before God and men that I have labored twenty years under vices which I could not resist, and became free the very day I felt that Christ must be true. I received a fresh power. I could easily resist what I could not before, though with the strongest efforts of my will. I experienced such a change in my will that reason cannot possibly account for it. I felt free of my hardest oppressor. In a very short time I even felt free of the temptations. All through the name of Jesus Christ. Thanks and glory to the name of the Lord!

God, so that he becomes our aim of life. He therefore enables us to resign the will to God. The resignation is only the resignation of the will. When the will is resigned there is rest and peace in every state and circumstance of life. One may enjoy the allotments of Providence when the enjoyed object is not the aim of his life, when his heart, his will, clings not to the perishable but to the divine things. Sin is not objective but subjective; it lies not in the act or the object, but in the subject. One may sin by a certain deed while under other circumstances the same deed would be no sin. Sin is in the will. For instance, love of money is a low sin which makes the man more foolish than the animal, but the sin lies not in the money but in the love. It is even a duty, a necessity to work for money, and so it is with everything; if my will aspires upwards and is subjected to God I elevate the enjoyed thing to me, and when I have no other object in life, but in the enjoyments of this world I make myself low with the thing I enjoy. In short, in loving Christ we enter his spirit and we feel a love and a thirsting for God as expressed by King David, God becomes all in all, our aim and motive, and we are enabled to will and to do, as we are prompted by the love of God. God himself becomes an enjoyment. I only state a fact, not an argument, and millions of true Christians can testify to it. A love of God like that of King David, is the consequence of believing in Christ. This is an experience of the heart, and one need only take the testimony of millions of Christians in order to believe it.

From this fact we have a logical proof that Christ has a divine character. For since we find that Christ converts by love to his person, therefore he is a remedy against our depravity. For our depravity is only that we are not converted to God. Now, he is the one who converts, and if he is that he is our religion, which must be given by God. For if man could make the religion himself then he would not be depraved, the doctrine of the depravity includes the fact that man cannot help himself. If he cannot help himself naturally, then only God can help supernaturally. And again we find that Christ is the help; then he is the supernatural help of God. We only have to believe what the Jews do, that man is depraved, and therefore God reveals himself for our salvation, and then we see the fact that Christ converted so many millions to the God of Israel through his name only, and we find the conclusion that he must be supernatural.

Again, when we find that Christ imbues with a love to the things divine, and changes our heart, then we must conclude that the law is abolished in his love. For I only needed a law because I did not love. Love is a radical cure for the disease against which the law is intended. Love elevates the nature above the law. The law is not revoked, it exists. The Christian only does not need it. As the honest man needs no law not to steal, his honor forbidding it, so one whose heart is moved by the love of God needs no law whatever. The law was necessary to be before Christ in order to teach me that there is a God of Israel, a God of holiness who gives me means for my sal vation. How could I believe Christ if I knew nothing of the God of Abraham, the God of holiness, and that he wants me to do his will? I could not expect that the God of nature and history would send a supernatural redemption. What would I see in Jesus if not that he is given to the holy God of Israel and converts to him? Everything in the Old Testament was necessary in order to teach me what Jesus ought to be, to point to him in the law, especially in the sacrifices, and finally to predict him. We do not follow Jesus and give ourselves to him because multitudes followed him, but because he followed and was given up to God. We do not believe him as a founder of a new religion, but as the fulfiller of the old. And I would not have known this God, nor could I have appreciated Jesus without the law. How could we understand what Jesus is without the Old Testament? The law was the way to Christ; when I reach the aim I do not need the way any longer. As long as one believes with the mind only he needs a law, but when one feels God through Christ's love he wants no law. Law is for the mind, love from the heart. Moses drew a people chosen in the seed, to give them the freedom of this world only, and he had to give them a law. Christ draws his people chosen in the Spirit from all the corners of the earth, and gives them the freedom of the soul to follow God by love. The staff and miracles of Moses were visible to his people near and around him, but Christ's love is enthroned above the sun and seen all over the world by every brokenhearted man who turns his eye towards heaven. Moses commanded the law and Christ proclaims freedom, because his love makes the law superfluous and us the more free. I am free when my actions are prompted by my love, but a slave and tempted when I am compelled to work by law.

So far I have spoken only of the experience of the Christian heart in finding a love of God and strength of will through Christ. But there are other experiences in consequence of the belief in Christ. As I said before, the love of God makes the will resigned to him; this causes rest and peace of heart and soul. One may deny it, but it is still true that men have no inward rest without Christ. Besides this, Christ gives consolation and hope. The belief in Christ gives a sure hope in God as Christ reveals God to us as a loving friend, and his name and sufferings are a consolation in our sufferings. Christ *ministers* to-day as much as he did when he walked on earth. He still heals the heart which is wounded, he has a cooling balm for the one which burns. From his own gaping wounds springs a fountain of life and love. When your hard fate presses tears from your eyes, he bows over you to wipe them away; when your face burns he cools it with a drop from his own eye milder than the dew from heaven. He changes tears into pearls, the expression of sorrow and pain into a smile of gladness. The face of a storm-beaten sinner he transfigures into that of an angel-like infant, laughing in his dreams. His sorrow and self-denial, his wounds and cross, they are an everlasting source of consolation. Many noble hearts have beaten on earth, but there is only rest at *his* bosom. Leaning on him all sorrow is gone, for you love . . . . The roaring billows of this raging world subside, no storm roars, the soul breathes. He closes the wounds of the heart, he raises you above yourself, you weep again and the tears are tears of love. .... Only Christ enables us to love really and calmly. Love is consolation, and hope and life and manna, and everything; but you must love God.

Another consequence of the belief in Christ is the loss of fear of death, which is caused by our depravity. He quiets conscience and his love casts out fear. Love gives confidence in God. How can I be afraid when I believe that God has shown us so much love; that His Christ is the greatest sufferer. The belief also gives satisfaction. This yearning without an aim, of which I spoke in the chapter on depravity, this love without knowing the object, without finding satisfaction; this longing which the beauty of nature causes in our breast; all these indescribable emotions of the soul find their aim and satisfaction in finding Christ. We have yearned for the all, for the omnipresent divinity, which is too high, unattainable for us; in Christ it is connected with the man, and we can reach it. The divine spirit is, so to speak, concentrated so that we can embrace it. In finding Christ, we recognise the object for which our soul yearned in vain; we find that we did not know what we wanted. Every human soul yearns and longs to find rest in his love, but the man knows it not. In Christ we find a satisfaction which has no end; it is the death of the flesh, and life and freedom of the imprisoned soul. The flesh causes our misery as long as our will is clinging to it; in Christ the will turns to God. It is the awakening of the soul which was slumbering in fetters. Christ awakens the consciousness of man's soul.

In short, I have given a description of the heart's experiences which are caused by the human depravity, (and no man who is honest with himself can dispute the correctness of my description.) Christianity removes all those hard experiences, and gives joy and happiness to heart and soul. The Christian finds living water for his soul; he finds cooling for his burning heart. What the inner man needs is found in Christ. Shall we bring better proofs than this? If a Christian can not bring the least evidence for his belief, he is still as much convinced of it as he is of the fact that bread satisfies hunger, without understanding why. One who has tasted the love of God through Christ is not surprised at the heroism of the early martyrs; he knows that there is a sweetness in loving God which enables us to give one's life for it with delight. Though all the philosophers in the world rage, they cannot shake a man who has tasted Christianity. The religion of the heart can not be shaken by the mind. Though all the world say we are hypocrites and fools, we feel and know what we have. We know that we are depraved, and must expect the consequences in a future world, but in Christ we find God, the only salvation. Just as one man could convince another that it is foolish to drink water when he is dry, so he can convince a Christian of the error of the Christian religion. The unbeliever misunderstands the Christian religion; it is a something which cannot be argued; it is love, and love asks not for reasons. And so are many who think that they belong to the Christian church, and have nothing but the belief of the mind. The belief of the heart is seen in the man's works. Our works can not be good enough to justify us before God, but the works show and testify. Some German writer has rightly said, "It takes more spirit to believe than understanding to disbelieve."

The Kingdom of Heaven is like unto a magic castle, from whose interior come forth the sweetest strains of seraphic music; streams of life flow from its midst; the most fragrant flowers of joy grow on its grounds; everlasting peace and rest are found in its rooms; its tower offers a safe refuge against all powers destructive to real life; it is adorned with the banner of love; the noblest flag waves from its top—the flag of the all-loving, Almighty Jehovah, the God of Israel. Many pass by this castle and look upon it with contempt. But the weary soul, which yearns for rest, which is drawn by its charms and desires to place itself under the protection of the God of Israel, finds no door. Every way which seems to lead to the castle terminates with an insurmountable obstacle. There is only one magic name to be called— "Jesus Christ"—and the doors open. It is not reasonable, but it is a magic castle, and as soon as you are in you cannot be moved by those who pass by and look upon you and the castle with contempt. There is a power in this name which defies all reason; but it brings into the castle, it gives the love of God.

The less reason can account for the fact that Christ's love leads to God, the more proof it is for his supernatural character. There is God with him, who alone can give the experience of safety to the heart. There is a supernatural connection between the believer's heart and God.*

I do not mean to enter into any philosophical discussion about the experiences of the Christian heart. I simply state the facts. I only know it as a fact, that the believer is drawn to the living God; that Jesus is a principle with him which guides and gives power to be good; that the heart finds peace and satisfaction; therefore I believe in him. Miracles are occurrences which convince the mind of God's supernatural interference, because they happen against the laws of nature so that reason can not comprehend them. Could the miracles be understood, then they would prove nothing, as I said above. So the experiences of the Christian heart are facts which are not according to psychology, and therefore they convince the heart which has such experiences. Every worldly joy leaves the heart burning and hollow, but Christ gives satisfaction and the fullness of God. When men are tempted to sin, they will find it harder to resist when they are guided by the moral and the divine law than when they have Jesus as a principle to guide them, and look for no law. And when they all resist, it is a hard burden for the man who has a legal measure for his actions, but the one who follows Jesus is

---

*I must say here that, besides the above cited experiences of the heart, there is a supernatural experience which can not even be described. The baptism with the Holy Ghost is not a phrase but a fact. It is surely nothing visible or perceptible by the senses, but still many have experienced such an inward perception. If it is only an experience of the heart it still convinces of the existence of supernatural things; it was so the case with me. This, my assertion, caused some to pervert my words as if I had said that I had a revelation of Christ in the flesh. And so it was promptly circulated by the Jewish press.

prompted by love. Here we see that Jesus is a principle which replaces the law, and does even more.

Unbelievers do not oppose Christ's doctrines, but his person. They may deny that he had a divine character, but they cannot dispute that there are men for whom he is a principle; whom he places above the law; whom he gives satisfaction of life; whom he imbues with a love to God, so that death becomes something desirable, as the means to come to the beloved. Consequently we may ask, how could a man become a principle, a religion, a satisfaction of the heart, a moving power for every thing good, the end of all hopes; how can he become all that, except God be with him? Since we see that he is a mediator between God and man in pleading the cause of God before men with such a matchless success, why shall we not believe that he also pleads the cause of men before God? I do not say that philosophy can account for it. I do not claim to be able to defend it philosophically. I even believe that according to reason the pantheists are right. No miracle can be defended by reason; but still the Bible is true. So the Christian experiences have no reason, and therefore Christ is true. If he was not true, he could not possibly work such miracles in the heart. He is true because his greatest miracle is leading human hearts to God. This miracle I see at this day.

In conclusion, we find that every one who sees the miracles of the heart will be convinced of the religion of the heart, and then he will find that all the doctrines of the world can not make atonement between man and God, but Christ himself. Even Christ's doctrines are of no avail, when we have not *him*. He is our only help according to the Bible, as we shall find in the next chapter. All those who misunderstand his religion will find problems in history. They try to show how Christianity originated, in order to remove the problems. All they show is only how it *might have* originated, but not how it *did* originate. If one knows where the holiness of God originates, he may also claim to know where Christ's religion originated. For true Christianity is the holiness of God. And we have our evidences irrefutable for mind and heart. We only have to examine now whether that which we find in Christ is according to the Jewish Bible.

CHAPTER XIII.

THE MESSIAH OF THE BIBLE.

Hear ye this, O house of Jacob, which are called by the name of Israel, and are come forth out of the waters of Judah, which swear by the name of the Lord, and make mention of the God of Israel, but not in truth, nor in righteousness. Is. xlviii: i.

If Israel's Messiah was not to come in order to give worldly glory and riches; if we consider it the greatest riches to have the heart turned to the living God in love; if God is a God of mankind, and the Messiah was to bring nations to God, then we cannot dispute that Jesus is the Messiah, since we see that he brought many nations to the God of Israel. We have no more ground to dispute that Jesus is the Messiah than we have to say that the Emperor William is not the Emperor of Germany while he actually reigns.

How many millions of people believe in the God of Israel through the name of Jesus Christ! How many thousands of buildings have Gentiles erected and dedicated to the service of the God of Sinai, because they believe in Jesus the Christ! Many thousands of churches testify, their stones cry, and say: " Jesus is the Messiah." Those heaven-pointing church-spires are witnesses, they speak loud that Jesus is the Christ. If we believe or reject him, we still see that he is the Christ; he actually reigns. The civilized world is called by his name.

It is only left to us to examine whether and how the Bible promised a Messiah, whether Christ's reign was promised by the God of Israel. I shall only cite the most striking passages.

When God blessed Abraham he said:

Gen. xxii: 18. "And in thy seed shall all the nations be blessed."

Is there any reason to say that the nations were blessed in Abraham's seed, if not in Jesus Christ? Can this prediction, with any plausibility, be applied to any man in Israel? You say the Bible is the blessing. True, but the Bible is only understood by the nations in the Christian sense, and they have only accepted it through the name of Jesus by his Apostles. I have already said that the Gentiles did not receive the Bible from the hand of any Jew unless he was a follower of Christ.

Also Noah's blessing to Japhet.

Gen. xl; 27: "God shall enlarge Japhet and he shall dwell in the tents of Shem,"

can only be considered as fulfilled in Christianity, which Japhet's children received from those of Shem.

Jacob in predicting to his sons what shall befall them in the last days says:

Gen. xlix: x: "The scepter shall not depart from Judah, nor a lawgiver from between his feet, until Shiloh come; and unto him shall the gathering of the people be."

The Jews never doubted that Shiloh means the Messiah. Both Thargums and all the rabbinical literature agree to this. They never thought of any other interpretation. Now we see that Judah existed as a state with a government of its own, until Christ came, and soon after the crucifixion Jerusalem was destroyed. If Jesus is not the Christ, then this prophecy is not fulfilled. Centuries after Christ some Jewish interpreters, seeing that this passage is an irrefutable evidence for Christ, maintained that Shiloh means not the Messiah. Aben'Ezra says that the prediction, that the scepter shall not depart from Judah until Shiloh come, is fulfilled in the fact that after the death of Joshua the tribe of Judah was going at the head of the army in the war, (according to Judg. i.) until David came, when the holy ark was removed from the place Shiloh. I need not show how Aben Ezra tortures the language of this verse. I leave it to any honest Hebrew scholar to say whether Aben Ezra's interpretation has the least plausibility. Rashbam also perceiving the consequences of this verse, says that "until Shiloh come" alludes to King Rehoboam's coming to Shechem, where the tribes refused him obedience, and means "until the King of Judah will come to Shiloh." But Rehoboam did only come to Shechem, not to Shiloh, therefore Rashbam thinks that Jacob called Schechem Shiloh because the two places were not a great distance apart. Thus, Jacob predicted that nations will bow in humility before David and Solomon until Rehoboam will come to Schechem, which may also be called Shiloh, as it is not very far from it. This interpretation speaks for itself; there is surely no necessity to waste one word in refuting it. The fact is, that any unbiassed Hebrew scholar sees very plainly that "Shiloh" is a person, for it says afterwards, "and to him shall the gathering of the people be." The prophecy is not fulfilled with David or Solomon, for it is predicted that "the scepter and law-giver shall not depart," and Judah had its government until Christ. The fact that excellent Hebraists, like Rashbam and Aben Ezra, could force themselves so much as to give such absurd interpretations proves how strong an evidence for Christ the plain interpretation is, and that it is impossible to translate "Shiloh" as anything but a person, else the above commentators would have found an interpretation not so queer. The Middrash, also perceiving that there is a difficulty for the Jews, says that scepter and law-giver allude to the Patriarchs "*Nessiim*," who existed in Palestine after the destruction of Jerusalem, (and were descendants of Hilel, for whose mother the descent from David is claimed,) and to the Heads of the exile, "*Rosh Galutha*," in Babylon, as these were a kind of clerical heads of Israel. Besides that these Patriarchs and Heads of exile never had any scepter or legislative power, they could not have been meant, since they lasted but a comparatively short time. Who is the Shiloh then? He did not come after them. Now, the Rabbis supposed that the scepter did not depart from Judah, but remained with him until Shiloh shall come, since there were Patriarchs and Heads of exile. What could these Rabbis answer now, since these do not exist and their expected Shiloh did not come? Are the predictions of Jacob not fulfilled? If the Rabbis had not known for certain that this Shiloh means the Messiah, they would not have found consolation in the Patriarchs and Heads of exile. Well knowing what a proof it is for Christ, they would have denied that it alludes to the Messiah. They could not, for it was a living truth known to all Israel. All efforts to give a different interpretation fail, for the simple meaning of the passage says that "Shiloh" is a person and not a place. The language compels to this interpretation. And the Jewish nation, who preserved the Hebrew language with the Bible, knew that this person Shiloh means the Messiah, to whom the nations shall gather. And this we see fulfilled in Christ, while we also find that the scepter and the lawgiver have departed from Judah since Shiloh—Christ came. The Christian interpretation is so obviously correct that this verse alone ought to be a sufficient biblical evidence for Christ. Rationalists must necessarily maintain that this prophecy was fulfilled in David or Solomon, and that Shiloh means a place. But this cannot satisfy them since it would still be a prophecy which is fulfilled, and they do not believe in any prophecy. They say, therefore, that Jacob's predictions are altogether a poem, written in Solomon's time and put in the mouth of Jacob. According to this the Bible is an imposition. This is surely not a Jewish platform, but still there are men teaching such doctrines and still occupying a rabbinical chair, and who claim that Israel was chosen, and a blessing to the nations, because the world received the Bible from Israel. What a blessing such a Bible would be!

When the Prophet Ahijah predicted to Jeroboam that

on account of Solomon's sins the kingdom of the ten tribes should be taken from David's seed, he said:

I Kings, xl, 39: "And I will for this afflict the seed of David, *but not forever.*"

If Christ is not the King, then David's seed is afflicted forever.

Is. xlii: "Behold my servant whom I uphold, mine elect in whom my soul delighteth, I have put my spirit upon him and he shall bring judgment to the gentiles. He shall not cry nor lift up, nor cause his voice to be heard in the street. A bruised reed shall he not break, and the smoking flax shall he not quench he shall bring forth judgment unto truth. He shall not fail nor be discouraged till he have set judgment in the earth. And the isles shall wait for his teaching. Thus saith God the Lord, he that created the heavens and stretched them out, he that spread forth the earth and that which cometh out of it, he that giveth breath unto the people upon it, and spirit to them that walk therein. I the Lord have called thee in righteousness, and will hold thine hand, and will keep thee, and give thee for a covenant of the people, for *a light of the gentiles.*"

There is no necessity of showing that this prophecy is fulfilled in Christ, since he is actually A LIGHT OF THE GENTILES (Or Goyim). By whom are the civilized nations drawn to the One God of Israel? Who makes every knee bend and every tongue swear to Him? Who taught the Gentiles to call Jehovah "My light and my salvation?" Who destroyed the temples and altars of idolatry? Who opens the human heart to cry "Father" to the Creator? Is it not Jesus Christ? Israel mocked at this claim and crucified him, but we see that he prevailed. He IS *the light of the Gentiles.* His light shines and shows the inhabitants of the remotest islands where Zion lies. It is a fact; we see it. Some servant was promised who is described to be lowly and meek. "He shall not cry," etc., and at the same time shall be a *light to the Gentiles.* Is there any other name in whom one could reasonably claim that the above prophecy is fulfilled? Jews may claim that Israel is the servant alluded to, but are they the light of the Gentiles? I have already said that the nations received the Bible only from the hands of the Apostles of Jesus.

Is. lv: " O every one that thirsteth come ye to the waters, and he that hath no money come ye buy and eat: yea come, buy wine and milk without money and without price. Wherefore do ye spend money for that which satisfies not, hearken dilligently unto me and eat ye that which is good, and let your soul delight itself in fatness. Incline your ear and come unto me. Hear and your soul shall live, and I will make an everlasting covenant with you, even the *sure mercies of David.* Behold, I *have given him* for a witness to the people, a leader and commander to the people."

This chapter speaks too plainly to need any further interpretation. If the Prophet Isaiah lived at this day, he could not speak any plainer. The Jewish religion is the bread which satisfies not. What benefit do you derive from it? Is there any consolation in God, any hope, any joy offered in the synagogue? And what a fountain of living water Christ offers! what a satisfaction and joy in God! "Joy in God" is not a phrase with the Christian, it is an actual joy (*Chedvath Adonai.*) Wherefore do you spend your money for that which is no bread? and your labor for that which satisfieth not? Since there is such a thing as a religion given by God, we ought to find its aim, its object. "Hearken, and ye shall have the *sure mercies of David.*" For, says the Prophet, in the name of God, you see that *I have given* him for a witness to the people, a leader and commander to the people. You see that Christ does lead the people, he *is* the leader, you *see* it. What else can you expect of the Messiah if not to lead nations to God? You see the hand of God in the fact that the despised and crucified Christ conquered the civilized world; history testifies to this. You see that the Prophet predicted him as he is now; why shall we not believe then that this pure, loving Jesus was God's Messiah? Has any man ever been nearer to God? Concerning our reasons for refusing to believe anything against nature, the Prophet continues in the very same chapter and says:

"My thoughts are not your thoughts, neither are your ways my ways, saith the Lord. For as the heavens are higher than the earth, so are my ways higher than your ways, and my thoughts than your thoughts."

Can we understand God's ways?

Can an impartial man possibly believe that the above cited passage alludes to Israel and not to the Messiah through whom we receive "*the sure mercies of David?*" Is Israel the commander of the nations? In the name of our Fathers, my Jewish brethren, I adjure you to take the Bible and examine. Just this chapter is sufficient to convince you that Christ is the promised servant of God, who is also promised to be God's "*salvation to the end of the earth,*" in ch. xlixv : 6. Indeed, the last twenty-seven chapters of Isaiah are nearly all predictions of Christ. They promise the consolation and peace which are only found at Christ's cross, they predict that the name of the God of Israel will be glorious among the heathen, and this will all be accomplished through the chosen servant. We see it fulfilled. God wipes away men's tears, he lifts man above himself, makes him able to despise his troubles, gives freedom to the soul, and this all through the name of Jesus; shall we still refuse him? It is true that in the same chapters the Israelitish nation is also sometimes mentioned as the "servant," but we can distinguish where the Prophet speaks of a servant in such circumstances that it cannot possibly allude to the Israelitish nation. For instance:

Is. ch. xlix: "And now saith the Lord that formed me from the womb, to be his servant, to bring Jacob *again* to him, though Israel be not gathered, (or, according to K'ri, that Israel may be gathered) yet shall I be glorious in the eyes of the Lord, and my God shall be my strength. And he said, it is a light thing that thou shouldst be my servant, to raise up the tribes of Jacob and restore the preserved of Israel : I will also give thee for a light to the Gentiles."

Here we see that the servant is to restore Israel and to be a light to the Gentiles. And so we find at other places. For instance:

Is. ch. xliii: 10: "*Ye* are my witnesses, saith the Lord, *and* my servant whom I have chosen."

Thus " ye " does not mean the servant. We only need

to read the prophecies in order to find that they speak of a servant besides Israel.

It is perfectly absurd to say that the Prophet himself was meant in those chapters, for he did not accomplish what is promised. The prophet did not destroy the idols, and was no light to the Gentiles. There is always something dark in all prophecies, but we see it too conspicuously that the Prophet sometimes speaks of Israel, who refuses to believe, sometimes of the Israelites according to the belief, and sometimes of the servant who converts to the belief. It is very easy to distinguish every time to whom the Prophet alludes. Speaking to the children of Israel, he never ceases to rebuke them. For instance, the last part of ch. xlii, and xliii; also the beginnings of xlviii and l.

While the Prophet laments over the destruction of Jerusalem in ch. lxiv, the Lord answers in ch. lxv: "I am sought of them that asked not for me; I am found of them that sought me not. I said, behold me, behold me, unto a nation that was not called by my name. I have spread out my hands all the day unto a rebellious people, which walketh in a way that was not good, after *their own thoughts.*"

In short, we find that the Prophet speaks, firstly, of Israel, who refuses to believe, and declares that it is the consequence of not obeying God, and going after their false teachers. This Israel the Prophet rebukes and exhorts and asks them to believe. But he predicts that the time will come when they will believe; when God will forgive their sins and hardness of heart for His own sake, and then they will be glorious. Secondly, of Israel in the spirit, those who believe God and cling to Him in love. And accordingly he speaks of two Zions, the visible and the spiritual. Thirdly, of his chosen servant, who shall restore Israel and be a light to the Gentiles, and through whom idolatry will fall, and salvation will be given. And every one of these three persons, namely: Israel according to the flesh, Israel according to the spirit and the Messiah, is called "my servant." This is so obvious that no impartial reader can deny it. The last part of Isaiah is all very intelligible if we are guided by this true principle. In the first part we also find prophecies of the same character. Especially in ch. xxviii we find a nice picture of Jewish orthodoxy, of the worship of the lips and the accumulation of laws; "here a little, there a little." Isaiah gives such a true picture of Judaism as it is. after Christ, and breathes so much of the spirit of the New Testament, that if the Bible had no other evidences for its divine origin, this shows it sufficiently. Only God could predict the two religions, and describe them so perfectly, centuries before they existed..

The question whether the last twenty-seven chapters of Isaiah were written by this Prophet or by another, in a later period, is of no consequence for us, since they were surely written before Christ, and are in the Old Testament canon. Whoever wrote them was a Prophet, for he foresaw the two religions. No matter how much the two parts of Isaiah differ in the character of their language, we see the same prophecies concerning Judaism and Christianity. In the first part we even find the Prophet pointing more to the distinction between the religion of the mind and that of the heart. In the following chapters we shall have occasion again to cite the same Prophet.

Jeremiah xxxi, 31: "Behold, the days come, saith the Lord, that I will make a new covenant with the house of Israel and with the house of Judah, not according to the covenant that I have made with their fathers in the day that I took them by the hand to bring them out of the land of Egypt, which my covenant they brake, although I was a husband unto them saith the Lord. But this shall be the covenant that I will make with the house of Israel, after those days saith the Lord. I will put my law in their inward parts and write it in their hearts, and will be their God and they shall be my people," etc.

Do we not find this covenant in the love of God with which Jesus imbues the heart of the one who is drawn to his person, and which places a man above the law? Is not the glowing love to everything spiritual and divine, with which Jesus alone can fill the human heart, a law which is written in the heart?

Ez. xxxvi: 26: "A new heart also will I give you, and a new spirit will I put within you, and I will take away the stony heart out of your flesh, and I will give you a heart of flesh. And I will put my spirit within you, and cause you to walk in my statutes, and ye shall keep my judgments and do them."

Does not God give a new heart and a new spirit to the Christian, and cause him to walk in His statutes, when He moves his heart to everything good by love? There can be no stronger evidence for Christ than the fact that the above described experiences are promised by the Prophets Jeremiah and Ezekiel. The Christian *feels* the fulfillment of the above prophecies. Every truly converted Christian can testify to this, before God and men.

Ez. xxxiv: 22 : "Therefore will I save my flock, and they shall no more be a prey: and I will judge between cattle and cattle. And I will set up one shepherd over them and he shall feed them, even my servant David; he shall feed them and he shall be their shepherd. And I the Lord will be their God and my servant David a prince among them.."

Reformers deny that a Messiah from the house of David is promised. Since Ezekiel prophesied in the exile, therefore he could not have alluded to any of the Kings of the house of David who reigned before the destruction of the temple. To-day we cannot even tell whether there are any children of David living; no Israelite can prove his pedigree. Must not this prophecy be fulfilled in Christ? It is especially very interesting to compare Ezek. xxxiv, with John x and Math. xxxv.

Hosea iii : 4 : "For the children of Israel shall abide many days without a king, and without a prince, and without a sacrifice and without an image (or monument) and without an ephod, and without theraphim. Afterwards shall the children of Israel return and seek the Lord their God, *and David their king*, and shall fear the Lord and his goodness in the latter days."

In this passage we find a prediction of the condition of Israel as it is now, lasting more than eighteen centuries, with the sure promise that they " shall *return and seek* their God and *David* their King." Consequently the King David is not to come to them, but he *is* the King and they have to *return* and *seek* him, when they return and seek their God. Can this passage be interpreted in any other sense than that Jesus is their King and they left him when leaving their God? Do we not see it? Who else is the King to whom they shall *return and seek him?* The Bible is true, and every one of my people will return to their King, as Paul also affirms. May they do it soon.

Haggai ii: 6: "For thus saith the Lord of hosts; yet once, it is a little while, and I will shake the heavens, and the earth and the sea and the dry land. And I will shake all nations, and the desire of all nations shall come: and I will fill this house with glory, saith the Lord of hosts. The silver is mine, and the gold is mine, saith the Lord of hosts. The glory of this latter house shall be greater than of the former, saith the Lord of hosts, and in this place will I give peace, saith the Lord of hosts."

The Prophet Haggai encouraging to build the second temple, says that the "*desire of all the nations*" shall come, and the house shall be filled with glory. Also that the glory of the second shall be greater than that of the first temple. And in the second God promises to give peace. The second temple was destroyed. Where is the desire of all the nations, the glory which is to be greater than that of the temple of Solomon, and the peace, if everything is not fulfilled in Christ? This passage is too plain, it cannot even be perverted. Must we not see in Christ the promised desire of all the nations, the greatest glory of God, and the given peace? Is not everything fulfilled in Christ?

Haggai, ii : 21 : " Speak to Zerubabel, Governor of Judah, saying, I will shake the heavens and the earth, and I will overthrow the chariots and those that ride in them, and the horses and their riders shall come down every one by the sword of his brother. In that day, saith the Lord of hosts, will I take thee, O Zerubabel my servant, the son of Shealthiel, saith the Lord, and will make thee a signet, for I have chosen thee, saith the Lord of hosts."

Again the Lord by the mouth of Haggai speaks of shaking heaven and earth, and then He will take His servant Zerubabel and make him a signet, for he is chosen. Where is this prophecy fulfilled, if not in Jesus, the son of Zerubabel, the son of David ?

Zech. iii : 8 : " Hear now, O Joshua the high priest, thou and thy fellows that sit with thee, for they are men wondered at; for behold, I will bring forth my servant the *Branch* (Zemach.)

" ch. vi : 12 : "And speak unto him, saying, Thus speaketh the Lord of hosts, saying, Behold the man whose name is the *Branch*, and he shall grow up out of his place, and he shall build the temple of the Lord. Even he shall build the temple of the Lord, and shall sit and rule upon his throne, and the counsel of peace shall be between them both."

We find that the Thargum, the Rabbis and Philo consider this *"Branch"* (Zemach) to be the promised Messiah. In Jeremiah we also find this *"Branch"* promised. He is to be a king and still a *priest* upon his throne. This agrees with the Christian doctrine.

Zech. ix : 9 : "Rejoice greatly, O daughter of Zion, shout, O daughter of Jerusalem, behold thy King cometh unto thee ; he is just and having salvation, lowly and riding upon an ass, and upon a colt, the foal of an ass. And I will cut off the chariot from Ephraim, and the horse from Jerusalem, and the battle bow shall be cut off, and he shall speak peace unto the heathen; and his dominion shall be from sea even to the sea, and from the river even to the ends of the earth. As for thee also *by the blood of thy covenant I have sent forth thy prisoners out of the pit wherein there is no water.*"

This passage is considered a prediction of the Messiah also in the Rabbinical literature. It is a perfect marvel how they still could refuse Christ. (*As I said, nothing convinces but the love of God.*) This passage is a full description of Christ. A joyous thing for Zion, the King comes, poor and lowly still the King, just and having salvation, (a helper or saviour,) will speak peace to the *heathen*, and reign to the ends of the world. In the midst of the joyful tiding the Prophet speaks, though, of cutting off the chariot from Ephraim and the horse from Jerusalem, (alluding to Israel's unbelief.) And then, speaking of this glorious and poor King, he says, "As for thee, (or better, 'and also thou,') *by the blood of thy covenant,*" etc., predicting the crucifiction and atonement. Is it not a wonderful blindness that a people who own the Bible, who brought it from God, and see the history of Christ and his government, still refuse him in spite of such a passage. The poverty of the King who speaks peace to the heathen teaches very plainly that the Messiah is the spiritual King. Indeed, that this passage is alluding to the Messiah is a thing which is obvious to every reader. Dr. Strauss says that the Evangelists invented that Christ rode on an ass into Jerusalem, because it was according to this prophecy that he should do so. So that the prophecy is not fulfilled but in the invention of the writers of the New Testament. But what does Mr. Strauss answer to the prediction, "and he shall speak peace unto the heathen, and his reign shall be from sea even unto the sea"? That Jesus rode on an ass is a thing which no one can prove, and Mr. Strauss can claim that it was an invention. But this is a fact, which Mr. Strauss cannot and does not deny, that Jesus speaks peace to the Gentiles, and that his reign *is* from sea even to the sea. We see, therefore, that this *prophecy* is fulfilled in him, and the whole thing cannot be an imagination. Then it is not reasonable to suppose that the occurrence with the ass was an invention, when the words of Zechariah *are* a prophecy, and the Evangelists *are* the servants of the one promised. If there is something supernatural about it then we see that we have to believe. And it must be supernatural, for how could Zechariah predict the coming of one who will reign from sea to sea without having a supernatural revelation. Or, is the fact that Jesus reigns from sea to sea, and speaks peace to the Gentiles, also an invention of the Evangelists?

Daniel ix. 1. "In the first year of Darius the son of Ahasuerus, of the seed of the Medes, which was made king over the realm of the Chaldeans:

2. "In the first year of his reign, I Daniel understood by books the number of the years, whereof the word of the Lord came to Jeremiah the prophet, that he would accomplish seventy years in the desolations of Jerusalem.

3. "¶ And I set my face unto the Lord God, to seek by prayer and supplications, with fasting, and sackcloth and ashes:

4. "And I prayed unto the Lord my God, and made

my confession, and said, O Lord, the great and dreadful God, keeping the covenant and mercy to them that love him, and to them that keep his commandments:

5. "We have sinned, and have committed iniquity, and have done wickedly, and have rebelled, even by departing from thy precepts and from thy judgments:

6. "Neither have we hearkened unto thy servants, the prophets, which spake in thy name to our kings, our princes, and our fathers, and to all the people of the land.

7. "O Lord, righteousness *belongeth* unto thee, but unto us confusion of faces, as at this day; to the men of Judah, and to the inhabitants of Jerusalem, and unto all Israel, *that* are near, and *that are* far off, through all the countries, whither thou hast driven them, because of their trespass that they have trespassed against thee.

8. "O Lord, to us *belongeth* confusion of face, to our kings, to our princes, and to our fathers, because we have sinned against thee.

9. "To the Lord our God *belong* mercies and forgivenesses, though we have rebelled against him:

10. "Neither have we obeyed the voice of the Lord our God, to walk in his laws, which he set before us by his servants the prophets.

11. "Yea, all Israel have transgressed thy law, even by departing, that they might not obey thy voice; therefore the curse is poured upon us, and the oath that *is* written in the law of Moses the servant of God, because we have sinned against him.

12. "And he hath confirmed his words, which he spake against us, and against our judges that judged us, by bringing upon us a great evil; for under the whole heaven hath not been done as hath been done upon Jerusalem.

13. "As *it is* written in the law of Moses, all this evil is come upon us: yet made we not our prayer before the Lord our God, that we might turn from our iniquities, and understand thy truth.

14. "Therefore hath the Lord watched upon the evil, and brought it upon us: for the Lord our God *is* righteous in all his works which he doeth: for we obeyed not his voice.

15. "And now, O Lord our God, that hast brought thy people forth out of the land of Egypt with a mighty hand, and has gotten thee reknown, as at this day; we have sinned, we have done wickedly.

16. "¶ O Lord, according to all thy righteousness, I beseech thee, let thine anger and thy fury be turned away from thy city of Jerusalem, thy holy mountain: because for our sins, and for the iniquities of our fathers, Jerusalem and thy people *are become* a reproach to all *that are* about us.

17. "Now therefore, O our God, hear the prayer of thy servant, and his supplications, and cause thy face to shine upon thy sanctuary that is desolate, for the Lord's sake.

18. "O my God, incline thine ear, and hear; open thine eyes, and behold our desolations, and the city which is called by thy name: for we do not present our supplications before thee for our righteousness, but for thy great mercies.

19. "O Lord, hear; O Lord, forgive; O Lord, hearken and do; defer not, for thine own sake, O my God; for thy city and thy people are called by thy name.

20. "¶ And while I was speaking, and praying, and confessing my sin and the sin of my people Israel, and presenting my supplications before the Lord, my God for the holy mountain of my God;

21. "Yea, while I *was* speaking in prayer, even the man Gabriel, whom I had seen in the vision at the beginning, being caused to fly swiftly, touched me about the time of the evening oblation.

22. "And he informed *me*, and talked with me, and said, O Daniel, I am now come forth to give thee skill and understanding.

23. "At the beginning of thy supplications the commandment came forth, and I am come to shew *thee;* for thou *art* greatly beloved; therefore understand the matter, and consider the vision.

24. "Seventy weeks are determined upon thy people and upon thy holy city, to finish the transgression, and to make an end of sins, and to make reconciliation for

iniquity, and to bring in everlasting righteousness, and to seal up the vision and prophecy, and to annoint the Most Holy.

25. "Know therefore and understand, *that* from the going forth of the commandment to restore and to rebuild Jerusalem, unto the Messiah the Prince, *shall be* seven weeks, and threescore and two weeks: the street shall be built again, and the wall, even in troublous times.

26. "And after threescore and two weeks shall Messiah be cut off, but not for himself: (or and hath nothing) and the people of the prince that shall come shall destroy the city and the sanctuary; and the end thereof *shall be* with a flood, and unto the end of the war desolations are determined.

27. "And he shall confirm the covenant with many for one week: and in the midst of the week he shall cause the sacrifice and the oblation to cease, and for the overspreading of abominations he shall make *it* desolate, even until the consummation, and that determined shall be poured upon the desolate."

Daniel, in the exile, looking for the redemption of Israel, made a confession of sins, and offered a most fervent prayer for his people. He must have expected the full redemption by the Messiah after the seventy years which were to be the duration of the exile according to Jeremiah. This we understand from the answer to his prayer by the angel Gabriel. For he tells him "seventy weeks are determined to finish transgression," etc., *i. e.*, the redemption for which thou hast prayed will not come as thou thinkest in seventy years, but in seventy weeks, or seventy times seven years. After seventy weeks, or four hundred and ninety years, the thing for which thou prayest will come, namely, the end of sins and reconciliation. For we must expect the answer of the angel to be in accordance with the request. Now,

the angel predicts the end of sins, the coming of the
Messiah and his being cut off shortly before the end of the
appointed period, which will terminate in desolation.
Thus the hope of Israel will be fulfilled in a time of desolation, not in outward glory. The question is, now,
when those four hundred and ninety years terminate.
They begin with the going forth of the commandment to
restore and to build Jerusalem. The commandment of
Cyrus in the first year of his reign, 536 B. C., was only
to build the *temple* not *Jerusalem*, according to Ezra i.
The same is the case with the commandment of Darius
Hystaspes, 516 B. C., according to Ezra vi. But in the
seventh chapter of Ezra we find that Ezra went up to
Jerusalem, and the letter which Artaxerxes Longimanus
gave him the seventh year of his reign, 457 B. C., makes
mention of *Jerusalem*, and endows him with civil authority to appoint magistrates and judges. There can
be no doubt but that Ezra had authority to build the walls
of the *city*, not of the temple only, for in his prayer in the
ninth chapter he says, "Our God has not forsaken us in
our bondage, but hath extended mercy unto us in the sight
of the kings of Persia, to give us a reviving, to set up
the house of our God, and to repair the desolations
thereof, and to give us a *wall* (Gader) *in Judah and Jerusalem.*" This makes it sure that Ezra had authority to
build the wall of *Jerusalem*. We also find in Nehemiah i.
that Hanani, who came back from Jerusalem, brought the
report to Nehemiah that the *wall of Jerusalem* was
broken down and the gates thereof were burned with fire,
and that Nehemiah wept over this report. This shows
plainly that Nehemiah thought that the walls were rebuilt.

For he knew of the destruction of the walls by Nebuchadnezzar without Hanani's report. Consequently we see that the commandment to build Jerusalem went forth in the seventh year of Artaxerxes, 457 B. C. From this to 33 after Christ is exactly 490 years, which fills out the period of seventy weeks. Thus sixty-nine weeks, or 483 years after the commandment to build Jerusalem went forth, "Messiah was prince," that is, Christ came forth and commenced his work according to the angel's prediction. And after these sixty-nine weeks, *i. e.*, somewhat later, the Messiah was cut off, the crucifixion taking place A. D. 30. About three years later the persecution of the church commenced, and the Apostles were banished from Jerusalem, A. D. 33. This is the beginning of the desolation according to the angel. We see therefore very plainly that the angel's prediction is all fulfilled according to the appointed time. The division of the sixty-nine weeks into seven and sixty-two may allude to the first fifty years after the return of Ezra till law and order and the old canon were established. The seven weeks are the first division of the seventy, consequently they must allude to the first forty-nine years after Ezra's return. Sir Isaac Newton wrote a work in defence of this system, but I have not had the opportunity of seeing it.

Some Christian scholars take the twentieth year of Artaxerxes, when Nehemiah went up expressly to *build Jerusalem* (according to Nehemiah ii.) to be the time of the going forth of the commandment. They try to show that the seventh year of Artaxerxes was before the 457th B. C., but they seem to fail in their chronological calculations. Besides, we have seen from Ezra ix. and Nehemiah i. that the commandment to build Jerusalem must have been given when Ezra went up.

As the book of Daniel so explicitly points out the time of Christ, there is no room left for the opposition, and one may ask how it was possible that a man should refuse to believe in both Testaments after he sees so clearly that the predictions of the Old are fulfilled in the New. But since God wanted to make the belief a means of salvation, he left stumbling-blocks in Scripture, so that the unbeliever always finds a way to pervert the word of God. Isaiah said, "He shall be a sanctuary and a stone of stumbling." Hosea said, "The ways of the Lord are right and the just shall walk therein, and the transgressor shall fall therein" (or better, "shall stumble thereat)."

Indeed the predictions of Daniel are too plain, and therefore this book was subjected to the severest criticism, and became the object of more attacks than any other book of Scripture. There is a full literature written about this book. Opposers try to show that everything which this book predicts was fulfilled within the period of time between Daniel and the Maccabeans from about 540 to 164, B. C. Rationalists, who would not admit that a special prophecy ever was fulfilled, must therefore try to show that the book was not written until after 164, B. C. The writer, say they, wrote down past occurrences of history in the form of prophecies, which he ascribed to Daniel. Thus the whole book is an imposition. Orthodox Jews would excommunicate one for such an assertion about any book of the old canon. The Jewish nation is a witness for the genuineness of every book of their Bible. Sincere Jews, that is, such who are not inconsistent, but really believe their Bible, will look with contempt upon a critic who tries to prove the Bible an imposition. The consciousness of the genuineness of their Bible lives in their hearts. The testimony for this book is sealed up with the blood of millions of Jewish and Christian martyrs. The fearful curse of blindness and madness with which this book cursed my unhappy nation, and which is fulfilled in them, is certainly evidence enough for the Bible. Look at the mad Talmud and the phantom called reform, and say that they are not a curse to the children of Israel. I have nothing but contempt for such hypotheses as would make an imposition of the Bible of God. Thanks to the living God of my fathers that these hypotheses which they call science do not move me now. If all the sciences could really prove that the Bible is an imposition, then they would themselevs altogether be an imposition, but God's word is true. "Thy word is a lamp unto my feet, and a light unto my path."—Ps. cxix: 105. But surely no science proves anything against the Bible. The rationalists only make hypotheses, which they call science, because they would not believe. They would not accept the greatest fortune which the Bible offers.

When I cite evidences of the Old Testament, I do it only for those who believe it. It is not my object here to refute the rationalistic critics, and I would not waste one word here in showing their error. But since highly esteemed, learned and faithful Christians, like Ewald, Delitsch and others were caught in the net of the rationalists concerning the book of Daniel, and defend the system for those who maintain that its prophecies were all fulfilled before 164, B. C., therefore I shall just mention some points of their system, and leave it to the reader to decide whether this system is not a perfect blunder.

At first their strongest proof that the book was written at the time of the Maccabeans is *the mentioning of some Grecian names for musical instruments.* But this is no proof, for the Perso-Grecian wars commenced not a very long time after Daniel, and the first occasion for these wars was given by the Grecian colonies in Asia, so that Grecian settlers certainly existed in Asia in Daniel's time, and very naturally some artists came to the court of Babylon and introduced some musical instruments there, which were known by their Grecian names. Secondly, we find the character of the language of the book of Daniel to be the very same with that of Ezra and Nehemiah, so that they *must* have been written at about the same time. But the above cited chapter ix is of itself a strong proof for the genuineness of the book. We have seen, above, how the predictions of the angel is perfectly fulfilled in Christ, and how exactly the time agrees. We shall now see how the other side explains the fulfillment of Gabriel's prediction of seventy weeks.

According to them, the time of the seventy weeks terminates at about 164, B. C. Some say that Seleucus Philopater, who was killed, was the Messiah who was to be cut off, and others maintain that it was some High Priest. Now, we ought to find that about 490 years before 164, B. C., some commandment was given to build Jerusalem, for the angel appointed this as the beginning of his seventy weeks. If the year 164 is the termination of this period, then 654, B. C., must be the beginning of it, but this year falls in the reign of Josiah, King of Judah, when Jerusalem was still flourishing. They take, therefore, the fourth year of Jehoiakim, 606, when Jeremiah predicted the seventy years of exile (Jeremiah xxv and xxix) to be the beginning of the seventy weeks, and Jeremiah's prophecy to be the commandment for rebuilding the city. But Jeremiah never speaks one word about rebuilding Jerusalem; he only prophesied that they shall be in exile seventy years. Secondly, Jeremiah's prediction was made only 442 years before anno 164, B. C. and there is no period of seventy weeks between the beginning and the end of the appointed period. Some of them say, therefore, that the seven weeks were included in the sixty-three, so that the period appointed by the angel was to last only sixty-three weeks altogether. But the angel said explicitly that *seventy* weeks were determined, and then he divided them into three unequal parts of seven, sixty-two and one. Thus the seven can not be included in the sixty-three. In short, no system but the Christian can show that the angel's prophecy was fulfilled according to the appointed time. Besides this, any man who is familiar with the Jewish literature will find the idea absurd that Seleucus Philopater, or even a High Priest, was understood under the word Messiah. It is true that every High Priest and every King of Israel was called Messiah, since they were annointed. "Messiah" is the word for " the annointed" in the Hebrew language, like "Christos" in the Greek. But whenever in the Jewish literature the word Messiah is mentioned alone, not alluding to any certain king or priest, it surely means the expected Messiah. Whenever a rabbinical scholar meets a passage speaking of the Messiah he never dreams that it can possibly allude to any other than the expected Redeemer, Goël. The Mishnah was written about 160, A. C., and speaks of the Messiah without giving any closer definition, but takes it for granted that any reader will know who is meant. This shows that it always was a standing expression in Israel as it is now. The first Christians also understood by the word Messiah the Redeemer. It is especially most absurd to suppose that this wicked idolater, Seleucus, was called "Messiah." We find that the Lord called Cyrus "My Messiah," alluding to his being God's chosen to restore the temple. This gives no reason to think that we can call any heathenish King Messiah. If one could name any King or priest with the name Messiah, then this word could never have become the common expression for the Redeemer.

But, besides all the objections I have cited above, which I believe must convince every reader, we can not suppose that the angel predicted only such things as were fulfilled within 164, B. C., since this would be no answer to Daniel's prayer, Daniel looked for the redemption of Israel, and the angel answers him that Seleucus or some priest will be killed. Especially, what has the Syro-Maccbean war to do with the finishing of transgressions and sins and reconciliation for iniquity, of which mention is made in the twenty-fourth verse? Where is the everlasting righteousness to be brought in, as the angel promised? And what an importance the angel placed upon his message! There is no sense whatever in the angel's answer to Daniel if he did not allude to Christ. Look at the whole chapter and common sense will compel to see a Messianic prediction in it, else it would make nonsense. Therefore, this very passage proves that the prophecies of Daniel are not fulfilled before Christ.

This passage is so plain a prediction of Christ that it refutes rationalism of itself; we see that it must be the words of an angel, since it can allude to no one else but to Christ. And if it had been an imposition, not a prophecy, then it had to be written after Christ, and every man will admit that the Jews kept their Bible so that no sensible man will suppose that the Christians could impose any spurious passage upon them. Notwithstanding that the language of the angel remains dark, especially the last verses, it is still clear enough that it is the plainest prediction of Christ. The time of the seventy weeks can not be explained in any other way than in the one I have cited.

The strongest corroboration for our explanation we find again with the Jews. (How wonderful that they are always the strongest witness), for, about 50 years after the destruction of Jerusalem, the Jews organized a gigantic revolution against Rome under the leadership of Bar-Kok'ba who claimed to be the Messiah. Rabbi Akiba, who was the greatest authority and the most influential Rabbi of this time, followed this impostor. The reason why he followed him is said to be erring in calculating the time after Daniel (Shetaah becheshban Daniel). There we see that the Jews who knew well enough that Daniel is genuine did not suppose that all was fulfilled.

They knew that this passage alludes to the expected Messiah, but they expected him to come later. I must say that we see a special punishment of God in this. Since they believed their Bible, any reader may ask, how could they miss Christ after the book of Daniel so particularly points out the time? But their error was not in misunderstanding the prophecy nor in taking the time of the termination to be earlier than it was; they were only confused in the chronology of their own history. It is a most wonderful phenomenon that the Jews lost over a century and a half of their history. And this all within the period of the second temple. They reckon less than five hundred years between the destruction of the first and that of the last temple, while there is a period of six hundred and fifty-eight years between the two disasters. Thus when Christ came they must have thought that there was about a century and a half to the end of the seventy weeks. Consequently, when Bar Kok'ba was successful about one hundred and twenty-four years after Christ's birth, Rabbi Akiba thought that the end of the seventy weeks was near, and he followed him. A good many things indicate that the Jews expected the Messiah after the destruction of the second temple, else they would not have had so much courage as to undertake their revolutions. We see that since they became influenced by the narrow spirit of Phariseeism they lost all sense for history, they did not even write a history of their own people. Everything they relate of their history is mixed up with fables and tales, without any chronological order whatever. The result was that they lost a century and a half out of sight, and their crazy chronicles, which were written later, show less than five hundred years between the destruction of the two temples, and so it is copied in their calendars (Luäch) to this day. All this was caused by their haughty belief in their own human authority. For the Rabbis considered everything they said as belonging to the oral law. They not only thought that their ordinances and perverse doctrines were the laws of God, *i. e.*, the oral law, but they also believed that all they spoke were holy words, and were also the law of God. And since the oral law was not permitted to be written, they did not write *anything*, not even their history. Thus their haughtiness and self-reliance caused their error in missing the appointed time of the Messiah, as well as the misunderstanding of his character. They went after their own thoughts. The common chronology is pretty sure and reliable up to Cyrus, and we can therefore see in the failure of R. Akiba that our passage predicted Jesus as the Christ according to a right chronology.

There are a good many other points which prove the error of those who consider the prophecies of Daniel all fulfilled within 164 B. C., especially of those who deny its authenticity. It is especially very clear that the four kingdoms, of which Daniel speaks in other chapters, allude to Babylon, Persia, Greece and Rome. Josephus also mentions the book of Daniel in connection with the pre-maccabean history.

Thereis no room here to say any more about the book of Daniel. But I believe, that every thinking man will find the best proofs for its authenticity in the books of its opponents, notwithstanding that great Christian scholars like Ewald and Delitsch follow the opposition. Every man is liable to err, and we go after no human authority. Just the fact that the Jews err in their chronology, and looked for the Messiah considerably later, shows sufficiently what the angel predicted. Also the fact that rationalists maintain that our citation from Gen. xlix, and the book of Daniel were impositions, written later, and were only ascribed to Jacob and Daniel, shows that they found irrefutable evidences for Christ in those predictions; that is, if they would admit them to be authentic they could only interpret them in the Christian sense; therefore they must make efforts to show that these sure predictions are only an imposition. For if they were not impositions then Jesus is Christ. But as Daniel could not have been written after Christ, since it is a Jewish book, therefore they must also show that all of Daniel was fulfilled 164 B. C. Their unbelief caused them difficulties, and they have to seek such explanations of the Bible as agree with their unbelief. It is the same as with their historical researches about the origin of Christianity; unbelief prompts their researches in history and in the Bible. Take the Bible as it is, simply as the Bible, and there is no reason for any such studies. If we believe the Bible as we ought to do, we find nothing odd, no difficulty nor problem. They make themselves difficulties and problems where there are none, because they *would not* believe the simple truth. But they cannot prove their hypothesis, their systems have no ground.

Of all the passages cited thus far we see that the Bible predicts a Messiah, a Son of David, and that his kingdom is spiritual only, for he was described to be poor and lowly. In Isaiah, Hosea and Zechariah we even see it predicted that the children of Israel will not believe in him. Besides that the character of Jesus is according to the description given by the Prophets, and besides that we actually see him reigning from sea to sea, as the promised light of the Gentiles, speaking peace to them, we find the surest evidence that he is the hope of Israel, in the fact that he did come at the time appointed by the Bible.

It is yet to be remarked that every single passage which we cited is considered to be Messianic, also by the Rabbis, so that the contest is only about the person of Jesus. Against the fact that the scepter departed from Judah since Christ came, the Rabbis only maintained that it did not depart, since they had some clerical heads; but now that these do not exist, they have no answer whatever.

Having now cited scriptural passages sufficient to prove that Jesus is the Messiah according to the Jewish Bible, I shall devote the following chapter to the doctrine of incarnation, or the divine character of the Redeemer.

CHAPTER XIV.

THE DIVINE REDEEMER.

"Thus saith the Lord, the REDEEMER of Israel and his Holy One, to him whom man despiseth, to him whom the nation abhorreth, to a servant of rulers, Kings shall see and arise, princes also shall worship, because of the Lord that is faithful, and the Holy One of Israel, and he shall choose thee."—Is. xlix: 7.

"And the REDEEMER shall come to Zion, and unto them that turn from transgression in Jacob, saith the Lord."—Ch. lix: 20.

Before citing any biblical passage to prove the divine character of Christ, I find it necessary to give a short explanation of this doctrine, since it is very much misunderstood. The Jews think that believing in Christ's divinity is believing that a man was God. This misapprehension leads them to think that the Christians have a corporeal God. Indeed, such a belief would not only be idolatry, but even illogical, as it is inconsistent with the first and main doctrine of Christianity, which is, to believe in One invisible, omnipresent God, the mysterious Holy God of Israel. To make people believe in the only One God of Israel, with all their heart and soul, was the only object of Christ's life. This belief is the only aim of Christianity. Since the *man* Jesus was visible to the eyes of man, it is illogical to say that he was the invisible God. Christianity could therefore never teach any such a thing. Nothing can be considered a Christian doctrine which is not taught in the New Testament, and one needs only to read this book in order to see that Christianity teaches only the One God of Abraham. No man is converted to Christ if he does not feel himself drawn to this One God through Christ. (I have shown above that the doctrine of the Trinity does no more interfere with the unity of God than the Jewish belief in the Shechinah.) The man Jesus only was visible to the eyes of some men at his time. The man Jesus was crucified, but the divine Jesus was visible only to the hearts of his followers; and so he is seen at this day. Jesus' body was created and visible, but his spirit is the spirit of the living God, who revealed himself in him. The suffering and tempted Jesus was a man, but the perfect, victorious Christ is God. The perfection of beauty and beauty of perfection, the beauty of holiness which we see in Jesus is the sweetness and beauty of God. In his heroic struggle with the world we sympathize with the man, but in his victory we see, not only his but God's victory, and we worship God. We admire the man, and become conquered by his self-denying love, until we see that in his self-denial he ceases to be a man, and in his universal love he shows us the love of God. Man's self is between him and God; in Christ the man is subdued, overpowered, and where the man ceases God commences. The obstacle which exists between man and God we see removed in his self-denial. He is perfect, and nothing is perfect but God. We commence to love the man; his lovely holiness makes our heart melt in contrition, his spirit of love consoles, reconciles and unites us with the spirit of love and harmony of the all, which is God. Our own self vanishes, we perceive the awe and unbounded greatness of the living God, until, like Moses before the burning bush, we hide our face, we stretch our arms, we feel that we are worms, our eyes cannot stand the splendor, the rays which radiate from the Holy God; we find that we are nearer, that we stand before the loving God, of whose nearnesss we are unworthy,—whose love we do not deserve. God enters our own hearts. . . . Oh, who can describe that! Who can describe the love and nearness of God!

Did Moses believe that a fire was God, when he hid his face before the burning bush? When we are impressed by the beauty and harmony of nature, when the rays of the moon elicit sighs from our breast, and we exclaim that we see God in nature, do we believe that the moon or stars or anything in creation is God? We only see God by the wisdom and harmony which we perceive in his works. So when we yield to Christ, when we see his divinity, we do not worship his body, but the revelation of God which we have in his character, in his beauty and perfection. We are drawn to God even through nature, but as the "I" separates us, we cannot reach him, we only see the Almighty, from whom we are so far, so far. We yearn, we love, we sigh, but we know not what ails us. When contemplating those silent stars, we feel as if something in us would sigh as if having a dark remembrance of better times, past in those higher spheres of calmness, rest and love. It is the poor soul's longing for her loving father. It is an insatiable love, the love without finding its object. In contemplating

Christ's character, in drinking consolation and life from his lips, the longing of our soul also awakens, the world of the higher spheres is also recalled in the dark memory of our soul, it is as if the gates of heaven were opened, and the still small voice, which Elijah heard on the Mount of Horeb, reverberated in our ears, the soul arises as if from a dream, the longing increases, she becomes amazed and finally it is as if she recognized the one after whom she thirsted. She finds the beloved, the Father, the friend, the dearest, God. . . . . She casts herself down, and prays, " Father forgive, for I have forsaken thy covenant, I am thy betrothed, and went after the love of the world." Tears drop, but they are a relief; the Beloved wipes them away. Sighs come forth, they are the sighs of love. The betrothed is in the arms of her Husband. The object of our soul's unknown love is found, recognized, the love is satisfied. The soul is reconciled to her God, the God of love.

When one sees God in nature, and perceives the divine existence through nature's beauty, he can only pity the atheist who mocks at him. So when one sees God in Christ and the world mocks, he has only the deepest compassion with the one who cannot see what he sees himself. And indeed, there is even more reason to see God in the character of Christ than in nature. The revelation of God in Christ is more conspicuous. In the revelation in Christ alone we see our Almighty Creator as the God of love. The revelation in Christ is the culminating point of monotheism. For here God is not only revealed as the personal God, but also as the living love. Monotheism is love. God as revealed in nature is rather the God of pantheism. Our weakness and blindness, which are caused by the flesh, our depraved nature prevents us finding any more than pantheism in the revelations of nature. It needed the supernatural, super-reasonable revelation of Sinai to teach us God's personality, and supernatural justice, which punishes and rewards after a law which is higher than the law of nature, after an incomprehensible law. Therefore one who does not believe in the personal God, or who refuses to believe what he cannot understand, cannot claim to be a Jew, for the Sinaitic revelation is supernatural, above reason, and teaches the personal God, whose love we see in Christ.

The Christian church teaches, therefore, that the man Jesus united with God is the Christ, that God was in the man, that a man alone cannot be the Messiah, the Saviour and Redeemer. God alone can save and redeem, but no man.

As salvation and redemption is promised to Israel through the coming of a Redeemer, then we must believe that God must be with the man who was to come. In Isaiah xliii, 11 : the Lord said, " BESIDE ME THERE IS NO SAVIOUR (MOSHIA.) Again in xlix, 6 : in speaking to the servant who is to restore the preserved of Israel, and to be the light to the Gentiles, he says, "THAT THOU MAYEST BE MY SALVATION (YESHUATHI) TO THE END OF THE EARTH." Also xlix, 7 : and in many other places, the Lord calls himself the REDEEMER, while in lix, 20 : we read : "AND THE REDEEMER SHALL COME TO ZION, AND UNTO THEM THAT TURN FROM TRANS-

GRESSION," etc. We see therefore that God must be united with the Redeemer who is to come. For if God himself is the Redeemer and Saviour how can a Redeemer come and be a salvation unless God is with him?

The mysterious connection between God and man, is not more incomprehensible than the belief of almost every man that soul and body are united in the man. On the same principle that men perceive and believe that there is an immortal soul united with their body, the Christian also believes that God Himself was united with Jesus. The man and God are one Christ. Men do not know any more of the substance of their own soul than they know of the substance of God. Many call themselves rationalists and refuse to believe anything supernatural, and yet they believe in the immortality of their own soul. Can they comprehend it? No matter how many books philosophers have written to prove the immortality of the human soul, it remains incomprehensible. Men only believe in their immortality because they perceive it, their conscience tells them of it, it is mysterious, incomprehensible. Also all the libraries which were written to bring metaphysical evidence that there is a personal God, prove nothing. The great Jew, the greatest, clearest and purest of all philosophers, Spinoza, excells them all, and teaches his own pantheism. Nothing can be proved but our conscience proves it. Men do not believe in a personal God because philosophy teaches so, but because they teach so themselves. The gods of the philosophers do not live long, one kills the other. Kant created his own god, and Hegel made a new one, and so those gods fight and eat each other up like the gods of the Olympus. Only the God of Israel, the God of the Bible, lives forever. Men believe in the immortality of their souls and in the personal God in spite of reason with its philosophy, only on account of conscience. So the Christian believes in Christ's divinity because he perceives, he feels it. He perceives the love of the God of the Bible.

We see, therefore, that even what we believe without the Bible is incomprehensible; why must we comprehend the religion, which is to be the supernatural help of God? Is the Sinaitic revelation comprehensible? The Reformers surely make it comprehensible when they deny it, but then they become incomprehensible themselves. Let a Jew who believes the Bible show me how the Old Testament is all comprehensible, then he may ask me to show how the New is according to reason. I have shown sufficiently that Judaism cannot claim to be comprehensible. If I could comprehend God I would surely need no religion; nay, I would be God himself. I have shown before that it cannot be our object to comprehend the religion; we only want evidences to believe that the things incomprehensible are credible.

If one feels only the helpless condition of his own poor soul he will find it easy to trust himself in the hands of Jesus. We are so weak, so helpless, and he is so strong, he is the greatest victor; he was victorious over himself. He is the greatest conquerer; he conquered his flesh, his earthly life, and if one conquers this he conquers death. Spiritual death is only the consequence of an earthly life. I struggle with myself; I can not overpower myself. I live an earthly life; I can not conquer it, and have to expect the consequences—death. The soul goes to the element by which it is attracted, and which it follows in this life. It goes to the hollow, burning, and cold joys of this world after it leaves the body, and it finds that there exists, not only a personal God, but also a personal Satan, the originator of these joys. And I am so weak, my flesh conquers me, *my life kills me*, and he is so strong. Shall I not allow my soul to be attracted by him? One who could manage himself and come out so glorious is also able to help me in my struggle with my life. I am so far from God; how far we are from God! He is so great and I am so little. He is so high and I am so low. He is so pure and I am so impure. He is loving and I am so selfish; everything is self in us. If I aspire to God I can not reach Him. And Jesus is so near to Him. There is nothing between God and Him. Shall I not cling to him? I am without hope or peace; I am restless, and he says, "Come unto me, all ye that labor and are heavy laden, and I will give you rest." Shall I mistrust him? When death approaches, when his mercyless hand will touch our shoulder, when a fearful chill will run through every one of our nerves; when the heart will tremble and the soul shiver; when the shadow of death lowers over the forehead, and we have to leave this world, we have to go alone. Nothing to cling to, nothing to take along. When the deeds and words and thoughts of our past life pierce our conscience; when our own life is so dark, will not then the life of Christ, which we love, be like a shining star over our death-bed? When all friendship and love is of no avail, will we not be proud of our love to such a purity like the character of

Jesus Christ? When we have to be ashamed of every one of our deeds and thoughts, is there no reason to be proud of thinking of and loving such a pure and holy life as that of Jesus? When our conscience finds us guilty, we shall still find some childlike innocence in our hearts, because we believed that living innocence—Jesus Christ? And must not God love the one who has the heart to trust and to believe in Jesus? Let one contemplate the life of Jesus, and say then that it can possibly be an error or a wrong to follow him, and to believe him in all his claims.

If Jesus' claim is idolatry, then the belief that God was on Sinai, or that he wrestled like a man with Jacob is also idolatry. An old Grecian philosopher, believing in one omnipresent invisible God, had just as much reason to consider Judaism idolatry or to say that the Jews believed in two Gods, because they believed that God was on Sinai or in a burning bush. The belief in Christ's divinity is only to believe that God chose the man to be a medium to reveal His divine love. And we shall see whether the Bible teaches that the Redeemer will have a divine character. Besides the above cited verses which show that the Messiah must be of a divine character, I shall cite the following passages, which teach it most plainly.

Is. ix : " The people that walked in darkness have seen a great light : they that dwell in the land of the shadow of death, upon them has the light shined. Thou hast multiplied the nation and not (or, *to him*) increased the joy : they joy before thee according to the joy in harvest, and as men rejoice when they divide the spoil. For thou hast broken the yoke of his burden, and the staff of his shoulder, the rod of his oppressor, as in the day of Midian. For every battle of the warrior is with confused noise, and garments rolled in blood; but this shall be with burning and fuel of fire. For unto us a child is born; unto us a son is given, and the government shall be upon his shoulder: and his name shall be called Wonderful, Counsellor, The mighty God, The everlasting Father, The Prince of Peace. Of the increase of his government and peace there shall be no end, upon the throne of David, and upon his kingdom, to order it, and to establish it with judgment and with justice from henceforth even forever. The zeal of the Lord of hosts will perform this."

These verses of the Prophet Isaiah form a prophecy of themselves. With the following verse another prophecy commences, as it is obvious to every reader. There are rabbinical passages showing that they took this prophecy to be an allusion to the Messiah. Also some of the oldest commentators interpreted it in the same sense. The Hebrew language does not permit any other translation than such as I have cited without coming in conflict with its grammar. We *must* see here a Messianic passage, for the Prophet promises peace without an end, an increased government, upon the throne of David *forever*. He also begins to speak of a *great light*, for those who are under the shadow of death, and of a great joy for breaking the yoke of his burden, the rod of his oppressor, why? Because a child is born who shall be called *Wonderful! Mighty God! Prince of Peace!* And the consequence is: peace without end. Who can be meant here if not the Messiah? Therefore we see it most plainly that he must have a divine character. And because it is too plain that a divine character is attributed here to a born child, therefore we can not doubt that it alludes to the Messiah, besides that the balance of the things promised in the passage can only be expected through him. Naturally the Jews must interpret the verse which gives divine attributes to a born child in a different sense. Some take it to be an exaggeration, but this is not natural in the language to exaggerate so much as to give such attributes to men. We find no other example of that kind in the Bible, but where it alludes to the Messiah. One commentator of the middle ages said that Wonderful, Counsellor, Mighty God and Eternal Father are all in the nominative, but Prince of Peace is in the objective. The translation would be then: "And he shall be called *by* the Wonderful, Counsellor, &c.: Prince of Peace." Others take the verb in the active form, *i. e.*, "And he shall call," not "and it shall be called." These interpretations are so obviously against the grammar that even Jews show the impossibility of such an interpretation. Besides that, it can not be my object here to enter into any philological discussions, which could not interest the reader, there is no necessity of doing it since I can allude to Dr. Herxheimer, and other good Jewish authorities in the language, who show that our translation is the only one according to the grammar. The idea of taking the first four names in the nominative is so obviously against the language, that any Hebraist must find it perfectly absurd. And the fact that a commentator could try to pervert the language so absurdly shows how clearly he saw how the simple interpretation is a true prediction of Christ; but as his standpoint *is* taken, he must oppose him, therefore he will rather pervert the Bible, for he must contrive something to show that the Bible teaches not Christianity, when it *does*. Such perversions show that the Bible did not prevent the Jews accepting Christ, but on the contrary, they would not follow the Bible, and so try to make the Bible follow them. Exactly as the rationalists cast history after their own pattern, because the plain history contradicts them, so the Jews do with the Bible. I only ask every man who understands a little Hebrew, is it possible that any commentator, (whoever he is, being entirely without books; I do not recollect what one it is, either Redak or Rashi), would pervert any other passage in such an absurd manner? Would he have tried such a perversion of this passage, if not that he saw the plainest Christianity in it? Therefore the fact that they so obviously and absurdly pervert the Bible indicates what the plain understanding of it would teach. A Mr. Leeser, who issued an English translation of the Bible in this country, gives this same perversion, and I believe also Dr. Philipsohn. I am not surprised at whatever Leeser said, but it is highly astonishing that Dr. Philipsohn, who is a scholar, could torture the language in such an absurd manner.

Jews, especially the Reformers, say that this passage alludes to King Hezekiah, and the divine attributes were only an exaggeration. I said above that we do not find such exaggerations in Scripture, but even the exaggerations would be accepted still it cannot allude to Hezekiah, for nothing of the passage can be applied to him. Where is the great light to be seen? Is the destruction of the Assyrian army, a great shining light? Where is the increased government, the peace without an end, and forever? Why is Hezekiah better than any other good king? We even read in II Chronicles, xxxii, 25 : "But Hezekiah rendered not again according to the benefit done unto him ; for his heart was lifted up ; therefore there was wrath upon him, and upon Judah and upon Jerusalem." Hezekiah's time was not so glorious to Judah. They were finally helped from the hands of Assyria, but they had trouble enough. We find nothing in the life of this king which could justify such attributes, even as an exaggeration. For instance, "*El Gibbor*" which means always Mighty God, they translate here, "mighty hero." Where do we find that Hezekiah was such a mighty hero? In his troubles he had to send to Isaiah to pray for him. Was he a hero because the angel killed the army of the enemy in one night? Let an impartial man, after reading the life of Hezekiah and this passage, say that it is possible that this extraordinary prophecy could allude to him. Let any one who ever read the Bible in Hebrew say that it is possible that a man could say "*El Gibbor*," meaning mighty hero. In the very next chapter, verse 9, we read, " The remnant shall return, the remnant of Jacob to the Mighty God *El Gibbor*." Shall the remnant return to the "mighty hero?" Jewish nation ! In the name of our God, how can you deceive yourselves so much? Our Bible is not only true, but given to us by our God with signs and wonders. We were chosen by the Creator of heaven and earth to receive this Bible, it offers us everlasting life for our souls, we have souls and deserve to go to destruction on account of our corrupted life, and this Bible offers us actually everlasting life. It shows the way to God. How can you be so indifferent? In the name of everything, for the sake of your children, see, open your eyes and see, it is not according to our reason, but it is in our Bible, ours, the Jewish Bible, it deserves to be believed, it must be believed, and it predicts a born child who is at the same time the Almighty God, it is a fact. No man can object to the above translation as being in the least against the Hebrew language. No one of the opposition, says that this translation is faulty, they only give their faulty translations in order to avoid belief in the plain Bible. The Bible cannot have any other meaning. Is it possible that the Prophet promises such a glory in connection with a born *child*? and this child was only Hezekiah. If Hezekiah had been such a great hero, there would still be no glory at his *birth*. The Prophet expresses so much joy because "*a child is born.*" Let it sound foolish, absurd, but it is God's will. Why shall you deceive yourselves? Every single other interpretation of this passage is not only false, but even absurd. There is only one effort made to give another meaning to this prophecy which does not sound absurd, but it is not less false. Some say, namely: that the names wonderful, etc., are only names, by which the child shall be called, but do not indicate his character. The passage alludes to the Messiah, and still does not allude to his divine character. This is not absurd, for we find an instance in Scripture, that Jacob named an altar " El Eloha Israel," " God, the God of Israel." Thus it could be possible that a child should be called by the name " El Gibbor," etc. But this could be supposed when a child born would have been called by these names, when the names would have actually been given to some person, but here it is a prophecy, it has to mean something. How can the Prophet predict a name when no one is ever called so? What are these words for if they mean nothing, nor is any one called by them? Besides, why are *five* such names given, and what sense would the whole passage have? It breathes so much joy about a child and then tells me his names, which have no meaning, and by which it never was called even. We see, therefore, that they must mean to assign the character, and if they do this then how can we refuse to believe in Christ's divinity, when we claim to believe our Bible? How can one call it idolatry if the Jewish Bible teaches it? For your life's sake, it is the most serious matter to examine.

The above passage would alone be sufficient to prove the doctrine of incarnation to be biblical, but we shall find others. Read Is. xi. where the Messiah, the branch of David is also promised, and the Prophet says, "The spirit of the Lord shall rest upon him." The Jews ask why the promise of peace, which it predicted in the same chapter, is not fulfilled. "The wolf shall dwell with the lamb," etc., and, "They shall beat their swords into ploughshares," etc. This chapter contains very plain promises that the wars shall cease. But when we have a sufficiency of other passages proving Jesus to be the Christ, then we can believe him concerning what he said about his second coming. Especially since we can see that the Christian doctrines contain the germ of peace. If all the nations would be true Christians, I believe that war would be impossible to-day. The trouble is that there are too few real Christians, the remnant of Israel is not numerous. And especially, Christianity is not really established until Christ's people, the Jews, have accepted him. They must show the Gentiles how to be in earnest with religion, how to believe Christ with the heart. The Gentiles cannot enter into the full spirit of the Jewish Messiah. It takes the Jewish nation, the people of God, the people with heart, to establish the right church. There is too much of aristocracy, too much of the foolish national conceit, too much of the thing called patriotism, which keeps the man on a platform of narrowness, and does not allow him to ascend the lofty platform of universal right and love, of humanity. The more they are Americans and Englishmen and Germans, etc., the less they are MEN. The Jews used to be accused of being no patriots, no soldiers, they denied it. But it is true, and I say it with pride, I am no patriot, the globe is my fatherland and I despise soldiership, and so does every Jew, who is genuine. We are no patriots, and we are able to see the wrongs and corruptions of our respective countries, for we are not blinded by partiality. We, the Jews, despise your hollow refinement, ye nations of the civilized world, ye people of diplomacy. Only in the unspoiled Jewish nation is yet the material to be found for the future Christian nation. There is no Christian *nation* in the world, nor ever shall be, besides God's people, and then wars will have an end. The Jews who are diplomats and brave soldiers to-day, are no genuine Jews, they are amphibious. The Jews, the full Jews, will establish the full church.

Jeremiah, xxxiii: 5: "Behold the days come, saith the
Lord, that I will raise unto David a righteous
Branch, and a king shall reign and prosper, and
shall execute judgment and justice in the earth.
In his days Judah shall be saved, and Israel
shall dwell safely, and this is the name whereby
he shall be called : *Jehovah our Righteousness.*"

In chapter xxxiii we find nearly the same words.
Some say that "Jehovah" is here in the nominative, but
it is shown that we cannot translate differently than the
cited translation according to grammar. The Thargum
interprets in accordance with it. Others admitting that
the passage teaches that the Messiah shall be called "Jehovah our Rightousness," claim that it is only a name,
as in Is. ix. We have seen that it is not reasonable. Especially since we find other passages teaching the divinity
of the Messiah, where we cannot say that it is a name.
There is no reason to force ourselves here.

Zech. xii : 8: "In that day shall the Lord defend the
inhabitants of Jerusalem ; and he that is feeble
among them at that day shall be as David ; and
the house of David shall be as God, as the angel
of the Lord before them. And it shall come to
pass in that day, that I will seek to destroy all
the nations that come against Jerusalem. And I
will pour upon the house of David, and upon the
inhabitants of Jerusalem, the spirit of grace and
of supplications: and THEY SHALL LOOK
UPON ME WHOM THEY HAVE PIERCED,
and they shall mourn for him, as one mourneth
for his only son, and shall be in bitterness for him,
as one that is in bitterness for his first born."

" ch. xiii : 7 : "Awake, O sword, against my Shepherd, and against THE MAN THAT IS MY
FELLOW, SAITH THE LORD OF HOSTS:

smite the shepherd, and the sheep shall be scattered, and I will turn mine hand upon the little ones." etc.

Can the crucified Christ be predicted more plainly? Who is the man, God's fellow? (Geber Emithi.)

Micah, v: 2: "But thou Beth-lehem Ephratah, though thou be little among the thousands of Judah, yet out of thee shall he come forth unto me that is to be ruler in Israel; *whose goings forth have been from of old, from everlasting.*"

This passage is considered Messianic also by the Jews.

Malachi, ii: 5: "My covenant was with him of life and peace; and I gave them to him for the fear wherewith he feared me, and was afraid before my name. The law of truth was in his mouth, and iniquity was not found in his lips: he walked with me in peace and equity, and did turn many away from iniquity. For the priest's lips should keep knowledge, and they should seek the law at his mouth; for he is the messenger (or angel) of the Lord of hosts. But ye are departed out of the way; ye have caused many to stumble at the law; ye have corrupted the covenant of Levy, saith the Lord of hosts. Therefore have I also made you contemptible and base before all the people, according as ye have not kept my ways, but have been partial in the law."

" ch. iii: 1: "Behold I will send my messenger, and he shall prepare the way before me: and the Lord, whom ye seek, shall suddenly come to his temple, even the messenger (or angel) of the covenant whom ye delight in: behold he shall come saith the Lord of hosts. But who may abide the day of his coming? and who shall stand when he appeareth? for he is like a refiner's fire, and like fuller's soap."

Malachi, the last Prophet, spoke in the time of the seccond temple, and prophesied of the coming of the angel of the covenant. I think there must be some rabbinical passages considering this prophecy of Malachi to be Messianic.

Ps. ii: 1: "Why do the heathen rage, and the people imagine a vain thing?

2. The kings of the earth set themselves, and the rulers take counsel together, against the Lord, and against his Anointed, *saying*,

3. Let us break their bands asunder, and cast away their cords from us.

4. He that sitteth in the heavens shall laugh; the Lord shall have them in derision.

5. Then shall he speak unto them in his wrath, and vex them in his sore displeasure.

6. Yet have I set my King upon my holy hill of Zion.

7. I will declare the decree; the Lord hath said unto me, Thou *art* my Son; this day have I begotten thee.

8. Ask of me and I shall give *thee* the heathen *for* thine inheritance, and the uttermost parts of the earth *for* thy possession.

9. Thou shalt break them with a rod of iron; thou shalt dash them in pieces like a potter's vessel.

10. Be wise now therefore, O ye kings: be instructed, ye judges of the earth.

11. Serve the Lord with fear, and rejoice with trembling.

12. Kiss the Son, lest he be angry, and ye perish *from* the way, when his wrath is kindled but a little. Blessed *are* all they that put their trust in him."

Some of the ancient Jewish commentators, and I think also the Midrash, take this to be a Messianic chapter. But yet, Jews call it idolatry to believe that the Messiah is the Son God, and here David says "KISS THE SON." The language of the chapter makes it very clear that no one can be meant but the Messiah, who is called the Son. Later, Jewish commentators, also the rationalists, say that this chapter speaks of King Solomon, and the expression "Son" is an exaggeration, because in Samuel the Lord said that Solomon should be to him *like* a son. It is a great difference, though, between saying, "*thou art my son,*" and "*he shall be to me LIKE a son* ("*beni atha*" and "*l'ben.*") Further we read, "*Kiss the son lest he be angry, and ye perish by the way.*" Obviously it alludes to the Son's being angry. But they say it means God will become angry. Even if we could admit this, yet we can not see why one shall perish if he does not submit to Solomon. Nor do we find that the nations raged against Solomon, but they did, and do yet rage against Christ. There is no need to show that this chapter can not allude to Solomon; the language speaks for itself. One of the old commentators, seeing that it is a Messianic chapter, and knowing that "kiss the Son" is the plainest Christianity, instead of becoming a Christian after such a conviction, he rather perverted the words, "Nashku bar," (which can mean nothing else but kiss the Son), into "be armed with pure hearts." The perversion is so childish that it shows that he was perfectly convinced that the plain translation teaches Christ, else he would not have thought of such a ridiculous perversion.

Ps. xlv: 1 : "My heart is inditing a good matter: I speak of the things which I have made touching the King: my tongue *is* the pen of the ready writer.

2. Thou art fairer than the children of men: grace is poured into thy lips: therefore God hath blessed thee forever.

3. Gird thy sword upon *thy* thigh, O *most* Mighty, with thy glory and thy majesty.

4. And in thy majesty ride prosperously, because of

truth and meekness *and* righteousness; and thy right hand shall teach thee terrible things.

5. Thine arrows *are* sharp in the heart of the King's enemies; *whereby* the people fall under thee.

6. Thy throne, O God, *is* forever and ever; the sceptre of thy kingdom *is* a right sceptre.

7. Thou lovest righteousness, and hatest wickedness: therefore God, thy God, hath anointed thee with the oil of gladness above thy fellows.

8. All thy garments *smell* of myrrh, and aloes, *and* cassia, out of the ivory palaces, whereby they have made thee glad.

9. Kings' daughters *were* among thy honourable women: upon thy right hand did stand the queen in gold of Ophir.

10. Hearken, O daughter, and consider, and incline thine ear; forget also thine own people, and thy father's house;

11. So shall the King greatly desire thy beauty: for he *is* thy Lord; and worship thou him.

12. And the daughter of Tyre *shall be there* with a gift; *even* the rich among the people shall entreat thy favour.

13. The King's daughter *is* all glorious within: her clothing *is* of wrought gold.

14. She shall be brought unto the King in raiment of needlework: the virgins her companions that follow her shall be brought unto thee.

15. With gladness and rejoicing shall they be brought: they shall enter into the King's palace.

16. Instead of thy fathers shall be thy children, whom thou mayest make princes in all the earth.

17. I will make thy name to be remembered in all generations: therefore shall the people praise thee for ever and ever."

The Thargum, Rabbi Saadiah, and I believe also the Midrash, take this chapter to be an address to the Messiah. And the psalmist addresses him: "*Thy throne, O God, is for ever and ever; the sceptre of thy kingdom is a right sceptre. Thou lovest righteousness, and hatest wickedness: therefore God thy God hath anointed thee,"* etc. The addressed person is God, and *at the* same time anointed by God. This is the plainest indication of the double character of the Messiah, who, as we have said in the last chapter, can be no one else but Jesus. All the unbelieving Hebraists, especially Gesenius, do all they can to pervert these two verses, but in vain. The language is so plain and decided that any kind of a perversion is obviously such. The rationalists say that the chapter is addressed to some king at his wedding, because it speaks of the king's bride and wife. The Reformers surely believe such things. As if this was the only place where the believers are called God's bride and wife! How many times God calls Himself the Husband. Such interpretations need no refutation; they are too much against the spirit of the Holy Book, and especially against this very chapter. It makes no difference whether such a learned man like Gesenius says it or not. It is only surprising to see that a venerable, estimable Rabbi like Herxheimer can copy such stuff.

Ps. xci: "He that dwelleth in the secret place of the Most High shall abide(or abideth)under the shadow of the Almighty. I will say *of* the Lord, He is my refuge and my fortress, my God in him will I trust," etc.

Who is the one who dwelleth in the secret place of the Most High, and is at the same time God, the refuge? This chapter cannot possibly be understood in any other way but that the first verse means Christ, and in the second he calls him God. The following verses describe the lot of the believer, and in the last three verses Christ answers:

"Because he has set his love upon me, therefore will I deliver him," etc. Taking the Hebrew text, we cannot make out the connection of the chapter in any other sense.

Ps. cx: 1: "A psalm of David. The Lord said unto my Lord, sit thou at my right hand, until I make thine enemies thy footstool. The Lord shall send the rod of thy strength out of Zion: rule thou in the midst of thine enemies. Thy people shall be willing in the day of thy power, in the beauties of holiness from the womb of the morning: thou hast the dew of thy youth. The Lord hath sworn, and will not repent. Thou art a priest forever after the order of Malkizedek," etc.

See Math. xxii : 43-45 : and Hebrews vi. and vii. The Messiah is not only King but also Priest, everlasting Priest, as is also indicated in Malachi II. The learned rationalists have no little trouble in trying to interpret the High Priest after the order of Malkizedek, who is at the same time a king sitting near God. Seeing such a plain Christian chapter they must claim that it was not written by David, but by some other person and only addressed to him. But the superscription is, "A psalm of David" (Mismor l' David). What psalm is written by David if this is not? Now, if it is only addressed *to* David they are embarrassed about the words, " *Thou art a priest forever after the order of Malkizdek,*" since David was no priest. They say therefore, that the word "*Kohen*" does not mean "priest" here, but servant, consequently Malkizedek was not a priest but a servant to the Most High. Not to speak of the violence which the Hebrew language suffers, I only feel sorry that my Forefather Abraham gave tithes of everything to Malkizedek who was no priest. Abraham must have made a big mistake in taking poor Malkizedek to be a priest.

There are many psalms having a special reference to Christ, indeed the spirit of all the psalms is a Christian spirit. No man can really understand David's yearning without Jesus. Ps. lxviii: 18–21: cannot be understood unless in the sense as it is interpreted in the New Testament."

Job, xix: 23: "Oh that my words were now written! oh that they were printed in a book. That they were graven with an iron pen and lead in the rock forever. For I know that my Redeemer liveth, and that he shall stand at the latter day upon the earth. And though after my skin worms destroy this body, yet in my flesh shall I see God."

This is plainly predicting that the Redeemer shall stand upon the earth, and also that there will be a resurrection of the body.

Proverb, xxx: 4: "Who hath ascended up into heaven, or descended? who hath gathered the wind in his fists? who hath bound the waters in a garment? who hath established all the ends of the earth? what is his name and what is his Son's name, if thou canst tell?"

The Bible, we see, speaks of the Son of God, and as I have mentioned above, the Jew Philo explains it in the same sense as the Christians do.

Dan. vii: 13: "I saw in the night visions, and behold, one like the son of man came with the clouds of heaven, and came to the Ancient of days, and they brought him near before him. And there was given him dominion, and glory, and a kingdom, that all people, nations, and languages, should serve him: his dominion is an everlasting dominion, which shall not pass away, and his kingdom that which shall not be destroyed."

Let all the world say that the prophecies of Daniel terminate with Antiochus Epiphanes, still this Son of Man, who came with the clouds of heaven, and received the everlasting kingdom, is no one else but the Son of Man of the New Testament who was crucified. Even some of the old Rabbis considered that this Son of Man is the Messiah. After Daniel saw the four governments of Babylon, Persia, Greece and Rome, he saw the Son of Man coming. Compare this chapter with Daniel II.

If one desires to see the truth, he can see enough in these passages of Scripture which I have cited. We have seen, that it is a historical fact that Jesus claimed to be the Son of God, and we also see that his claim was according to the Bible. If it is idolatry, then the Jewish Bible teaches to serve idols. If a man finds Christ he knows though, how far it is from idolatry, and how near it is to God. I ask my people if it is possible that all these passages do not prophecy Christ?

As a conclusion, we shall speak of the Christian doctrine of atonement in the next chapter.

CHAPTER XV.

THE BIBLICAL ATONEMENT.

"I, even I, am he that blotteth out thy transgressions for mine own sake, and will not remember thy sins." Is. xliii : 25.

I have already said that the purpose of a religion can only be to make atonement before God. Since religion is only given to a sinning race, it must give us the means by which we can attain forgiveness of sins. I want a religion because I am a sinner. My sins are between me and God. If I was no sinner I should need no religion, consequently if the religion is not the way to remove our sins it is no religion. We have also seen that our religion must necessarily be incomprehensible, because if it only taught me according to reason then I would not need it. My nature is depraved, so that I cannot be with God if I have no other guide but reason, and I want a supernatural way from God because my reason does not suffice. Now if it is supernatural it is super-reasonable, for my reason is in nature. God would not tell me anything which I could find out myself, and if it was reasonable I could find it out by study and thinking. In short, God's revelation must give me something in addition to my reason, else there would be no need for His revelation. But how can I tell whether the supernatural teaching,— the thing given in addition to my reason,—is true? If it is not reasonable, how can I know that it is true? I must surely believe what I cannot understand, but I cannot believe everything. I said, therefore, that reason must find out which is the way given by God, so that we can believe without understanding it. In order to enable us to know which was His religion, God worked such stupendous miracles that we must see that they are from Him. He worked miracles until His religion was established. As soon as He had prepared and predicted His religion the miracles also ceased. The work is finished. In order to enable us to know that those miracles are true, He left witnesses in history so that we cannot help seeing that supernatural things must have happened. The witnesses are the children of Israel and the church, as we have seen. The proofs we have cited convince the mind that the Christian religion must be from God. And he who is convinced finds also the best evidence in his own heart; he finds the atonement in his heart. Therefore when the Lord spoke from the burning Sinai he said, "I am the Lord thy God, *which brought thee out of the land of Egypt.*" Ex. xx: 2: He did not say, which created heaven and earth, but "*which brought thee out of the land of Egypt.*" That is, I give you a religion which must be believed, not on account of philosophy, because you can see there is a God from your own reason. No, what your reason teaches suffices not. I give you my law which you cannot understand, but you must *believe*, because I have brought you out of the land of Egypt.

God brought the children of Israel out of Egypt with signs and miracles, by a supernatural working. He even hardened the heart of Pharaoh, that He might show His signs. Did God work miracles, did He redeem us from Egypt in order that we should be Reformers, and say, "do not believe what you cannot understand"? Does He preserve the Jewish nation in order that we may know that He created heaven and earth? No, He said to Moses "that thou mayest tell in the ears of thy son, and of thy son's son, what things I have wrought in Egypt, and my signs which I have done among them; that ye may know that I am the Lord." Ex. x: 2. A great number of times the Lord emphasizes that He is God who worked the miracles. To believe in the God of Israel, means to believe that God worked and taught things above reason. This is the sum of what we find in this book.

Now, the redemption from Egypt and the other miracles are not religion yet, they were only the introduction, the proof that we may believe the law. The religion, as I said, is only the way of atonement. After the redemption of Egypt He said, "I am the God who brought thee out," and then gave His religion. We have already seen that God only promised atonement through the blood of the sacrifices. It is by no means comprehensible, but God revealed a mystery, that he cleanses from sin by blood. We cannot expect to comprehend it. Now, as the law was only given to Israel, and God, as the Father of mankind, finished His religion by sending a Saviour for every man who accepts him, and we find in Daniel ix. that the end of sins is promised with the Messiah, and as this Messiah is the law embodied, therefore we find in the blood of this Messiah the finishing of the redemption, as much as we found the sacrifices to be the integrity of the Mosaic law. I do not try to find any reasons why God needed the blood, it is enough to know that He said so. To Moses He said, that He gave the *blood* for a cleansing, and to Christ he said:

Zechariah ix: 2: "As for thee (or, also thou) by the blood of thy covenant I have sent forth thy prisoners from the pit wherein is no water."

We see, therefore, that the blood is called "the blood of thy covenant," and is the only means to give freedom to the soul. Just as much as the law could not give justification without sacrifices, so Christ had to die in order to give us redemption. He took our sins upon himself, according to the Prophet.

Isaiah liii: "Who hath believed our report? and to whom is the arm of the Lord revealed?
2. "For he shall grow up before him as a tender plant, and as a root out of a dry ground: he hath no form nor comeliness; and when we shall see him, *there is* no beauty that we should desire him.
3. "He is despised and rejected of men; a man of sorrows, and acquainted with grief: and we hid as it were *our* faces from him; he was despised, and we esteemed him not.
4. "¶ Surely he hath borne our griefs, and carried our sorrows; yet we did esteem him stricken, smitten of God, and afflicted.
5. "But he *was* wounded for our transgressions, *he was* bruised for our iniquities: the chastisement of our peace *was* upon him; and with his stripes we are healed.
6. "All we like sheep have gone astray; we have turned every one to his own way; and the Lord hath laid on him the iniquity of us all.
7. "He was oppressed, and he was afflicted, yet he

opened not his mouth: he is brought as a lamb to the slaughter, and as a sheep before her shearers is dumb, so he openeth not his mouth.

8. "He was taken from prison and from judgment: and who shall declare his generation? for he was cut off out of the land of the living: for the transgression of my people was he stricken.

9. "And he made his grave with the wicked, and with the rich in his death; because he had done no violence, neither *was any* deceit in his mouth.

10. "Yet it pleased the Lord to bruise him: he hath put *him* to grief: when thou shalt make his soul an offering for sin, he shall see *his* seed, he shall prolong *his* days, and the pleasure of the Lord shall prosper in his hand.

11. "He shall see of the travail of his soul, *and* shall be satisfied: by his knowledge shall my righteous servant justify many: for he shall bear their iniquities.

12. "Therefore will I divide him *a portion* with the great, and he shall divide the spoil with the strong; because he hath poured out his soul unto death: and he was numbered with the transgressors: and he bare the sin of many, and made intercession for the transgressors."

This chapter is not only the most striking evidence for Christ, so that it has even brought conviction to a good many Jews, but it also teaches plainly that the Lord has laid upon him the iniquity of us all. As much as Christ's love replaces the law, so does his blood replace the sacrifices. The blood of the sacrifices was only cleansing temporarily, and had to be renewed, but in Christ the work is finished, his blood is the everlasting sacrifice. He is the everlasting King, and High Priest, and sacrifice, according to the passages of Scripture I have cited.

There is no necessity of saying much now in order to

show that ch. liii. of Isaiah can allude to no one else but to Jesus. The chapter of itself speaks too plainly. The Jews claimed that it alluded to the Jewish nation. Did the Jewish nation *bear the sins of many?* The Prophet says in the name of the Lord, "*my righteous servant shall justify many: for he shall bear their iniquities,*" or "*with his stripes we are healed.*" Can this be applied to the Jewish nation? In verse 8, the Prophet says, "for the transgressions of MY people" (*Mipesha Ami*) this makes us understand that for the sins of Israel, *my* people, he was smitten. Any man who is honest with himself will see that this passage cannot possibly allude to the Jewish nation.

We even find that modern opposers of Christianity, Jews and Gentiles, have abandoned this impossible perversion and claim no more that this chapter refers to the Israelitish nation; they try therefore to find a person in the Jewish history to whom they could apply this prophecy. Necessarily they make great blunders. For surely, there is no one but Jesus to whom this chapter has any reference. Some say that this chapter alludes to Jeremiah. There is a passage in the Talmud (Soteh) which applies it even to Moses. But there is no one to be found upon whom "the Lord has laid the iniquity of us all." Read the chapter and it will tell you of itself to whom it refers.*

---

* A number of years ago I came to the conclusion that Isaiah could not have predicted any one else in this chapter but Jesus. My reason refused to accept any other interpretation. This, my opinion, I communicated to a Jewish friend, who also understood the Hebrew language. He read the chapter carefully, and I showed to him that common sense does not suffer any other interpretation. The poor man saw that I was right; he turned pale and said, "What shall we do?" I laughed at

Returning to the doctrine of atonement, we find that the law which was necessary before Christ taught us that we must subject our lives to God, and to this subjection we are brought afterwards through Christ. We also had sacrifices against sins; this we have now in the blood of Christ.

Reformers say that this doctrine of atonement through Christ's blood is a perfect outrage on common sense. It is proxy. How can I forgive one man's sins by punishing another man? Consequently God can not do it. I say myself that this doctrine is perfectly against common sense, but in comparison to the old sacrifices, that the blood of an animal cleansed from sin, this appears even reasonable. As I said, the belief of the mind is an entirely blind belief. Christ's sacrifice has considerably more sense than that of animals. At first we see Christ's perfection is in overpowering the world, the flesh. We can see that Christ had to die; the perfect Christ had to move and to win us to God by his innocent blood. And then if I enter the spirit of the crucified Christ I crucify my flesh morally. If he is my greatest glory what value can my life have for me then? The sacrifice

---

him, and thought that he must be very foolish if anything could disturb him concerning Christ. If Isaiah teaches Christianity, continued I, then I do not believe him either. I considered Christianity to be idolatry, and nothing in the world could move me to believe. Such is the blindness of my people. While I was a Jewish minister I said once that the Christians show their religion predictad in Daniel, but Daniel is an imposition. I said so with the greatest thoughtlessness. I *believed* everything which the rationalists wrote without examination. But after I was converted it was like a blindness falling from my eyes. I at once saw the errors of all systems in perverting Scripture. I knew before that Christianity is taught in the Old Testament, but this did not move me. It is evident, though, that a kind providence prepared me since many years.

of the religion of the heart is also a sacrifice for the heart. It means to seek no glory but in the spirit. As much as Christ himself becomes as a principle to his followers, so his cross becomes a state of life to the one who accepts it. To accept the cross means to crucify the flesh in the will, to despise it, and by this become free. Thus it is even reasonable in comparison with the old sacrifices. Secondly, why must it be reasonable? If a judge would punish one man for another it would surely be an outrage, because the humane judge must deal according to reason, but God is not obliged to act according to my reason. His reason is higher than ours. It is enough for us to know that blood expiates sin according to His will.

Besides the Bible, the Lord teaches even in history that the shedding of blood is necessary. The God of love shows his sword in history. The steps of mankind leave marks of blood behind them. Before a nation makes any progress it is baptized with blood. Abraham worked the first work in the cause of freedom, when he went to rescue his nephew Lot, and he had to shed blood. History dips her pen in blood to write her annals, from the death of Abel to the last German war. Why does not Providence let mankind progress without blood? Do we not see something like proxy when the young men die in the battle-field for their country? God's ways are incomprehensible, even without the Bible.

After all our proofs from history and Scripture, I think I may close this book and express my hope that every man, who listens to the voice of his conscience will seek to find the true atonement, which he can reach by following the prescription of the Jewish Bible. I believe that every reader who is honest with himself will admit that Christianity is even more *reasonable* than Judaism. Every man can see that the Old Testament alone is a foundation without a building. Christians have good reason to be astonished at the Jews, who claim to believe the Old Testament and still refuse Christ, who is so plainly predicted in it. The fact is, that very few know what a love of God there is in Christ, and hardly any read their own Bible. Those who do not study the Hebrew language surely do not read it. And the students accept any perversion, since they know not Christ. They think that Christianity teaches idolatry, and are not even to be moved to examine. Especially are most Jewish scholars used to perversions of Scripture since they also study the Talmud. I have shown a few examples of their interpretations; the most learned Gentile unbelievers have no better interpretations. During eighteen centuries greatly learned scholars have written on both sides. There is a large literature written about the Messianic passages of the Old Testament. And the Jews believe everything which is written without examining. Why is there so much written? It is not because these passages are dark. There are really very dark, difficult passages in Scripture, but the Messianic passages are just the clearest, smoothest of the Old Testament. The Christian finds no difficulty; there is nothing obscure. But the unbeliever tries to make them obscure, because he will not believe. Their standpoint is taken to oppose Christ, and they have to write books to make out some intelligible meaning, when they refuse the clear, simple interpretation. I have used the common English version for my citations. It is true that this version is very imperfect if one wants to do justice to the Hebrew language. But concerning our object it suffices. No scholar can say that our citations are against the grammar. It is impossible to translate in any other sense without coming in conflict with the language. The great Gesenius, who has perhaps not found his rival as a Hebraist, works and struggles with the language to make out some other meaning to Scripture, but all in vain. If one desires to do the will of God he will soon find the plain truth. No Jew ever refused Christ really on account of the Bible. I must again cite the words of Christ: "My doctrine is not mine, but his that sent me. If any man will do his will he shall know of the doctrine, whether it be of God, or whether I speak of myself."

www.ingramcontent.com/pod-product-compliance
Lightning Source LLC
Chambersburg PA
CBHW031336230426
43670CB00006B/342